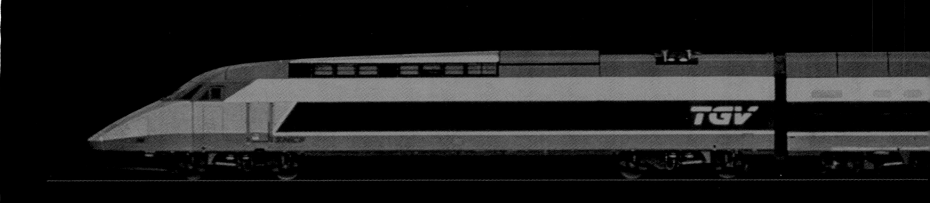

TRAINS

FROM STEAM LOCOMOTIVES TO HIGH-SPEED RAIL

WHITE STAR PUBLISHERS

TRAINS

FROM STEAM LOCOMOTIVES TO HIGH-SPEED RAIL

Text
FRANCO TANEL

Editorial Director
VALERIA MANFERTO DE FABIANIS

Editorial Coordinator
LAURA ACCOMAZZO
GIORGIO FERRERO

Graphic Designer
MARIA CUCCHI

THE PUBLISHER WOULD LIKE TO THANK GIANFRANCO BERTO,
EDITOR OF tutto TRENO, FOR HIS INVALUABLE HELP

© 2007 White Star S.p.A.
Via Candido Sassone, 22/24
13100 Vercelli, Italy
www.whitestar.it

Translation: Davide Arnold Lamagni and Glenn Debattista

ISBN: 978-88-544-0277-5

Reprint:
2 3 4 5 6   12 11 10 09 08

Color separation: Chiaroscuro, Turin
Printed in China

INTRODUCTION

The passing of a train no longer arouses any curiosity today. It's an event taken for granted like many other aspects of our daily life. But half a century ago, the birth of the railway had a revolutionary effect. For the first time the transport of people and goods via land no longer needed animal traction which, had always dictated its means and speed. Suddenly, distances grew shorter and the diabolical machine – as the steam locomotive seemed to some – allowed many people to travel at little cost.

This cheaper method of transport was a profound social development in a time when most people never traveled far from their homes for their whole lives. The Industrial Revolution in Europe would not have been possible without a railroad system capable of carrying goods anywhere. The United States of America might never have become the giant economy it is if it wasn't for the railroad.

Year after year, tracks and locomotives spread to every corner of the Earth. To narrate their development is a little like rerunning the history of European contemporary civilization: that is how integral to our history is this means of transport.

The first two rudimental steam locomotives were rapidly replaced by more powerful and faster models. In 1825 Stephenson's Locomotion carried the English at 14 mph (22 km/h), only 27 years later, in 1852, the French Crampton locomotives reached 70 mph (112 km/h). A speed which was prodigious at the time for those used to travelling by horse-drawn coaches, if not those drawn by oxen. The primitive wagons first used were replaced with especially designed carriages and at the beginning of the 1900s routes were already run by comfortable international trains. Thousands of goods cars, thanks to the increasing network, transported products of all kinds. These were years of rapid development but also great political instability. The great world conflicts of the last century affected the railroads enormously and they proved of great military and strategic importance.

Steam traction was eventually replaced by electric and the diesel power during a problematic modernization of the system after the Second World War. However, the railroads were unable to resist the spread of motorization, both in the transport of people and goods. Road transport with its flexibility and low costs put the railroads of the world in crisis. This was a period when authoritative economists theorized the total disappearance of the railroad system and state administration. To face the growing deficit, thousands of miles of track were closed. Car, coaches and trucks, thanks to the low cost of fuel, seemed to be the only sensible means of transport and the railroads were destined for a marginal role.

However, at the beginning of the 1980s there was a shift against the dominance of road transport. The first great oil crisis in 1974 had already led to a road transport model which was obviously unsustainable in the long run. In the following years a greater awareness of environmental concerns also boosted railway use. There is still no means by which so many people can be carried at such a relatively low cost and with a minimal impact on the environment.

After years of uninterest, governments have begun investing in railroad infrastructures again. The railway has caught up with the times: on average and long distance it has become competitive thanks to the introduction of high speed trains. At first at speeds of 135-150 mph (217-240 km/h) and now up to 220 mph (350 km/h). Local and regional transport has been modernized with special trains for commuters and the development of intermodal freight services, i.e. combined integrated road/rail services, which are extremely efficient. Traffic management and control systems will soon be managed by satellite.

There has been a boost in tourist use too, as more and more people choose trains for trips and excursions of all kinds. Railroads and locomotives are often not only a "different" means of transport, but the objects of cultural and leisure interest. This is born witness by the hundreds of historical and tourist railways which are now found in all corners of the world. It is possible to choose between going to China on a vintage steam train or to cross a continent in the comfort of a luxury train. In both cases, the journey, thanks to the train, becomes an event, an experience to be appreciated and not a simple means of getting from one place to another. Of course, the percentages of people and goods moved by rail are still low, but railroads are increasingly recognized everywhere as an invaluable and essential method of transport, and often unsurpassed as a less stressful and often more human way traveling.

The whole subject of trains and their networks is a complicated and difficult one to understand, but is fascinating nonetheless. Historical, economic, technological and social changes are all reflected in the evolution of the railroads, with varying stories across nations and continents. It is an impossible task to cover the subject in just one volume, but by concentrating our attention on fundamental facts and the most representative trains we have attempted to give an overall account, a general impression of the story of the railroads. We have not tried to provide encyclopedic completeness, but rather a sincere and passionate attempt to transmit the charm of this often unknown world.

2-3 An engine driver rinses a locomotive used on the Durango & Silverton Narrow Gauge Railroad line, in Colorado.

4-5 A freight train hauled by a steam locomotive crosses a Jitong Railway's bridge, in the north of China.

6-7 A steam locomotive in India traveling in the vicinity of the Taj Mahal, at Agra.

9 The Union Pacific's "119 Pride of The Prairie" locomotive, a reconstruction of an 1869 model, moves towards Promontory, Utah.

10-11 A Dining Car forming part of the luxurious Eastern & Oriental Express train.

12-13 The Union Pacific's "The City of Los Angeles," which, since 1936, connected Chicago to Los Angeles, was the company's most prestigious train.

14-15 The high-speed Japanese train, Shinkansen, crossing a bridge.

& ORIE

THE FIRST LOCOMOTIVES
PAGE 18

THE FIRST RAILWAYS IN THE WORLD
PAGE 50

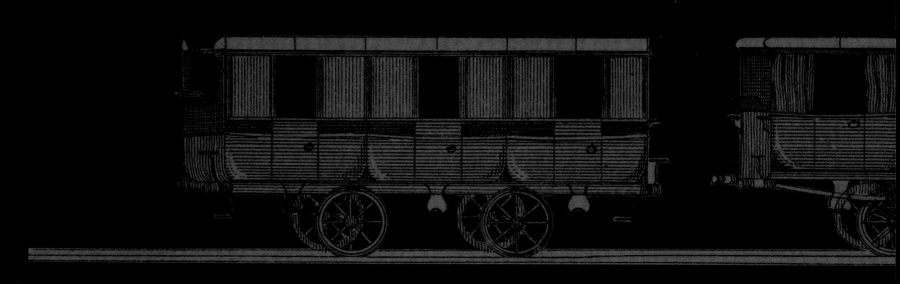

THE RAILWAY IS BORN
1830 - 1880

THE FIRST LOCOMOTIVES

Cows will stop producing milk! Such speed is dangerous to people's health! It is an instrument of the devil! The appearance of steam engines and the first railways in the English countryside and cities at the beginning of the 19th century generated enthusiasm and curiosity, but also fear and ancient prejudice. In truth, it could not have been any other way as this was an invention which was about to radically change the transport of people and goods in just a few years – a major driving force of the Industrial Revolution.

Like most innovations, the steam engine and the railways did not appear overnight, but were the fruit of the combined effort of many different people, often working well behind the scenes. The technological advance involved the convergence of diverse experiences and discoveries, ancient knowledge and a fortunate alchemy of historical and economic conditions. Thanks also to the contribution of a few men of genius, this invention was to change the course of history.

> *The invention of railway was fundamental for the development of the industrial revolution.*

Since ancient times, man knew that wheels worked best on flat and smooth surfaces. The Romans thus paved their main highways, firstly in Italy and then in the rest of Europe. They used two rows of stone slabs the same distance apart as the wheels of their chariots. It is interesting to notice how the grooves left over time by the wheels of these chariots, measured in Pompeii, are only a fifth of an inch closer together than the normal railway standard, called the gauge, which is the distance between the internal sides of the rails.

In the 17th century, the Alsatian miners of Leberthal transported the coal from the mines on carts with flanged wheels that ran on wooden rails. The use of these technical expedients to alleviate miners' work was to spread quickly in the following decades, especially in England. In 1676, Roger North described with particular detail this technological breakthrough. He pointed out how just one horse was able to pull four or five wagons, each weighing about a ton. This is possible because the reduction in the pulling power necessary to move a vehicle is proportional to the drop in friction between the wheels and the ground. Rails with their perfectly smooth and uniform rolling surface carry out this task perfectly.

19 TOP TROLLEYS, WHICH MOVED ON SIMPLE WOODEN RAILS INSIDE THE MINES, WERE ALREADY BEING USED IN 1700, AS CAN BE SEEN IN THIS PERIOD ENGRAVING WHICH ILLUSTRATES DIFFERENT STAGES OF COAL MINING.

When the steel industry began to develop, it was logical to substitute the wooden rails, which would deteriorate quickly, with metal ones. These metal rails were first made from cast iron and then iron. In 1776 in Sheffield, England, they began to make rails with an L-shaped cross-section: the wheels of the wagons sat on the horizontal part and were kept in place by the vertical flange.

Perhaps it was because these first railroad tracks were made for the already existing wagons that the normal distance between rails was set at four feet and eight and a half inches. This became the normal gauge of English railways and then of the rest of the world. Rails were then to take on the mushroom shape, which we all know today (probably the first were those made by William Jessop in the Loughborough mine in 1789).

The system first developed inside the mines and then from the mines to the river ports with teams of horses pulling the loads along.

1803 was an important year in railroad history: on July 24 the Surrey Iron Railway was inaugurated, becoming the first public railway in the world with parliamentary concession. The commission was in favor of the Croydon, Merstham and Godston Railway and dated May 1, 1801. It granted permission for the construction of a railway powered by animals from Wandsworth Wharf on the Thames to Croydon. The service was meant for goods alone, but on the occasion of what we would now call a test run, a single horse managed to pull a convoy weighing 60 tons along the six-mile (10-km) track, carrying over 50 people. The chronicles of the time do not, however, tell us in what condition the poor creature arrived.

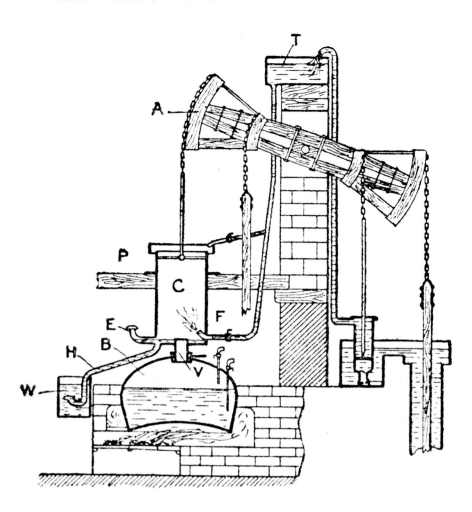

and realize another ancient human aspiration, that of making inanimate objects move by themselves. That was how Frenchman Nicolas Joseph Cugnot in 1769 came to build his "steam wagon." It looks like a jalopy to us today but at the time it must have seemed a technological wonder. His steam wagon had a spherical copper boiler under which two cylinders operated in direct connection with the wheels. The vehicle rested on three wheels and was rather difficult to handle. In fact, on the day of its public presentation in Paris, it went out of control and crashed into a brick wall, thus quashing any hopes for glory its unfortunate inventor may have had.

22 TOP IN THIS PERIOD DRAWING, THE WORKINGS OF THE STEAM MACHINE, INVENTED BY THOMAS NEWCOMEN, ARE SCHEMATICALLY ILLUSTRATED. THE PISTON'S ALTERNATIVE MOVEMENT ALLOWED THE PUMPING OF WATER FROM MINES.

So far, we have seen how the railway came to be, but the invention was not to become revolutionary until they found a way to substitute animal power. This is where we have to take a step back. At the beginning of 1700 Thomas Newcomen, by applying the studies of Frenchman Papin on the transformation of the energy contained in vapor into mechanical work, was able to build the first true steam machine, whose main elements were a boiler, a cylinder, and a rocker arm. The vapor produced by the boiler would lift the piston in the cylinder, which would then be hit by a jet of cold water which rising, it allowed in below. This would draw it down again, thus causing the rocker arm to oscillate. This rudimental machine was immediately applied in mines where it was used to pump out water. Thanks to this practical application its use became widespread in a short time, unlike many unused experiments.

Much later on, in 1765, a certain James Watt was asked to repair one of these machines, kept in the Glasgow University Museum, in Scotland. Watt, however, didn't stop at getting Newcomen's machine back into working order. After four years' work, he developed a much more efficient and economical prototype, capable of performing four times more work with the same amount of fuel. Watt's steam engine left the mines and became widespread in many factories all over England, contributing substantially to the take off of what would then be called the Industrial Revolution.

It was inevitable that amid this fervor of innovation, curiosity, and experimentation that someone would try to use Watt's steam engine to try

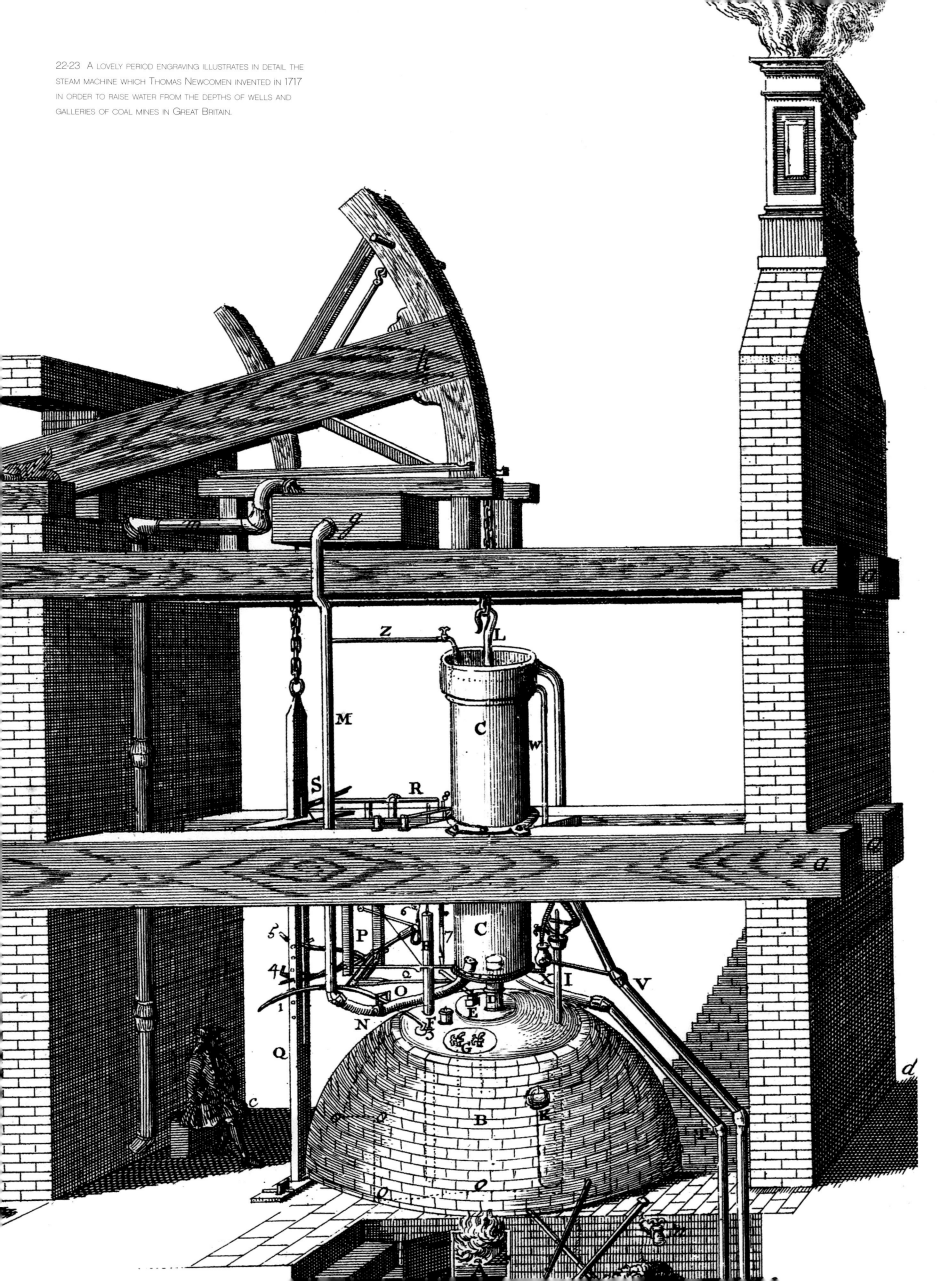

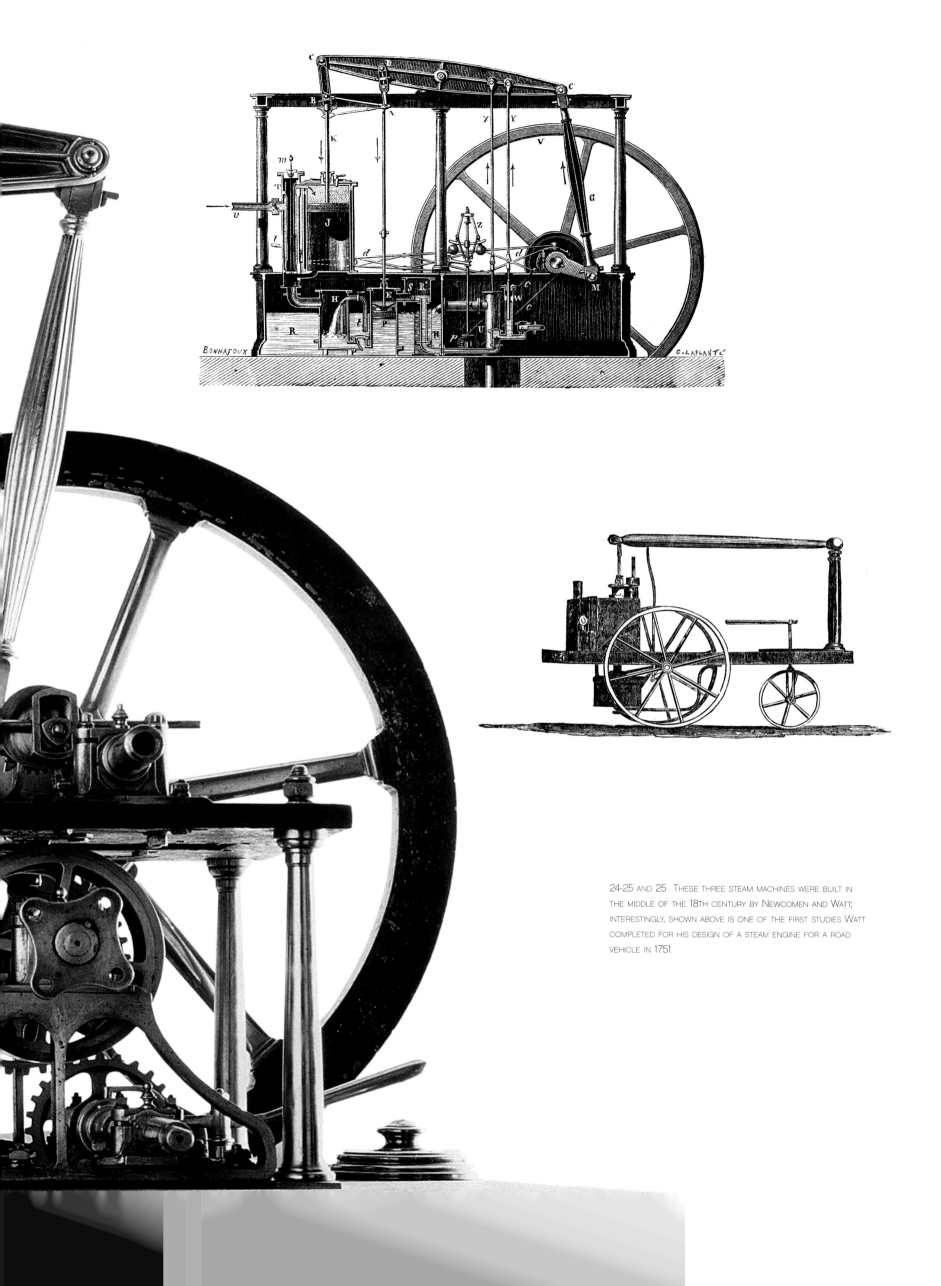

24-25 and 25 These three steam machines were built in the middle of the 18th century by Newcomen and Watt; interestingly, shown above is one of the first studies Watt completed for his design of a steam engine for a road vehicle in 1751.

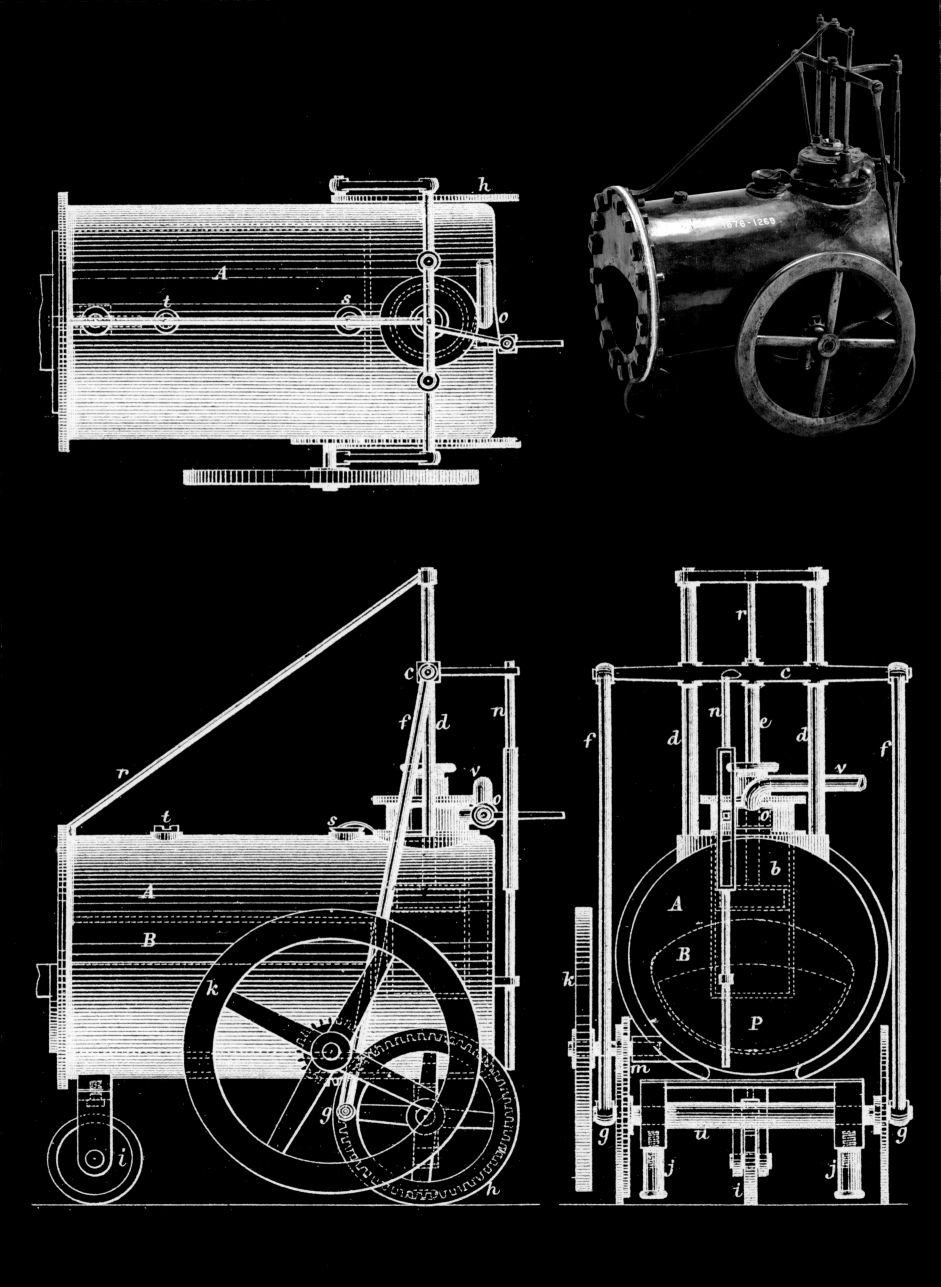

28 RICHARD TREVITHICK
DESIGNED, AT THE START OF
THE 1800s, VARIOUS STEAM-
POWERED VEHICLES, LIKE
THIS ROAD LOCOMOTIVE,
BAPTIZED KENSINGTON,
FROM WHICH THE SAME
INVENTOR CREATED A
PERFECTLY FUNCTIONAL
SMALLER MODEL.

29 TOP IN 1812, JOHN
BLENKINSOP DESIGNED THIS
LOCOMOTIVE WHICH MOVED
THANKS TO A RACK AND PINION
SYSTEM FOR THE MINES OF
MIDDLETON, CLOSE TO LEEDS,
WHERE HE WORKED. THE
MODEL, IN A SCALE OF 1:8,
IS AT THE NATIONAL RAILWAY
MUSEUM OF YORK.

29 BOTTOM THE RACK AND
PINION LOCOMOTIVE INVENTED
BY BLENKINSOP IS HERE
PORTRAYED AS IT HAULS
WAGONS LOADED WITH COAL:
THE SYSTEM ALLOWED THE
MOVING OF TRAINS WHICH
WEIGHED MORE THAN
100 TONS.

However, the success of the concept was undeniable, and in 1804, a few months after the opening of the first horse-led public railway in late 1803, Richard Trevithick presented the first true and proper steam railway locomotive. He had begun working on the project in 1800 and a year later had produced a prototype for travel on normal roads. The local inhabitants, in Cornwall, called it Capitan Dick's Puffer. In 1803 Trevithick had devised a locomotive for the Coalbrookdale ironworks, in Shropshire, but the project was never pursued. The vehicle must have been quite similar to that which a year later began regular service along the roughly 10 miles (16 km) of track at the Penny-Darren ironworks in Wales, where it happily drew loads of over 20 tons. Trevithick's engine had just one big cylinder and a huge flywheel, which, through a series of cogwheels, powered the left-hand wheels, leaving the ones on the right free. The driver did not board the vehicle but would walk alongside it.

To publicize his invention, the Cornish genius, decided to take it to London in 1808 and set up an attraction near the current Euston Square. So a

circular railway was built inside a fenced area. The new model demonstrated on this occasion ran at a good 13 mph (20 km/h), pulling a wagon adapted for the railway track. This new machine was called Catch-me-who-can. People could watch the show for just one shilling and even have a ride on it. The prodigious vehicle attracted thousands, but when one of the rails broke and the machine de-railed the exhibition was ended.

Trevithick, who was by no means a businessman, lacking confidence and financial means, at that point abandoned his research. But it is only fitting to point out that he is the real father of the steam locomotive. He was the first to use high-pressure steam and the turbulence of the vapor in the chimney to increase suction in the boiler and recover the steam. In the immediately following years, another two inventors made primitive steam locomotives which more or less worked. From 1812, Mattew Murray and John Blenkinsop assembled various advanced locomotive models using the combination of a cogwheel and a rack for the Middleton Colliery Railway.

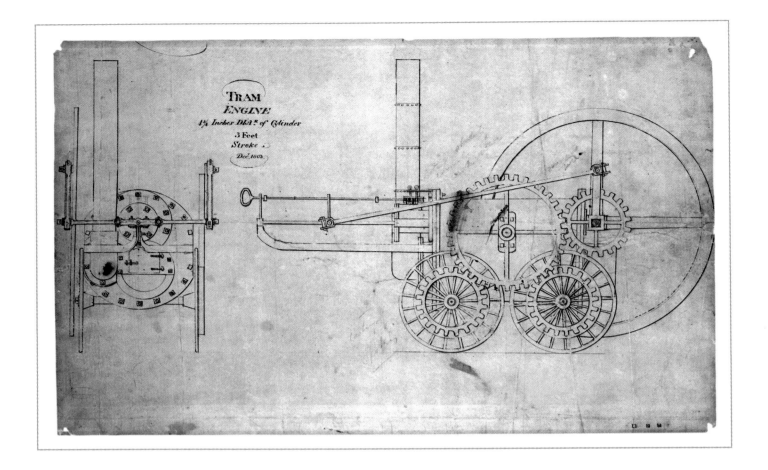

30 TOP, BOTTOM AND 31 TOP THREE ORIGINAL DESIGNS OF THE FIRST STEAM LOCOMOTIVES CREATED
AT THE START OF THE 1800 BY RICHARD TREVITHICK; THE CORNISH INVENTOR WAS THE FIRST TO USE
HIGH-PRESSURE STEAM, OVERCOMING THE TECHNICAL CONSTRAINTS OF THE BOILERS OF THOSE TIMES.

31 BOTTOM THE FIRST STEAM LOCOMOTIVE WHICH MOVED ON RAILS WAS THE ONE CONSTRUCTED BY
RICHARD TREVITHICK FOR THE IRON FOUNDRIES OF PENNY-DARREN IN WALES; THE MODEL WAS BUILT
USING SOME OF THE ORIGINAL DESIGNS MADE BY TREVITHICK IN 1803.

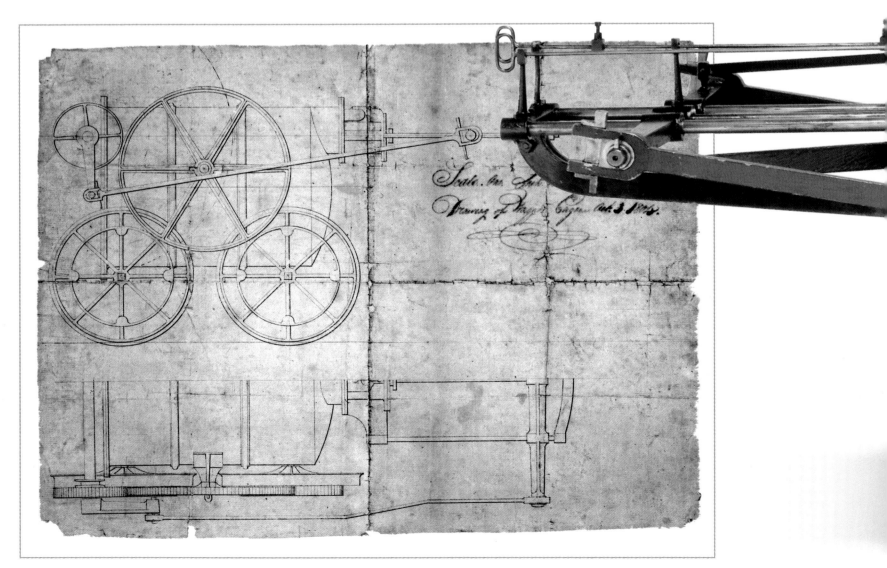

32-33 IN 1808, EUSTON SQUARE, LONDON, TREVITHICK CREATED A CIRCULAR TRACK WHERE, WITH HIS LATEST LOCOMOTIVE BAPTIZED "CATCH ME WHO CAN," HE HAULED A CARRIAGE ON WHICH ANYONE COULD RIDE BY PAYING A SHILLING.

32 BOTTOM EDWARD EVERETT WINCHELL'S DRAWING SHOWS RICHARD TREVETHICK AT THE CONTROL OF HIS STEAM LOCOMOTIVE "CATCH ME WHO CAN" WITH WHICH, FOR FOUR WEEKS, HE AMAZED LONDONERS AS HE TRAVELED ON THE EUSTON SQUARE CIRCUIT.

33 TOP A NEWSPAPER OF THE PERIOD ADVERTISES THE "PORTABLE" STEAM MACHINE OF TREVETHICK "CATCH ME WHO CAN" AND SUMMARIZED THE REVOLUTIONARY CHARACTERISTICS OF THE LOCOMOTIVE WITH THE SLOGAN "MECHANICAL STRENGTH SUBJUGATES ANIMAL SPEED."

33 BOTTOM THE NATIONAL RAILWAY MUSEUM DISPLAYS THIS 1:1 SCALE RECONSTRUCTION OF THE LOCOMOTIVE FOR WHICH RICHARD TREVITHICK, IN 1808, DESIGNED A SPECTACULAR CIRCUIT IN LONDON, NEAR THE PRESENT-DAY EUSTON SQUARE.

TREVITHICKS,
PORTABLE STEAM ENGINE.

Catch me who can.

Mechanical Power Subduing
Animal Speed.

THE "PUFFING BILLY" LOCOMOTIVE.

SCALE 1½ INCH: = 1 FOOT.

Side Elevation.

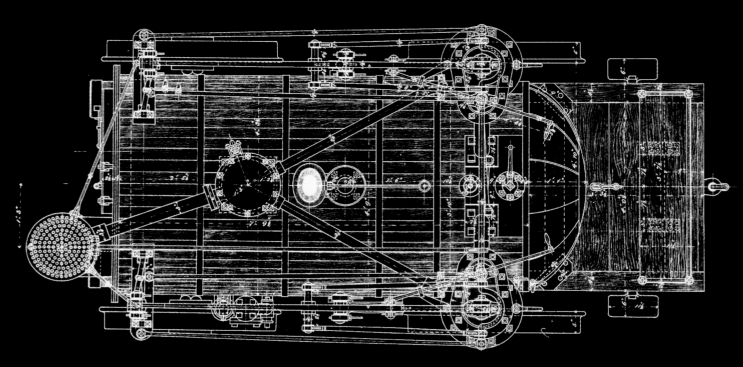

Plan.

Thomas Coates
22nd August 1892

William Hedley and Cristopher Blackett in 1813 built an engine for the Wylam Colliery Railway, which went down in history thanks to the nickname given it by the miners – Puffing Billy. The nickname was due to the puff of smoke and vapor that it would emit at every piston cycle. Hedley in fact immediately understood the advantage that using the suction through the funnel gave to the furnace. At variance with other pioneers, he was also, and rightly, convinced that the locomotive's traction could be transferred to the rails without having to use cogwheels and rail racks. The Puffing Billy is now kept in the London Science Museum after a long career. A photograph taken in 1862 shows it still in service.

34 THE TECHNICAL DRAWING IS OF "PUFFING BILLY," THE LOCOMOTIVE WHICH WILLIAM HEDLEY BUILT IN 1813 FOR THE FIVE-MILE-LONG RAILWAY WHICH CONNECTED THE COAL MINES OF WYLAM TO THE DOCKS AT LEMINGTON ON TYNE.

35 THE 1813 "PUFFING BILLY" IS THE OLDEST ORIGINAL STEAM LOCOMOTIVE STILL IN EXISTENCE AND IS PRESERVED AT THE NATIONAL RAILWAY MUSEUM AT YORK. IT WAS KEPT IN REGULAR SERVICE UNTIL 1861.

GEORGE STEPHENSON.

FIRST LOCOMOTIVE ENGINE.

Finally come to George Stephenson, generally credited as the inventor of the steam locomotive, to the point that he alone is awarded the honor and glory of this extraordinary discovery. Around 1814, the first locomotive built by Stephenson was working in the Killingworth colliery, running four miles uphill with a train of eight wagons carrying 40 tons of coal. The locomotive was baptized Blucher from the name of an important Prussian general also famous in England. But who was George Stephenson? He came from humble origins, learning to read and write at night school at 18. He soon showed a passion for mechanics and at age twenty was employed as an blacksmith in a Newcastle mine, doing odd jobs in his little spare time to improve on his meager salary. In the mine where he worked, there was a Newcomen steam engine used for pumping water out, which had been broken down for a long time. Well, in just five days, the young blacksmith got it working again. He was so impressed and fascinated by the machine that the encounter led him to become the most genial and capable locomotive builder of his time.

After his Blucher locomotive of 1814, Stephenson built other, better ones. But they all remained within colliery grounds until Edward Pease, a local mine owner asked for and obtained government permission to modify the 24-mile (38-km) horse-drawn railway between Darlington and Stockton on Tees for use with a steam engine. A public limited company was set up for the enterprise, funds were collected from the local population and George Stephenson was named chief technical officer of the operation.

On September 27, 1825 a crowd of curious on-lookers witnessed the departure of the first train, which was preceded for safety by a man on horseback. The convoy was led by a steam engine especially made by Stephenson and simply called "Locomotion." It was the first of a new breed. The journey was a success with the Locomotion personally driven by its inventor. Its average speed was 6 mph (9 km/h) with 33 small wagons loaded with coal and flour in tow, as well as a few hundred people who had enthusiastically climbed on the convoy. According to the chronicles of the time, the train weighed just under 100 tons and reached a peak speed of 15 mph (24 km/h).

A new era was born – railway travel. At this point, a brief description of the little Locomotion is necessary. It weighed just 8 tons and had a 0-4-0 configuration (technical term indicating the disposition of leading and driving wheels of railways vehicles). This numerical sequence indicates the succesin of leading whells and driving wheels starting from the front of the locomotive. Therefore 0 indicates no leading wheels, 4 the number of driving wheels, those moved by vapor power transferred via rods, 0 again stands for no rear leading wheels. The engine was made with two internal cylinders of 9.5 by 24 inches and the maximum pressure

in the boiler was only 50 lb per square inch. All in all, it was a locomotive, adopting technical solutions which were in part already surpassed at the time. The cylinders were still positioned vertically and the boiler was not tubular yet. Innovations that Stephenson introduced a few years later in his "Rocket."

Notwithstanding its initial success, though, the Stockton-Darlington service remained predominantly dedicated to the transportation of goods. The public still feared, with justification, that the locomotive might explode. So the passenger service still relied, in those years, on horsepower. Locomotion remained in service until 1846. All taken into account, the Stockton and Darlington became an organizational model that was to become typical of all railways in the word. It was divided into three divisions, rails and fixtures, locomotives and vehicles, and traffic. Within each division there was a rigid hierarchy establishing duties and responsibilities of each employee.

38-39 This impressive drawing dating around 1820, illustrates a conjoined study by George Stephenson and William Losh, proprietors of the iron foundries of Newcastle, for a steam locomotive still with vertical cylinders and balancers.

DESIGN of

LOCOM

LOSH and STEPHE...

...TIVE STEAM ENGINE

Scale of Feet.

BORN
JUNE 9TH, 1781.

DIED
AUG. 12TH, 1848.

Geo. Stephenson

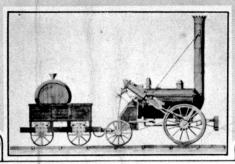

THE "ROCKET" BUILT BY R. STEPHENSON & Co. FOR
THE LIVERPOOL & MANCHESTER RAILWAY IN 1829.

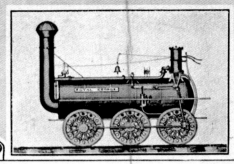

THE "ROYAL GEORGE" BUILT BY T. HACKWORTH
IN 1827. THE FIRST ENGINE WITH THE STEAM BLAST.

Stockton & Darlington Railway.

The Company's COACH

CALLED THE

EXPERIMENT,

Which commenced Travelling on MONDAY, the 10th of OCTO-
BER, 1825, will continue to run from *Darlington* to *Stockton,*
and from *Stockton* to *Darlington* every Day, [Sunday's excepted]
setting off from the DEPOT at each place, at the times specified
at under, (viz.):—

ON MONDAY,

From *Stockton* at half-past 7 in the Morning, and will reach *Darlington* about
half-past 9; the Coach will set off from the latter place on its return at 3 in the
Afternoon, and reach *Stockton* about 5.

TUESDAY,

From *Stockton* at 3 in the Afternoon, and will reach *Darlington* about 5.

On the following Days, viz.:—

WEDNESDAY, THURSDAY & FRIDAY,

From *Darlington* at half-past 7 in the Morning, and will reach *Stockton* about
half-past 9; the Coach will set off from the latter place on its return at 3 in the
Afternoon, and reach *Darlington* about 5.

SATURDAY,

From *Darlington* at 1 in the Afternoon, and will reach *Stockton* about 3.

Passengers to pay 1s. each, and will be allowed a Package of not exceeding
14lb. all above that weight to pay at the rate of 2d. per Stone extra.
Carriage of small Parcels 3d. each. The Company will not be accountable for
Parcels of above £5 Value, unless paid for as such.

Mr RICHARD PICKERSGILL at his Office in Commercial Street,
Darlington; and Mr TULLY at Stockton, will for the present receive any
Parcels and Book Passengers.

THE FIRST RAILWAY TIME BILL,
OCTOBER 10TH, 1825.

THE FIRST LOCOMOTIVE ENGINE EMPLOYED ON A PUBLIC RAILWAY.
THIS ENGINE WAS BUILT BY GEO. STEPHENSON IN 1825. AND CONTINUED
TO RUN ON THE STOCKTON & DARLINGTON RAILWAY UNTIL 1850.

BORN
JUNE 22ND, 1799.

DIED
FEB. 8TH, 1872.

OPENING OF THE FIRST PUBLIC RAILWAY THE STOCKTON & DARLINGTON.
SEPTEMBER 27TH. 1825.

THE "EXPERIMENT"
FIRST RAILWAY PASSENGER COACH 1825.

THE FIRST RAILWAY SUSPENSION BRIDGE
ERECTED OVER THE RIVER TEES IN 1830.

Published by the Proprietors
E. D. WALKER & WILSON, DARLINGTON.

PIONEER OF THE RAILWAY SYSTEM.

BORN
MAY 31ST. 1787.

DIED
JULY 31ST. 1858.

Edward Pease

PROGRAMME OF OPENING OF FIRST
PUBLIC RAILWAY. SEPT. 27TH. 1825.

PIONEER OF THE RAILWAY SYSTEM.

BORN
NOV. 30TH. 1785.

DIED
JUNE 11TH. 1867

OPENING OF THE FIRST ENGLISH RAIL·WAY BETWEEN STOCKTON AND DARLIN[...]

40-41 THE OPENING OF THE STOCKTON TO DARLINGTON RAILWAY IN 1825 WAS CELEBRATED WITH THIS ELABORATE LITHOGRAPH WHICH ALSO ILLUSTRATED THREE OF THE FIRST LOCOMOTIVES, THE LOCOMOTION, IN THE MIDDLE AND, ABOVE, THE ROCKET AND THE ROYAL GEORGE.

41 AN 1830 COLORED PICTURE DESCRIBES THE OPENING TO TRAFFIC OF THE FIRST RAILWAY LINE, THE STOCKTON TO DARLINGTON, IN 1825. THE DEPICTION TRANSMITS WELL THE ENTHUSIASM AND CURIOSITY OF THE SPECTATORS WHO ATTENDED THE HISTORICAL EVENT.

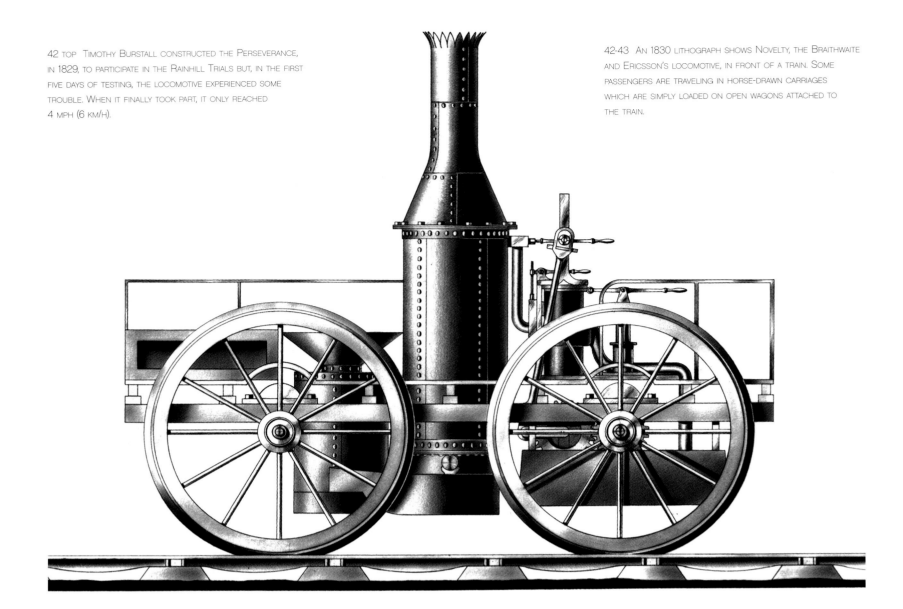

The first true and proper railway line, built for the exclusive use of steam locomotives, was the 1830 Liverpool-Manchester. In its construction archaic technical standards, typical of colliery railways, were abandoned. The flattest possible route was studied, with landfills and bridges to overcome natural obstacles and inclines. Not everyone was favorable to the use of steam locomotives in those years. Partly because there were still enormous technical problems and partly for economic reasons, for example, some categories of workers were afraid of losing their jobs. Just think of the boatmen (the railway was thought of explicitly to substitute the transport of cotton via the canal, being much faster than the barges) as well as coachmen and carters. To demonstrate the efficiency of the locomotives, in 1829 the famous Rainhill trials were organized, offering 500 pounds sterling for the winning machine.

The competition, which was the first public tender to choose the supplier of railway material, set only a few minimum requirements: it should reach a speed of at least 10 mph (16 km/h) pulling 20 tons, and not weigh more than 6 tons. The contest was held on October 6, 1829, in Rainhill, about four miles from Manchester with four steam locomotives and a horse-powered one.

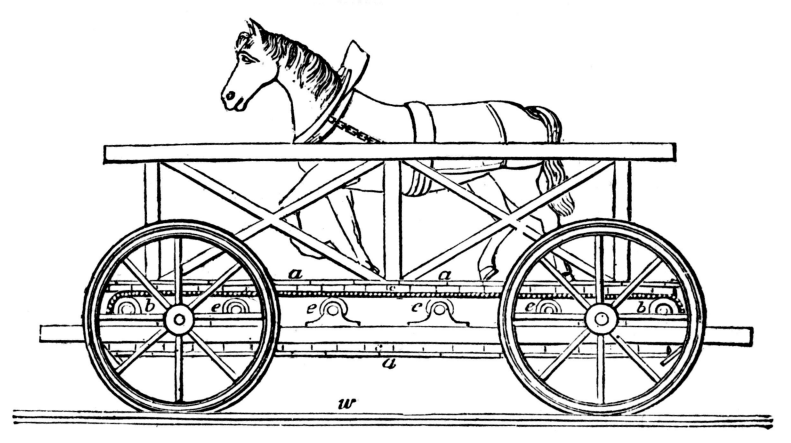

(Brandreth's Patent Cyclopede. 1829.)

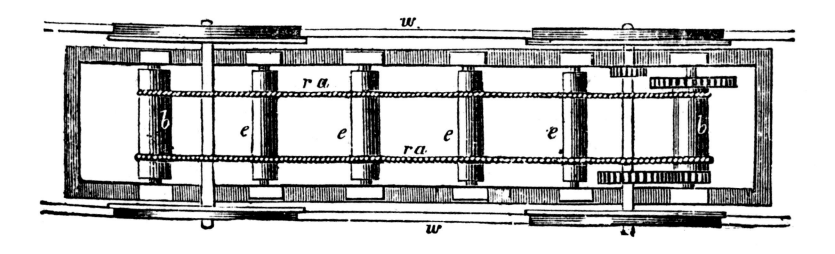

43 TOP AND CENTER CYCLOPED, THOMAS BRANDRETH'S HORSE-POWERED LOCOMOTIVE,
PARTICIPATED IN THE RAINHILL TRIALS, A COMPETITION TO SELECT THE LOCOMOTIVE TYPE FOR THE
MANCHESTER-LIVERPOOL RAILWAY, BUT OBVIOUSLY LOST AGAINST STEAM MACHINES.

44 top A color lithograph of that era shows "Rocket," George Stephenson's steam locomotive, winner of the Rainhill Trials which took place in 1829, surrounded by the curious and admiring spectators.

44 bottom and 45 The original 1829 "Rocket" is now preserved in the National Railway Museum of York; unfortunately, after it was saved from scrapping in 1862, the historic relic was in poor general condition, and its tender and several other parts were missing.

George Stephenson – helped by his son Robert – entered his new invention called the Rocket. John Braithwaite and John Ericsson participated with the Novelty. Timothy Hackworth with his Sans Pareil. Thimoty Burstall with Perseverance and Thomas Shaw Brandreth competed with his Cycloped, which was a strange machine using two horses on a kind of rolling carpet.

Both the Cycloped and the Perseverance didn't meet the required speed, whilst the Sans Pareil was over the permitted weight. That left only the Novelty and the Rocket. The latter was slower but it won the competition by proving to be far more reliable. The Rocket became the real forerunner of all steam locomotives, being the first to use all their fundamental mechanisms: the tubular boiler, the forced draught activated by the vapor exhaust, the distribution of vapor to the cylinders with a system of eccentrics.

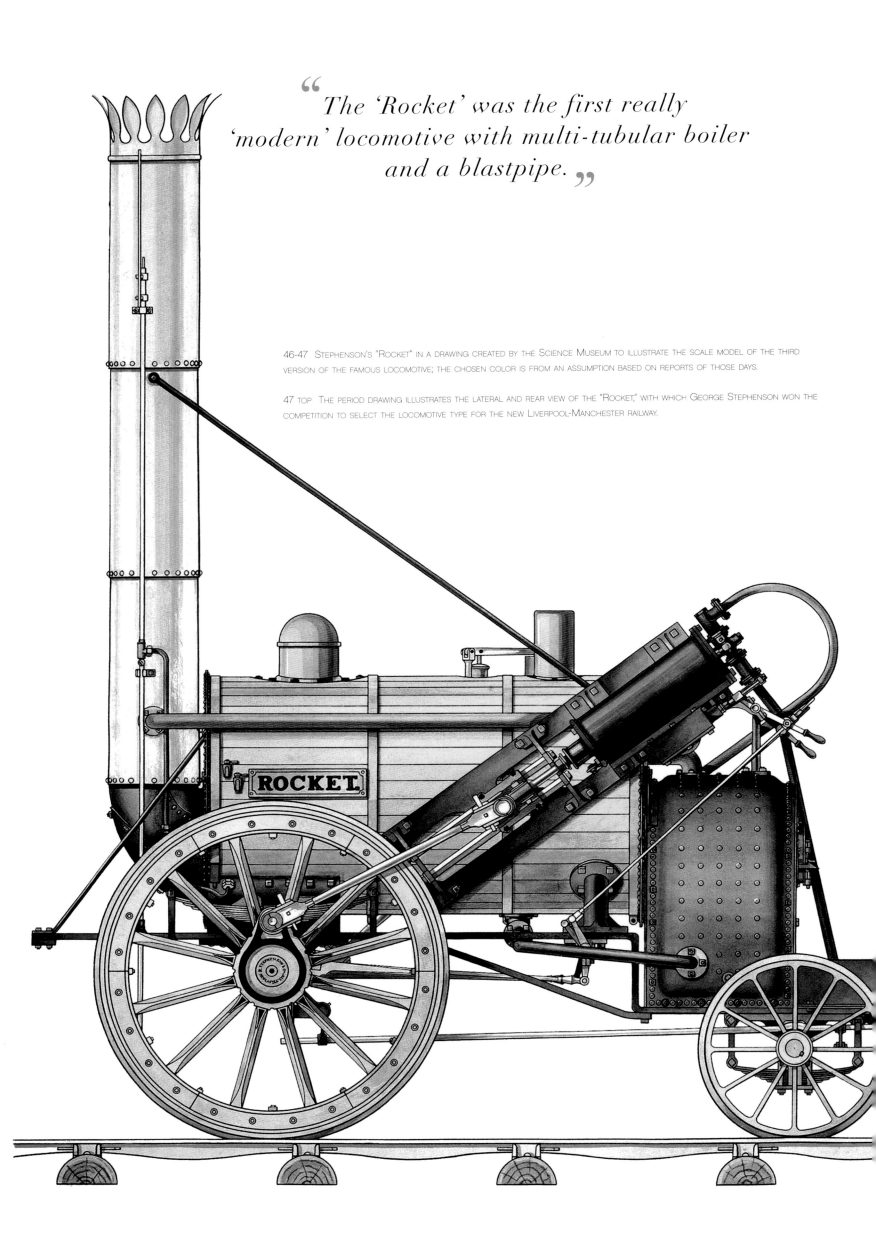

The 'Rocket' was the first really 'modern' locomotive with multi-tubular boiler and a blastpipe.

46-47 STEPHENSON'S "ROCKET" IN A DRAWING CREATED BY THE SCIENCE MUSEUM TO ILLUSTRATE THE SCALE MODEL OF THE THIRD VERSION OF THE FAMOUS LOCOMOTIVE; THE CHOSEN COLOR IS FROM AN ASSUMPTION BASED ON REPORTS OF THOSE DAYS.

47 TOP THE PERIOD DRAWING ILLUSTRATES THE LATERAL AND REAR VIEW OF THE "ROCKET," WITH WHICH GEORGE STEPHENSON WON THE COMPETITION TO SELECT THE LOCOMOTIVE TYPE FOR THE NEW LIVERPOOL-MANCHESTER RAILWAY.

ROCKET

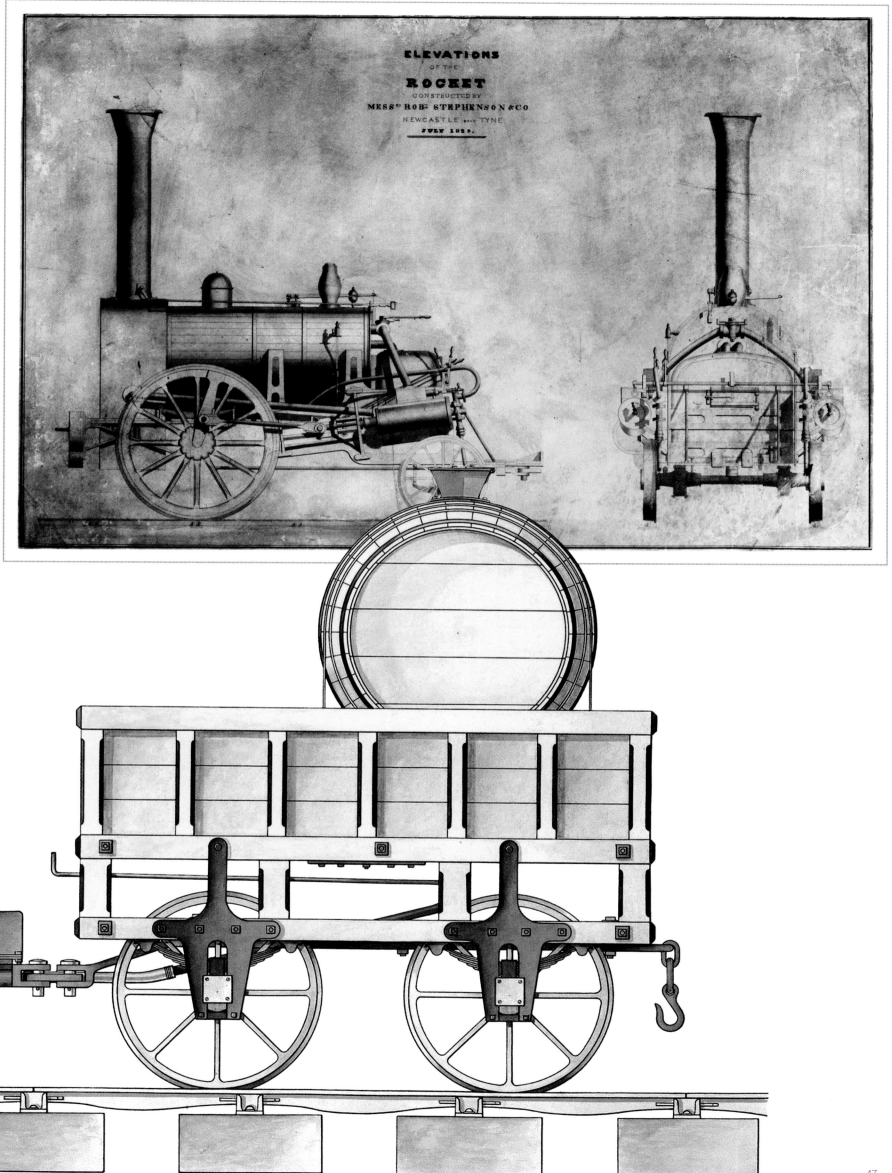

ELEVATIONS
OF THE
ROCKET
CONSTRUCTED BY
MESS^{RS} ROB^T STEPHENSON & CO
NEWCASTLE upon TYNE
JULY 1829.

A First Class Train, with the Mail.

A Second Class Train for Passengers.

A Train of Waggons with Goods &c.

A Train of Carriages with Cattle.

The Liverpool-Manchester line, inaugurated about a year after the Rainhill trials on September 15, 1830 was also the prototype of modern railway lines. The Stephensons were asked to design the route. This was made with extremely advanced techniques for the time: big stations, 63 bridges and viaducts, slopes of less than 3 to 1000 and even a tunnel two miles long. Unfortunately, the day of the inauguration was saddened by the first fatal accident in the history of railways: distracted by all the enthusiasm, a Member of Parliament, William Huskisson, crossed the track to speak to the Duke of Wellington just as the Rocket was arriving. He died in the accident.

After just one year of service, the number of passengers was ten times more than expected, earning its builders a good £14,000. All doubts about the future of railways vanished and in the space of just four years, 33 railway companies had been set up. By 1844 there were nearly 2500 miles of railroads, with another 5000 miles laid down in 1846 alone. By the end of the 1880s, there were about 18,640 miles of railroads in Great Britain..

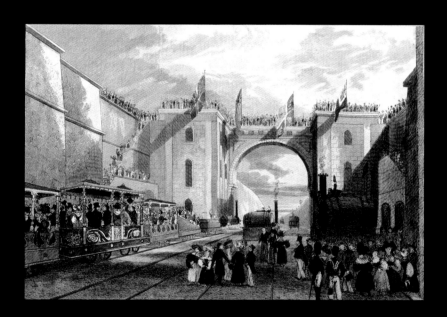

48-49 AN 1834 LITHOGRAPH SHOWS FOUR LIVERPOOL-MANCHESTER TRAINS; THE LOCOMOTIVES IN FRONT OF THE TRAINS ARE, FROM TOP TO BOTTOM, THE LIVERPOOL, THE FURY, THE NORTH STAR AND THE JUPITER. IN THOSE YEARS, EVERY LOCOMOTIVE WAS BAPTIZED WITH ITS OWN NAME.

49 IN A COLOR PICTURE PUBLISHED IN JANUARY 1ST 1831, A CURIOUS CROWD IS SEEN ATTENDING THE INAUGURATION OF THE NEW LIVERPOOL-MANCHESTER RAILWAY, THE FIRST ONE IN THE WORLD TO CONNECT TWO IMPORTANT CITIES.

THE FIRST RAILWAYS
IN THE WORLD

The success of the railways in Great Britain quickly crossed the Channel and they became widespread both on the European continent and in the New World. It would take dozens of pages to recount the detailed railway developments in each country, so we will limit ourselves to the most important and significant events that took place in those pioneering years.

In Europe, Belgium was the first country to build a line. On May 5, 1835 the 14-mile (22-km) Brussels-Malines line was opened. Its construction was begun in 1832, just two years after the Liverpool-Manchester.

Interestingly, the line was promoted and financed by the state with a law passed in 1834, unlike in Great Britain where it was all left to private companies. Since the beginning of railroad construction there has always been debate about whether state or private finance was the better system. The two organizational models were to be applied alternately in the following years across Europe in nearly every country.

In Belgium, in those years, the Cockerill Company was founded, becoming one of the most important European steam locomotive factories.

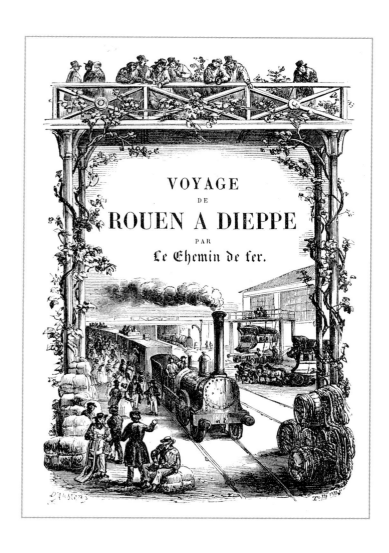

Also in 1835, the Kingdom of Bavaria (Germany wasn't unified until 1871) inaugurated on December 7 the first railway line between Furth and Nuremberg, which was only 4 miles (6 km) long. It was called Ludwigsbahn (Ludwig's Railway) in honor of King Ludwig I. The inaugural train was pulled by a locomotive built by Stephenson, baptized Adler (Eagle). It was to become very famous throughout Germany in the following years. In the German states of the time, the railway caused much interest and attention. In 1837 the Dresden-Leipzig line was opened in Saxony followed in 1838 by the Prussian Berlin-Potsdam line.

Prussia was the first to understand the strategic military importance of the railway and became the nucleus of that highly efficient German railway network, which set an international standard right up until the Second World War. Also in Berlin, in 1837, one of the most famous locomotive factories was established, the Borsig.

In France the first railway was running in 1837, with the opening of the Paris-Rouen line. But there was no particular fervor about the new means of transport. Only in the following years, thanks to a special law of 1842, did a network begin to spread out from the capital.

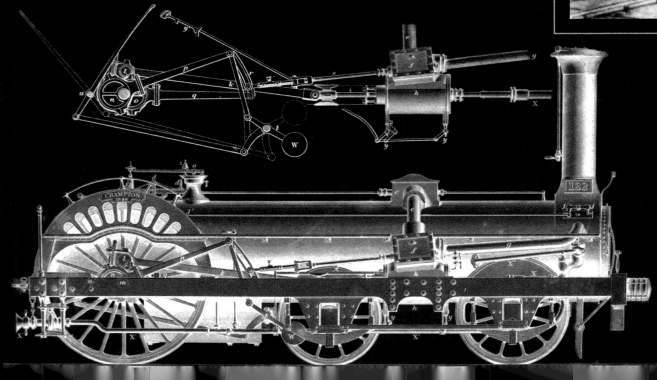

DEPICTED IN THIS PAINTING BY SALVATORE FERGOLA IS THE INAUGURAL TRAIN OF THE NAPLES-PORTICI LINE ARRIVING AT GRANATELLO STATION, WITH THE GULF OF NAPLES IN THE BACKGROUND. THE VESUVIUS LOCOMOTIVE WAS CONSTRUCTED IN BRITAIN.

In Italy the first train ran in the Kingdom of the Two Sicilies. It was October 3, 1839, when the Vesuvio locomotive chugged along the 4.5 miles (7 km) to Portici, then called Granatello. This stretch was the first functional trunk of the line which was supposed to reach Nocera, branching off from Torre Annunziata to Castellamare for a total of about 25.5 miles (41 km). Soon after that, in 1840, the Milan-Monza line opened in what then was the Lombardo Veneto region, and in 1842 the Padua-Mestre service began constructing the first stretch of the Milan-Venice line. Then came the Pisa-Leghorn line in the Grand Duchy of Tuscany in 1844 and the Turin-Moncalieri in 1848. One must naturally remember that in those years Italy hadn't been unified yet and the peninsula was divided up into various little states, most of which created their own rail networks with local

54-55 SALVATORE FERGOLA'S ILLUSTRATION OF THE INAUGURAL TRAIN OF THE NAPLES-PORTICI RAILWAY, WHICH WAS THE FIRST TO BE CONSTRUCTED IN ITALY IN 1839. THE TRAIN'S LOCOMOTIVE WAS THE VESUVIUS, EVEN THOUGH IT WAS LATER CONFUSED WITH ITS TWIN, BAYARD.

or, at best, regional structures. One exception was in the Kingdom of Sardinia, thanks to the foresight of Camillo Benso, Count of Cavour. In his role as head of government, he envisioned from the mid-1800s an organic network for the whole of the Italian peninsula. He understood the need for adequate connections with the other state networks. After 1861, the date of Italian unification, a complex operation of connection and adaptation of the various state networks was carried out. This resulted in the three main national lines running from North to South which to this day form the backbone of the Italian network: the Florence-Rome, the Adriatic, and the Thyrrenan lines. A progressive reduction in the number of railway companies also began and by 1885 there were just two networks, the Adriatic and Mediterranean, which divided the whole peninsula lengthways. The two companies (which, to be precise should also include the Sicilian Rete Sicula and the Ferrovie Reali Sarde in Sardinia) managed Italian railways until 1905, when the government decided to nationalize the whole network giving birth to the FS, the Ferrovie dello Stato. The years between 1885 and 1905 were very profitable all in all, laying the foundations for the "Italian school" which was to gain much success both in the construction of steam locomotives and in the introduction of electric traction for which Italy was the absolute world pioneer.

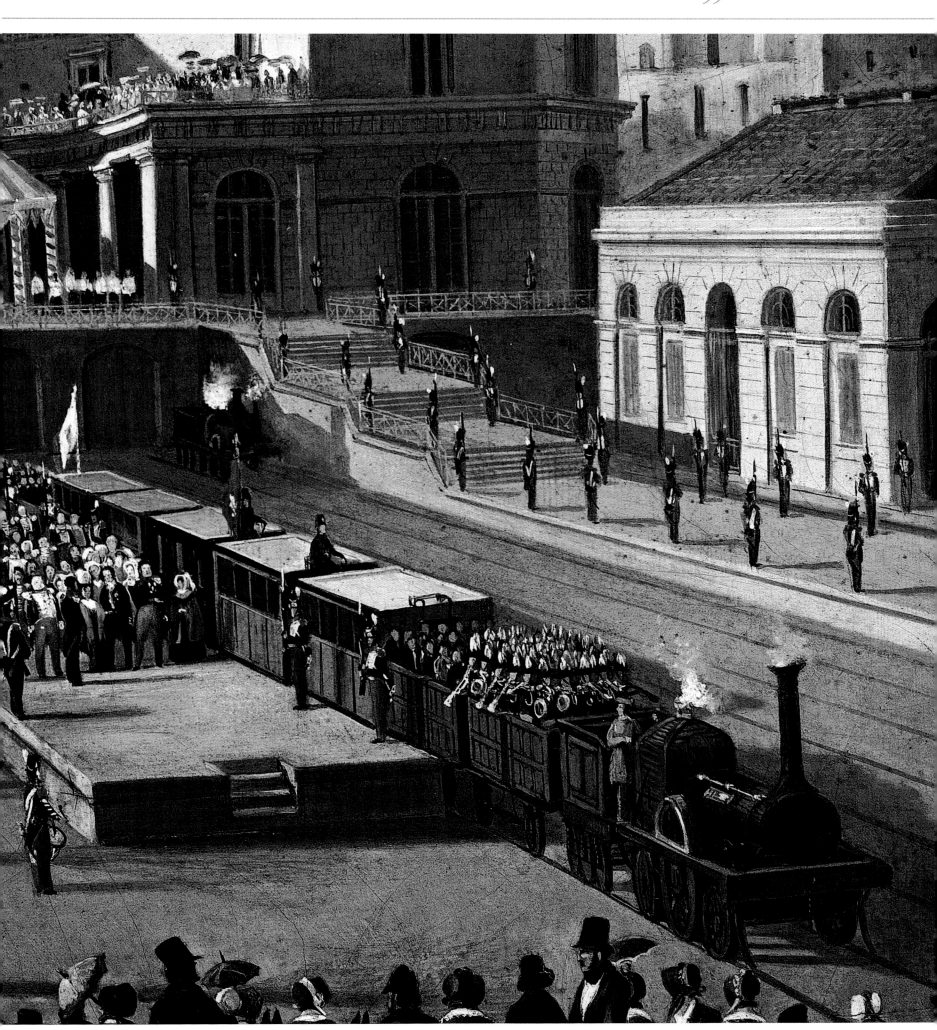

Ankunft der Dampfwagenzüge auf der Kaiser Ferdinands Nordbahn im Bahnhofe zu Brünn bei der Eröffnungsfahrt am 7ten July 1839.

56 TOP A LITHOGRAPH FROM THE PERIOD SHOWS THE ROYAL TRAIN ON THE OCCASION OF THE COMPLETION OF THE KAISER-FERDINANDS-NORDBAHN IN 1839, WHICH CONNECTED VIENNA AND BRNO. THE BUILDING OF THE LINE WAS FINANCED BY THE ROTHSCHILDS.

56-57 THIS COLOR LITHOGRAPH SHOWS THE BARCELONA-MATARO'S INAUGURAL TRAIN ON THE 28TH OF OCTOBER 1848. CURIOUSLY, TWO RAILWAY MEN SIT ON TOP OF THE CARRIAGES' ROOF, AS IF THEY WERE STILL TRAVELING ON A STAGECOACH.

In nearby Austria (still part of the Austrian Empire at the time) the railway began operation in 1837 with the opening of the Floridsdorf-Deutsch Wagram line. It was built and run by Salomon Rotschild. In 1848 the construction of the famous Semmering line began, whose objective was to connect Vienna to Trieste, then the most important port of the Empire. The work took just five years to complete and was a huge enterprise for the time, with a tunnel almost a mile long, and numerous bridges and viaducts.

In the same years, further east, railroads were spreading in Russia. The first line, of about 31 miles (50 km), connected St. Petersburg to Pavlovs. It had a particular characteristic in that the gauge was larger than usual at about 6 ft (1.8 m) instead of 4.7 ft (1.5 m). Experiments with wider gauges had also been carried out in other European nations. In Great Britain, before a government ruling set the gauge at the normal 4.7 ft (1.5 m), quite a network had developed using the wider gauge. The advantage was that of being able to have bigger locomotives with bigger furnaces and boilers, therefore more powerful and faster. On the other hand, wider gauges needed more ample bends, as well as bigger bridges and tunnels with their higher construction costs. The choice of the wide gauge was in those years influenced by military considerations. It had been understood that the railway would be a formidable resource in war, allowing the transport of troops and materiel at hitherto unthinkable speed. Connecting one network to nearby ones was perceived as an advantage for the exchange of goods and people, but a danger in case of war because the enemy could rapidly penetrate a country by using them.

Czarist Russia, therefore, opted for a larger gauge than the rest of Europe. In the construction of the Moscow-St. Petersburg line, which was finished in 1851, they chose a gauge of 5 ft (1.5 m). This was larger than standard, so as to prevent any direct connection with lines in Europe, but close enough to allow the transit of vehicles with a change in axles at special frontier stations. The 5-ft gauge of the Moscow-Petersburg line therefore became the gauge of unified Russia, even though the first connection between the Russian Empire and Europe, the Warsaw-Vienna line, was authorized and built with a normal gauge between 1839 and 1848. But Russia entered railway history with the realization of the fabulous Trans-Siberian Railway, the longest in the world with its 5856 miles (9424 km) of track between Moscow and Vladivostok. It was built between 1891 and 1903 through wild and extremely cold lands, where it was only possible to work a few months a year. An epic work that cost thousands of workers' lives. However, the Trans-Siberian Railway will be dealt with later in the book.

In Switzerland the railroads came much later with the opening in 1847 of the 18.5 miles (30 km) track between Baden and Zurich. This relative delay reflected the diffidence the Swiss had for novelties and in particular for the new method of transport. The locomotive that pulled the first train was a German-built 8-0-4, called the Limmat. But the Swiss remember it by the nickname the line soon acquired, "Spanisch-Brotli Bahn," literally the "Spanish sandwich train." The trains, in fact, delivered the sought-after Baden bakers' rolls to Zurich in just 30 minutes!

A year later, Spain joined the railway club, with the opening of the Barcelona-Mataro line, but it took another ten years for a true and proper network to develop.

In the United States, the development of the railroads was fast and furious. The "Steel Horse" was a fundamental element in the birth of the American confederation and its history is interlinked with that of the conquest of the West. The first steam locomotives to reach the US, in 1829, were built in Britain. They were imported by the Delaware and Hudson Company, in Pennsylvania, which had obtained the concession for building a railway line between Carbondale and Honesdale. The first train to enter commercial service was the Stourbridge Lion locomotive on August 9, 1929. But the debut was on weak rails and the overall construction was not the best. The excessive weight of the English engines caused the rails to break and the service was almost immediately suspended.

The following year, on August 25, the first American locomotive ran on the Baltimore and Ohio Railroad. The Tom Thumb built by Peter Cooper was little more than an experiment and much more primitive than the contemporary English locomotives. The first engine to successfully pull a train of four to five cars at a speed of 25 mph (40 km/h) was the Best Friend of Charleston in 1831, along the South Carolina Railroad, another of the very first private American railways. The first train left the Charleston station on January 15 of that year. Two years later, the track, extended to Hamburg, had reached the remarkable length of 135 miles (217 km), which was the longest track in the world at the time.

The "West Point," the Second Locomotive built i

58-59 TOP THE DE WITT CLINTON, OF THE MOHAWK AND HUDSON RAILROAD, WAS ONE OF THE FIRST LOCOMOTIVES, IN 1831, UNDER REGULAR SERVICE IN THE UNITED STATES. AS FROM 1853, THE RAILWAY LINE BECAME PART OF THE NEW YORK CENTRAL RAILROAD.

58-59 BOTTOM THIS 1877 DRAWING SHOWS THE LOCOMOTIVE "THE WEST POINT," THE SECOND STEAM MACHINE TO BE BUILT IN THE UNITED STATES BY THE WEST POINT FOUNDRY ASSOCIATION, OF NEW YORK CITY IN 1831, A YEAR AFTER THE "BEST FRIEND OF CHARLESTON."

he United States for actual service on a Railroad.

60 top THIS 1840 BALTIMORE AND SUSQUEHANNA RAILROAD'S POSTER ANNOUNCES A NEW DAILY CONNECTION BETWEEN BALTIMORE AND WRIGHTSVILLE; THE TYPICAL AMERICAN "COWCATCHER" ALREADY APPEARS IN THE DRAWING OF THE LOCOMOTIVE.

60 bottom THE DE WITT CLINTON LOCOMOTIVE, OF THE MOHAWK AND HUDSON RAILROAD COMPANY, WAS THE FIRST TO TRAVEL IN THE STATE OF NEW YORK FROM 1831. IT WAS THE FIFTH LOCOMOTIVE TO BE ENTIRELY BUILT IN THE UNITED STATES.

61 THE NEW YORK AND HARLEM RAILROAD ANNOUNCEMENT REPORTS THE CHANGES IN THE TRAIN SCHEDULE, STARTING FROM THE 10TH OF OCTOBER 1848. THE LOCOMOTIVE DRAWN ON THE NOTICE CLOSELY RESEMBLES THE DE WITT CLINTON OF SOME YEARS BEFORE.

NEW-YORK AND HARLEM RAIL ROAD,
DAILY.

FALL ARRANGEMENT.

On and after TUESDAY, OCTOBER 10th, 1848, the Cars will run as follows, until further notice.

TRAINS WILL LEAVE CITY HALL, N. Y., FOR

Harlem & Morrisania			Fordham & William's Bridge.		Hunt's Bridge, Under- hill's & Hart's Corners.		Davis' Brook, Plea- santville, Chapequa, Mount Kisko, Bedford, Mechanicsville, Pur- dy's and Croton Falls.
7 10 A.M.	12	M	7	A.M.	3 30 P.M.	9 A.M.	5 30 P.M.
8 "	2	P.M.	9 "	5 30 "		
9 "	3	"	12	M.	6 30 "	T'kahoe & White Plains	
10 "	4	"				7 A.M.	3 30 P.M.
	5 30	"				9 "	5 30 "
	6 30	"				7 A.M	3 30 P.M.
						9 "	

NOTICE.

Passengers are reminded of the great danger of standing upon the Platforms of the Cars, and hereby notified that the practice is contrary to the rules of the Company, and that they do not admit any responsibility for injury sustained by any Passenger upon the platforms, in case of accident.

RETURNING TO NEW-YORK, WILL LEAVE

Harlem & Morrisania		Hunt's Bridge.		White Plains.		Bedford	
7 08 A.M.	1 10 P.M.	7 50 A.M.	3 15 P.M.	7 15 A.M.	2 45 P.M.	7 55 A.M.	1 55 P.M.
8 "	3 "	Underhill's Road.		8 35 "	5 "		4 25 "
8 20 "	3 45	7 40 A.M.	3 06 P.M.	Davis' Brook.		Mechanicsville.	
9 "	4 "	Tackahoe.		8 26 A.M.	2 35 P.M.	7 45 A.M.	1 45 P.M.
11 "	5 "	7 35 A.M.	3 03 P.M.		4 55 "		4 15 "
	6 "	8 50 "	5 15 "	Pleasantville.		Purdy's	
Fordham & William's Bridge.				8 18 A.M.	2 20 P.M.	7 35 A.M.	1 35 P.M.
					4 48 "		4 05 "
6 45 A.M.	1 15 P.M	Harts Corners.		Mount Kisko.		Croton Falls.	
8 "	3 25 "	7 25 A.M.	2 50 P.M.	8 A.M.	2 P.M.	7 30 A.M.	1 30 P.M.
9 10 "	5 40 "				4 30 "		4 "

The TRAINS FOR HARLEM & MORRISANIA, leaving City Hall at 7,10, 8, 9, 10, 12, 2, 3, 4, and 6.30, and From Morrisania and Harlem at 7.08, 8, 9, 11, 1.40, 3, 4, 5 and 6, will land and receive Passengers at 27th, 42d, 51st, 61st, 79th, 86th, 109th, 115th, 125th and 132d streets.

The 7 A. M. and 3.30 P. M. Trains from New-York to CROTON FALLS and the 7.30 A. M. Train from Croton Falls will not stop between White Plains and New-York, except at Tuckahoe, William's Bridge and Fordham.

A Car will precede each Train 10 minutes, to take up passengers in the City; the last Car will not stop except at Broome street, and 32nd street

FREIGHT TRAINS leave New-York at 9 A. M. & 12 M.; leave CROTON FALLS 7 A. M. & 8 P. M.

On SUNDAYS an Extra Train at 1 o'clock P. M. to Harlem and Morrisania.

Nesbitt, Printer.

62 TOP A CLASSIC "AMERICAN" LOCOMOTIVE WITH WHEEL ARRANGEMENT 4-4-0 STABLING IN FRONT OF A FORT DURING THE YEARS OF THE AMERICAN CIVIL WAR. THE WAR HAD A CONSIDERABLE INFLUENCE ON THE HISTORY OF AMERICAN RAILWAYS.

" *The 'American Type' locomotives contributed in a substantial way to the birth of the United States.* "

The construction of new railroads took off at a remarkable pace after that. In 1840 the network measured a total 2783 miles (4478 km). In the next 20 years, on the eve of the American Civil War, it was more than ten times longer, reaching 30,457 miles (49,000 km). This rapid development had important consequences on the evolution of locomotives and wagons. In contrast to what was taking place in Europe, where builders were very attentive to the quality of the tacks, in North America these were often of poor quality, with cross ties simply resting on the ground with no regard for terrain and not being weighed down. The bends were designed without parabolic connections to the straight parts and without lifting the external rail.

The ride was thus rather bumpy and derailing occurred frequently. In 1832 builders began to examine the problem, working on the trains rather than the tracks, though.

John Jervis, a young engineer of the time, created the Experiment, the first steam locomotive with a leading swiveling truck connected by a fifth wheel. This truck, much freer to rotate and absorb the irregularities of the track than those with traditional loaded axles attached to the chassis, guided the locomotives into bends and improved the ride. A few years later the first steam locomotive with a leading two-axle truck and two engines was born. The 4-4-0, later dubbed the American Type, became the standard model for American locomotives of those decades. It became a part of the collective imagination as it appeared in hundreds of films and images. Perhaps the most memorable example is the film *The General* with Buster Keaton.

Thousands of the American Type were produced, about 25,000 from 1855 to the end of the century. The American railways almost immediately adopted the leading truck for freight and passenger carriages. In Europe, instead, two-axle vehicles were still built for quite some time. Another American invention was the system of automatic hooking between vehicles, which was devised in 1893. It was far more robust than the screw coupling still used today in the Old World. The automatic hooking allowed one to configure much heavier trains, eliminating the dangerous operations in the hands of shunters and replacing the traditional buffers. Also an American development was the compressed air braking system, devised in 1868 by George Westinghouse. This was then used throughout the world, with the exception of Great Britain where until 1960 they used the vacuum brake.

64 The American locomotives, with wheel arrangement 4-4-0, have been rendered famous throughout the world mostly thanks to Buster Keaton's acclaimed film "The General," filmed in 1927 but set in the years of the Civil War.

64-65 In a spectacular scene from "The General" the director and main protagonist, the American actor Buster Keaton, provokes the collapse of a large wooden railway bridge while the steam train is crossing it.

65 bottom The unmistakable Buster Keaton in one of the action-packed scenes shot on board the steam locomotive. In the movie, Keaton becomes involved in a long and spectacular chase between two locomotives.

Even though railroads developed rapidly in North America, it took the onset of the American Civil War in 1861 to bring about the first trans-continental line. Abraham Lincoln signed the decree authorizing its construction in 1862, because of the need to connect with California and the western territories. Two companies were assigned the colossal task: Union Pacific Railroad for the line from the East to the western frontier of the State of Nevada; and Central Pacific Railroad for the tract eastwards from California.

The construction, which began a few years late because of the civil war, was completed in record time and on May 10, 1869, the two lines met at Promontory Point in Utah where the event was celebrated with a joyous ceremony. Two American Type locomotives, Union Pacific's Pride of the Prairie and Central Pacific's Jupiter met there face to face. In the space between the two cowcatchers the celebrations were concluded with the placing of the last two nails in the last cross tie. One was silver, the other gold. The lines had finally met making the overall length of the track 1780 miles (2860 km). To favor the construction of the line, the two companies were given huge incentives, such as the ten miles (16 km) of land on either side of the railway and up to $ 50,000 for every mile of track laid down. Because of the scarcity of local labor, thousands of Chinese workers were brought over.

This first trans-continental line was soon followed by others which favored the integration of the western States. These were built by famous companies such as Burlington and Chicago and North Western. These, too, were richly sponsored by the central government.

In Canada reailroads also developed quickly, starting like in the US in the east and spreading westwards. The first railroad in public service dates back to 1836 when on July 24 the connection between La Prairie and Saint John was inaugurated. The line between the two main cities of the east, Monteral and Toronto was opened in 1856.

66-67 IN THIS HISTORIC IMAGE, WORKERS AND RAILWAY MEN CELEBRATE THE UNION BETWEEN THE CENTRAL PACIFIC AND UNION PACIFIC LINES AT PROMONTORY IN UTAH ON THE 10TH OF MAY 1869. THE FIRST NORTH AMERICAN TRANSCONTINENTAL RAILWAY IS COMPLETE.

68 THE EXPRESS TRAIN NO. 93 OF THE CANADIAN PACIFIC RAILWAY WAS CAUGHT IN THIS PHOTOGRAPH WHILE IT CROSSES THE MAGNIFICENT HORSEHOE TRESTLE (A WOODEN BRIDGE IN THE SHAPE OF A HORSESHOE) IN THE VICINITY OF SCHREIBER IN ONTARIO AROUND 1890.

68-69 A TRAIN LOADED WITH WORKERS STOPPED HALFWAY ALONG THE FRASE RIVER'S VALLEY IN BRITISH COLUMBIA. THE RAILWAY PRACTICALLY PASSES CONTINUALLY OVER HIGH WOODEN BRIDGES AND THROUGH LONG TUNNELS.

*"The transcontinental lines,
especially in the United States, paved
the way towards the West for the pioneers."*

70-71 A CANADIAN PACIFIC TRAIN STOPS AT A SMALL STATION ON THE WINNIPEG-CALGARY LINE IN 1883. THE ENGINE DRIVER, STANDING
IN FRONT OF THE COWCATCHER, TAKES THE OPPORTUNITY TO LUBRICATE.

Conversely, the spread of railroads was slower and more difficult in Central and South America. In Panama, in 1855, a line was inaugurated allowing goods to be moved from the Pacific to the Atlantic coast. It was a great success at the time because it was now possible to avoid having to sail around the South American continent. Its importance was completely obliterated by the opening of the country's famous canal in 1905.

In South America, thanks to both the hostile climate and political instability, railroads had a much harder time expanding. The construc-

tion of the main lines was possible thanks first to French and English then American finance and technology. A partial exception was Argentina, which had the advantage of its flat "pampas" lands. Although the first trans-continental line to Chile was opened as late as 1910.

In Africa the railway was obviously introduced by the nations then colonizing the continent, especially Belgium, France, Germany, and Great Britain. The lines were initially meant to connect the ports to the hinterland, so as to favor the export of raw materials to Europe. Among the countries to develop a significant rail network we mustn't overlook South Africa. Its first proper line connecting Cape Town to Wellington was opened in 1865, though a line had been constructed from Cape Town to Eersteriver in February 1862. Until recently, splendid and imposing steam locomotives were still used in South Africa for hauling goods and passenger trains. Another peculiarity of the South African system was its gauge of 3.5 ft (1 m), also called cape gauge.

In Australia, too, railroads arrived quickly. The first steam train on the continent appeared in the State of Victoria in 1854, running on a gauge of 5.25 ft (1.6 m). The first railway with a normal gauge opened the following year and connected Sydney to Granville. Especially in the first decades, the states adopted different track gauges, which created problems when they came to set up a national network. Only in 1910 did they ratify the normal gauge as the Australian standard. The first trans-continental line between Port Augusta and Kalgoorlie was completed on October 17, 1917. It is 1051 miles (1690 km) long and holds a

curious record: it has the longest straight section in the world at 309 miles (497 km), between Nurina in Western Australia and Watson in South Australia.

China today has an impressive railway network of over 43,500 miles (70,000 km). Until recently, before the country's conversion to a market economy, it was the main means of transport for both freight and people. The road network was very poor and nonexistent in some areas. The first train entered service quite late, however, in 1876, in Shanghai. Its story is rather an intriguing one. It is told that in 1865 a group of foreign businessmen had set up a company in Shanghai to build a railroad. The idea was not welcome by the Chinese, who perhaps rightly saw in that project an attempt at colonizing their country. The permission was not granted but as an alternative, they were allowed to build the military road from Shanghai to Woosung. The work was carried out precisely but the company then said that they wanted rails to be put down for a tram to also run on the road.

Once they had obtained permission, also thanks to the help of the British ambassador, in December 1875, to everyone's surprise a true and proper train service began. The line, five miles (8 km) long in all, was completed the following year notwithstanding the threat from the Chinese authorities to halt the works and the service. A dispute erupted between the English promoters and the Chinese authorities. It ended on October 21, 1877, when the Chinese completely reimbursed the work and took possession of the line with locomotive, carriage, and all

facilities. The last train was pulled by the two locomotives, Victory and Celestial Empire, watched by a large crowd. Then the whole railway was dismantled and shipped to Formosa where it rusted for years on the beach. Only 20 years later did railroads receive a warmer welcome in China.

73 TOP THE FIRST EXPERIMENT OF A RAILWAY SERVICE IN CHINA STARTED IN 1875 IN SHANGHAI, AS AN INITIATIVE OF A GROUP OF ENGLISH MERCHANTS, BUT IT WAS SOON INTERRUPTED DUE TO THE PROTESTS OF THE LOCAL AUTHORITIES.

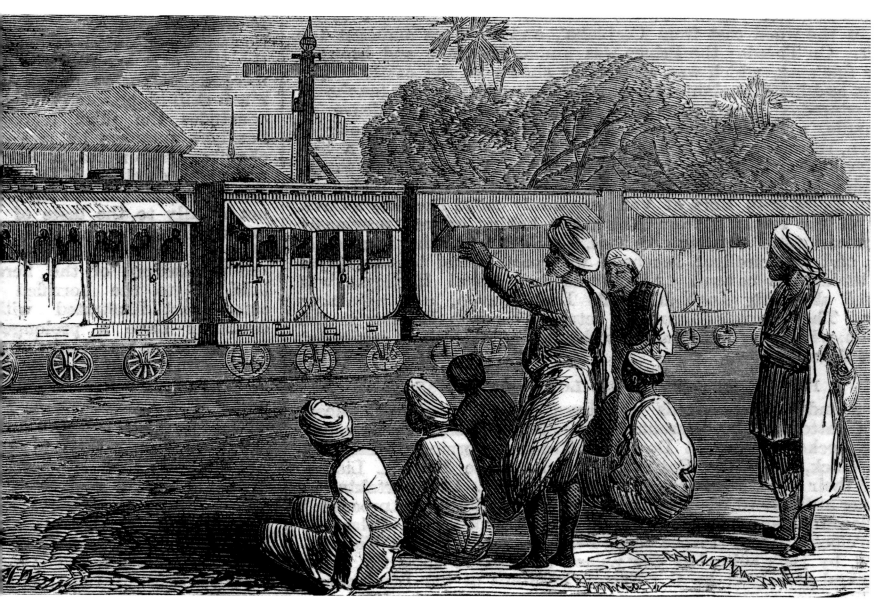

FROM THE ORIENT EXPRESS
TO THE TRANS-SIBERIAN

1880 - 1900

THE TUNNELS BELOW THE ALPS CONNECT THE NATIONAL NETWORKS

Italy played a vital role in the construction of the various train tunnels below the Alps that at the time were unique projects in the world. On September 17, 1871 the Frejus train tunnel was inaugurated (at the time there were talks about the Cenisio tunnel). This connected the Italian network to the French network; on May 23, 1881 the Gottard Tunnel was opened. This had been a joint Swiss, German and Italian project, constructed between Airolo in Ticino and Coschenen in Canton Uri. In 1889 work began on the Sempione Tunnel, from Domodossola to Briga in Switzerland. The project began on June 1, 1906 and was, at 12 miles, the longest train tunnel in the world.

The opening of these three tunnels had a fundamental importance on the development of international railroad connections. Italy had until then been connected to the centre of Europe essentially only by the Brennero Pass, which had been opened in 1867 more as an internal transport connection within the Hasburg Empire as a means of reaching the Po Valley. At the time the Italian border was in the Adige Valley near Rovereto, and it was only after the First World War that the border was brought to Brennero, transforming the railway into an international route.

The importance of the construction of these three great tunnels and the historical and technical ups and downs deserve a brief digression. The first studies for a train tunnel below the hills of Frejus go back to 1844 when Luigi des Ambrois, Minister of Carlo Alberto's government, awarded the project to the Belgian engineer Henri Mauss. In August of 1857, King Victor Emanuel II authorized the beginning of the project, directed by engineer Germain Somellier. At the time, to dig a tunnel of these proportions was a titanic undertaking and 200 workers were to lose their lives within those hills. Some of them accident victims, some killed by a typhus epidemic that burst out on construction sites around 1864.

The excavation was made possible by two inventions which completely changed construction methods. The first was the automatic air-compressed drill invented by Somellier himself. Holes were never again to be excavated manually, but with a new machine whose main system was situated outside of the tunnel. After having been used in the drill, the compressed air dispersed in the tunnel, maintaining the work environment free of poisonous emissions and continually ventilated. The second invention used on the Frejus project was dynamite. Invented by Alfred Nobel in 1866, it was immediately and successfully used instead of the traditional and much less effective explosives. The excavation of the eight-mile tunnel was completed on December 25, 1870. The entrance at Modane was later moved in 1881 to shore up the

instability of the rocks under which the tunnel was dug, bringing the length of the tunnel to eight and a half miles. The Frejus Tunnel today still connects Bardonecchia, at the top of the Susa Valley at Modane in French territory. The entrance on the Italian side is 3900 ft (1190 m) up, and then the two tracks rise to the peak of the tunnel, at 4380 ft (1335 m). The Modane entrance is a little lower at 4343 ft (1323 m) above sea level.

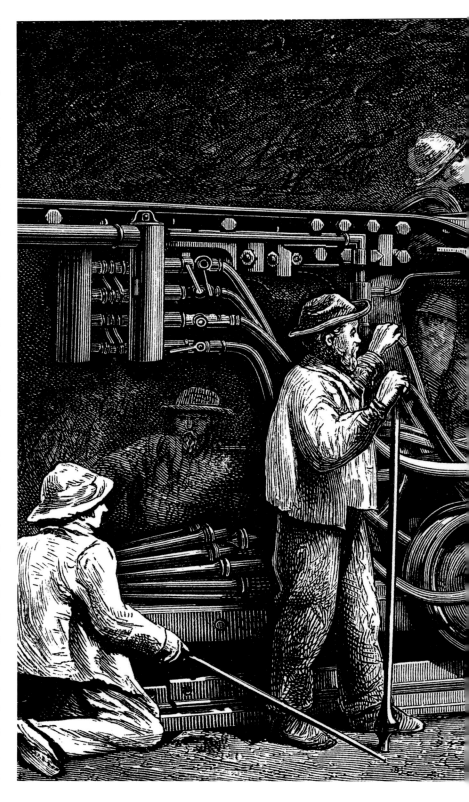

> *The completion of the Alpine tunnels was a fundamental stepping stone towards a European network.*

76-77 THE ENGRAVING SHOWS HOW THE AUTOMATIC PNEUMATIC BORER, INVENTED BY GERMAIN SOMELLIER, WAS USED. THIS INVENTION, TOGETHER WITH THE USE OF DYNAMITE, FACILITATED THE EXCAVATION OF THE MONT CENIS TUNNEL.

77 TOP ON SEPTEMBER 17TH 1871, THE INAUGURAL TRAIN OF THE MONT CENIS RAILWAY, PASSES THROUGH THE LONG TUNNEL UNDER THE ALPS. IT WAS BEDECKED WITH FLAGS FOR THE OCCASION. THE TUNNEL BETWEEN MODAINE IN FRANCE AND BARDONECCHIA IS 42,148 FT (12,847 M) LONG.

78 A GROUP OF WORKERS (TOP) IN THE SIMPLON TUNNEL AROUND 1906. BOTTOM, WORKERS POSE FOR A PHOTOGRAPH, NEAR A TRAIN YARD, IN THE LOCALITY OF GOESCHENEN, AT THE SWISS ENTRANCE OF THE ST. GOTTHARD TUNNEL.

79 THIS 1905 POSTER ADVERTISED THE GOTTHARD RAILWAY AND PROVIDES THE TRAIN SCHEDULE: THE MAP, WHICH ILLUSTRATES THE ROUTE, CLEARLY SHOWS THE FAMOUS RAILWAY'S EXTREMELY WINDING PATH.

Just as epic was the construction of the Gottard Ttunnel. Switzerland in 1860 already understood the necessity to create a connection through the Alps towards Ticino and Italy. They realized that they ran the risk of being totally cut out of the transport network between the north and south of Europe due to the Frejus Tunnel, to the east of Europe by the Brennero train pass, and to the west where two other tunnels were already under construction.

The governments of Ticino and Piedmont agreed therefore to fund the new project. For the Italian state it was important to be able to connect the port of Genoa with central Europe in the most direct manner possible, and without passing through the territories of the Austro-Hungarian Empire, who then relied on the ports of Venice and Trieste. In 1869 Switzerland, Italy and Germany set up an Economic Interest Group to fund and run the project.

Italy participated with 45 million lira, Switzerland and Germany contributed the equivalent of 20 million lira each. The project commenced in 1872 and was directed by Louis Favre, an engineer from Geneva, and ended in 1882 with a year of delays due to the financial problems the company encountered. Unfortunately, the loss of life during construction was high and once more some 200 workers died, many due to the poor living conditions they were forced to endure in the camps around the site.

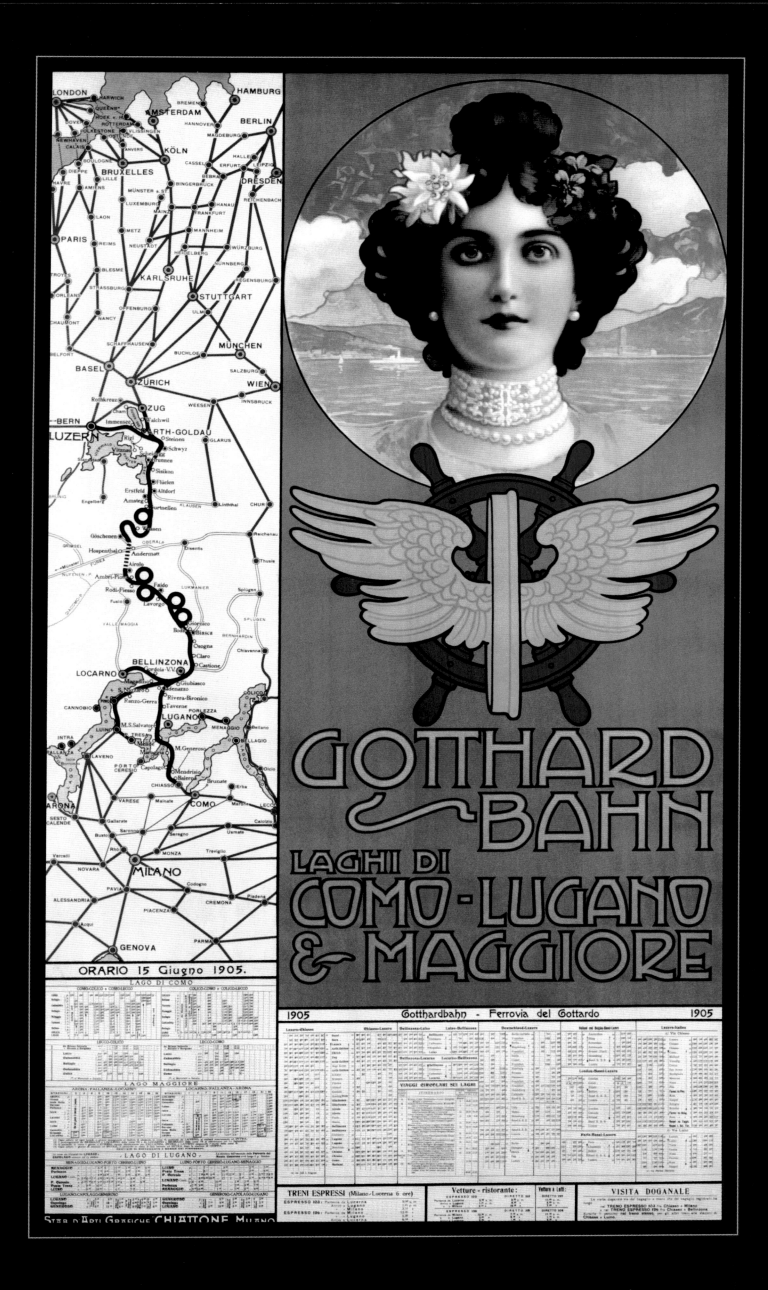

Lastly, but not least, the Sempione Tunnel was finished only in 1906. Its construction began in 1889 and was entrusted to a Prussian engineer, Carl Brandau. In contrast to the two other tunners, this one was constructed by excavating two parallel tunnels, approximately 55 ft (17 m) apart. The two tunnels were connected to each other by transverse tunnels, dug at regular distances. The difficulties encountered were considerable: rocks of various consistency, abundant water sources, temperatures inside the tunnel sometimes reaching over 113° F (45° C). The Sempione, however, significantly improved connections with Paris, Bern and Milan. The Orient Express for many years thundered through the impressive Sempione.

80-81 AND 81 TOP A GROUP OF MINERS AT WORK DURING THE EXCAVATION OF THE SIMPLON TUNNEL WHICH, UNLIKE OTHER ALPINE TUNNELS, WAS CREATED BY TUNNELING INTO THE MOUNTAIN WITH TWO PARALLEL TUNNELS, 55 FT (17 M) APART FROM EACH OTHER. ON THE RIGHT, THE WORKERS ROUND OFF THE TUNNEL'S VAULT WITH A STONE COATING.

81 BOTTOM THIS COMMEMORATIVE POSTCARD, PUBLISHED FOR THE OCCASION OF THE COMPLETION OF THE TUNNEL'S EXCAVATION WORKS, DEPICTS THE MAIN STAGES OF ITS CONSTRUCTION AND THE PICTURES OF THE DISTINCTIVE STATIONS ON THE TWO SIDES OF THE TUNNEL.

TRAINS BECOME HOTELS
ON TRACKS

82 Trains soon become, at least for the First Class, like real hotels on rail tracks: the image dates back to 1889.

83 top Even the President of the United States travels by train: this 1885 engraving shows Grover Cleveland with his wife, Frances, in their carriage.

The evolution and development of passenger cars made the realization of long-distance and international train journeys possible. Originally, passenger carriages were nothing more than wagons mounted on a flat train chassis, or for poorer travelers, just open cars furnished with benches. These last cars disappeared relatively quickly (in the UK their use was forbidden after several passengers froze to death), but it was still many years passed before the newly born railway industry built vehicles that were not directly influenced by the design of horse-drawn coaches.

One must right always remember that, from the beginning, passenger cars were grouped into two fundamental categories: those of English origin which were divided into compartments;

83 bottom The inside of the American First Class carriages reproduces, as much as possible, the typical luxury and décor enjoyed by the wealthy classes of that time; the floor is covered with carpets and beautiful decorative inlaid wood is everywhere.

and those of American origin with a corridor layout. Both designs evolved from horse-drawn vehicles for public transportation. The English passenger cars derived from the coach with side doors, whereas the American type is a sister of the omnibus, a vehicle for public use with access at the rear.

These two diverse design concepts gave life to different train cars: the European ones, for many years would have a structure divided in separated compartments, with two doors, one on each side, to allow for rapid getting on and off of passengers.

While the American cars from the beginning were characterized by a single large compartment with a central corridor, with at the fron and rear of the carriage is a platform or little terrace equipped with a small ladder to allow access.

Soon, railway companies realized that much better travel comfort was necessary to make life on board easier. The first lighting systems with wax or tallow candles were quickly substituted by gas ones, and then at the end of the 1800s the first functioning electric energy systems were installed. At the same time the vehicles became longer, thanks to construction techniques that allowed for more robust metal chassis and so cars went from having two to three axles. The increased length of the cars also allowed the railroad companies to improve comfort and facilities. Bathrooms were fitted in each carriage, where previously such facilities were either not present at all or were available only in the baggage area.

Also the heating system improved, initially thanks to mini heaters placed under the seats and filled with boiling water taken directly from the locomotive. However, at the end of the 19th century, steam heat began to be diffused along pipes passing along the entire train and fed directly by the locomotive's boiler. Interior design also evolved and, at least in the first-class cars, the seats were properly upholstered and the windows protected with heavy drapes.

With these improvements in comfort, considerably longer journeys could be made without excessive discomfort.

There were, however, still two further developments which would transform trains into true "hotels on tracks" – the sleeper and restaurant cars.

84-85 THIS IMAGE, TAKEN IN 1900, SHOWS HOW IT WAS TO TRAVEL IN A SMOKING CARRIAGE OF THE TIME ON AMERICAN RAILWAYS. IN EUROPE, ON THE OTHER HAND, CARRIAGES WERE NORMALLY DIVIDED INTO SEPARATE COMPARTMENTS.

85 TOP A CHEMIN DE FER DU NORD'S FIRST CLASS CARRIAGE IN THE SECOND HALF OF 1800; THE, TWO-WHEEL, VEHICLE HAS ONLY THREE COMPARTMENTS, EACH OF WHICH IS ACCESSIBLE FROM ITS RESPECTIVE SIDE DOOR WITH NO INTERNAL CORRIDOR.

85 BOTTOM THIS 1884 ENGRAVING SHOWS THE DIFFERENT ARRANGEMENTS FOR THE DAY AND FOR THE NIGHT OF A SLEEPING CARRIAGE OF THOSE DAYS. ONE SHOULD NOTE THE CURTAIN WHICH ALLOWED THE ISOLATION OF EVERY SINGLE BED AND THE SMALL PRIVATE BATH WITH A WASHBASIN.

THE FIRST SLEEPER AND RESTAURANT CARS BY GEORGE MORTIMER PULLMAN

We must at this point leave Europe and transfer to the United States, where, as mentioned earlier, from the beginning the rail car had a different evolution. In stark contrast to the Old World, where railroad companies offered a service subdivided into first, second and third classes (a reflection of social classes), in the United States, probably due to the origins of the country itself, the train car was a public place completely accessible to anyone. This openness was immediately apparent by the large, single sitting room in which everyone sat.

In the US, trips were on the average much longer than in Europe and the huge availability of space allowed the construction of much longer vehicles, and also much wider ones which were easier to transform. The first identifiable sleeper car can be dated as early as 1838. It was used by the Cumberland Valley Railroad, had a cloth ceiling, a candle lighting system, a bathroom in the women's compartment and an iron stove for winter heating.

In 1855, Illinois Central, and thereafter Burlington, introduced sleeper cars in their trains. In 1857, Theodore Woodruff constructed a representative model of a sleeper car which he proposed to various railroad companies. The single-roomed vehicle was furnished with small two-seat sofas placed face-to-face along the central corridor. The small sofas, with a leverage system, could be transformed into a sort of couchette on which passengers could sleep, isolated from the rest of the car with a curtain. But a few years later it was Mortimer Pullman who filed the patent for what, in the collective imagination, was to become the sleeper car *par excellence*. George Mortimer Pullman (1831-97) without doubt forever associated his name with the history of railway transportation, and above all, to the evolution of passenger cars. Contrary to what is believed, he was not a genial inventor but a very good entrepreneur, capable of seiz-

ing the innovative elements of other inventions and transforming them into extraordinary business successes.

After prospering from the American Civil War, he instinctively understood that railroad travel would explode in the years to come and in 1863, with a partner, began constructing carriages and designed a day-night car. However, this vehicle was similar to others already in use, and he wanted to have a design that was markedly different from the rest. And so in 1865 the "A" car was born, baptized "Pioneer." Actually, from a technical point of view, it was not very different from the others. The real difference was made by the dimensions and the maniacal attention to detail and interior finishings. Some internal furnishing solutions were even patented and exploited by a very good advertising campaign. This culminated in the transportation, with an appropriately equipped carriage, of the corpse of Abraham Lincoln after his assassination in April 1865. Over the period of a very few years Pullman monopolized the entire sector to the point of convincing the railroad companies to adjust the moulds of bridges and platform roofs for his enormous cars. The comfort level and luxury of his vehicles set the standard for rail travel worldwide.

86 THIS 1865 COLOR LITHOGRAPH SHOWS THE LUXURIOUS INTERIOR DÉCOR OF THE FIRST SLEEPING CARRIAGE DESIGNED BY GEORGE MORTIMER PULLMAN, WHICH SOON BECAME A POINT OF REFERENCE FOR ALL THE OTHER DESIGNS OF THOSE DAYS.

87 PULLMAN HAS BECOME A SYNONYM FOR COMFORT AND LUXURY ON RAILS: THIS 1910 POSTER ADVERTISED THE PLEASURES AND AMENITIES OF THE JOURNEY ON BOARD THE DINING CAR ON THE CHICAGO AND ALTON RAILROAD.

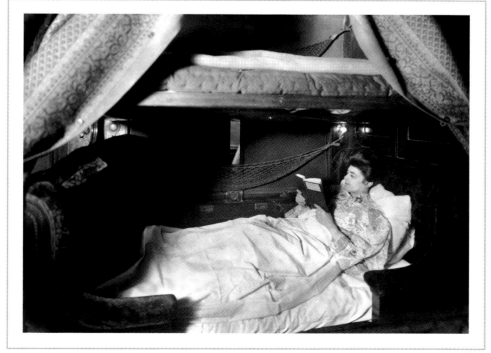

88 PULLMAN ROUNDED OFF IN LUXURIOUS WAY, NOT ONLY THE SLEEPING CARRIAGES, BUT ALSO THE NORMAL LOUNGES, LIKE THIS ONE PHOTOGRAPHED IN ILLINOIS AT THE START OF THE 1900S. THE LAMPS ALONG THE CENTRAL CORRIDOR APPEAR PARTICULARLY ELABORATE.

89 TOP THIS SLEEPING CARRIAGE OF THE CANADIAN PACIFIC RAILWAY APPEARS MORE AUSTERE THAN THE ONES PRODUCED IN THE UNITED STATES BY PULLMAN: *ON THE RIGHT*, THE OPENING MECHANISM OF THE SIMPLE BERTHS IS QUITE VISIBLE.

89 BOTTOM THE STRICT DECORUM OF THE TIMES REQUIRED THAT WOMEN IN PARTICULAR MUST SLEEP AND REST IN COMPLETE PRIVACY. THE HEAVY CURTAINS THAT PROTECTED THE BED FROM PRYING EYES ARE CLEARLY VISIBLE IN THIS PHOTOGRAPH.

90 THE FAMOUS BRITISH ILLUSTRATED MAGAZINE "THE GRAPHIC," IN JANUARY 1870, DEDICATED ITS COVER TO THE DINING CARRIAGE IN SERVICE ON THE UNION PACIFIC; IN EUROPE SUCH A SERVICE DID NOT EXIST YET.

91 AN ADVERTISING POSTER, OF THE CINCINNATI, HAMILTON AND DAYTON RAILROAD, GLORIFIES THE COMFORT AND SERVICES OF THE PULLMAN DINING CARRIAGE: HUNDREDS OF BLACK AMERICANS WORKED AS WAITERS AND PORTERS ON THE TRAINS IN THOSE DAYS.

92-93 THE "HOLYROAD" DINING CARRAIGE OF THE CANADIAN PACIFIC RAILWAY, BUILT IN 1885, WAS USED, IN 1886, FOR THE FIRST CANADIAN TRANSCONTINENTAL PASSENGER TRAIN. IT IS A HOTEL ON RAIL TRACKS.

93 A NORTHERN PACIFIC RAILROAD'S NOTICE BOARD ANNOUNCED, IN 1883, THE START OF THE RESTAURANT SERVICE, WITH THREE CARRIAGES SPECIFICALLY BUILT BY PULLMAN CAR WORKS, AND FIXES THE LUNCH PRICE AT 75 CENTS PER PERSON.

THE GRAPHIC

AN ILLUSTRATED WEEKLY NEWSPAPER

VOL. I—NO. 9
Registered for Transmission Abroad.

SATURDAY, JANUARY 29, 1870

PRICE SIXPENCE,
OR SEVENPENCE STAMPED

Pullman also revolutionized the concept of the restaurant car. In the United States in 1835 they were already carriages offering snacks and drinks on board, but they were not equipped with a real kitchen. In 1866 Pullman introduced vehicles, called "hotel-cars," in which he added a small kitchen to a sleeper car in the centre in order to be able to serve the two salons. The service was called "The President" and aimed to re-create on trains the same impeccable service as deluxe hotels. In 1869, in order to avoid the trouble that the kitchen in the middle of the two rooms created for passengers, he proposed a restaurant car specifical-ly only for the consumption of meals. A few years later, the final design was achieved, which is still in use today: a kitchen at one end of the car and a corridor connecting to the room where there were tables along the walls next to spacious and bright windows.

The cars were managed by the Pullman Palace Car Company (which he himself had founded in 1867) and offered an on-board service un-thinkable for the time. Every passenger had an usher at their disposal; a black ex-slave who served as a waiter, butler and porter. Pullman was convinced that black ex-slaves were the best combination of submis-sion, training and fine physical appearance that one could find for that job. And even though such thinking is indeed racist, one must also re-member that at that time, the job offered by Pullman was a great oppor-tunity for a black man in the United States.

In those years, Pullman also invented a collateral business that showed his remarkable intuition. He rented out his sleeper and restau-rant cars, parked at stations, for political and large associations' conven-tions and meetings. The participants at these meetings ate and slept in Pullman's car instead of at hotels. On some occasions, such as the Knights Templar Rally in Saint Louis, nearly 200 cars were used.

At the height of his success, in 1890 the Pullman Palace Car Compa-ny operated 2135 cars practically on all of the 100,000 miles of the Amer-ican network. The sleepers accommodated approximately 100,000 peo-ple per night, more than all of the American deluxe hotels put together. In order to efficiently maintain this incredible organization, the company had over 12,000 employees.

PULLMAN Compartment Cars

CINCINNATI, INDIANAPOLIS, CHICAGO.

CINCINNATI HAMILTON & DAYTON R.R.
CH&D
CINCINNATI
INDIANAPOLIS CHICAGO DAYTON TOLEDO DETROIT

THROUGH TRAINS

CINCINNATI, DAYTON, TOLEDO, DETROIT.

INTERIOR OF DINING CARS ON THE CINCINNATI, HAMILTON & DAYTON R.R.

THE CIWL IS BORN: INTERNATIONAL COMPANY FOR SLEEPER CARS

The history of the railroads often reads like a romance novel. Belgium, 1867: George Nagelmackers was a young civil engineer graduate, son of a prestigious family of bankers very close to King Leopold II's court. The boy fell seriously in love with his older cousin but his feelings were not reciprocated. For this reason his family thought about a trip abroad, both for him to forget about his love and for him to complete his professional studies. Nagelmackers departed for the United States and in ten months traveled all over the nation, often on Pullman's newest cars. In those same years, there were already 50 vehicles sold by the Pullman Company in operation.

The young engineer was struck by the technological innovations introduced by Pullman and he instinctively saw the potential for their use in Europe. He was Belgian and from a family who had most of their financial investments in railroads. Nagelmackers also met George Pullman to propose a type of collaboration but the two did not hit it off and the talks came to nothing.

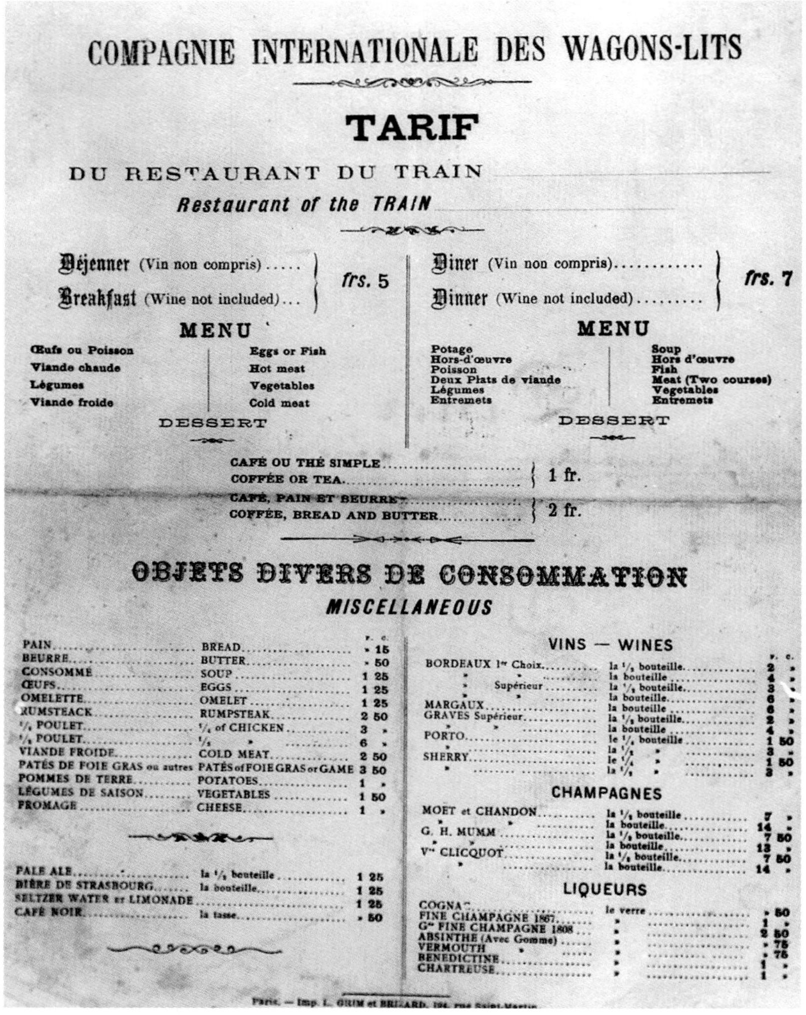

Back in Europe the Belgian engineer pursued his ambitions and in 1870 published a document with the significant title "Installation project for sleeper cars for the continent's railway." In the same year, though, the Franco-Prussian War broke out and the atmosphere was definitely not the most appropriate to propose deluxe international rail travel.

When the hostilities ended, the tenacious Nagelmackers once again resumed his project and submitted his plans it directly to the Belgian king. He obtained a concession to establish a service with sleeper cars from Ostend to Brindisi. By linking these two ports meant connecting the UK to the Orient (where at the time the English colonies were already quite vast) via the Suez Canal, which had been opened in 1869. Steamships already joined that port with Brindisi. A London-Brindisi connection was already activated, continuing by sea through Suez to Bombay, which was used above all for mail and was known as the "Indian Suitcases."

Nagelmackers, however, understood that simply transferring the American model to Europe would not have been successful. His cars would have the same level of comfort and luxury as their American counterparts, but the interior layouts had to be in tune with the tastes and fashion of the time. The idea of having the couchettes arranged on the sides of a central corridor, with both sexes only separated by a curtain was certainly unthinkable. It would have been absolutely scandalous at that time in Europe. The enterprising Belgian engineer therefore designed a car with a lateral corridor and closed cabins arranged one after the other, guaranteeing as such private compartments. The trains also had seating cars, living rooms in which to spend the daytime hours of the trip in company, and restaurant cars. Improvements were also developed for the suspension devices and brakes.

COMPAGNIE INTERNATIONALE DES WAGONS-LITS

TARIF

DU RESTAURANT DU TRAIN
Restaurant of the TRAIN

| Déjenner (Vin non compris) ..... | frs. 5 | Diner (Vin non compris) .... | frs. 7 |
| Breakfast (Wine not included) ... | | Dinner (Wine not included) .... | |

MENU

Œufs ou Poisson	Eggs or Fish	Potage	Soup
Viande chaude	Hot meat	Hors-d'œuvre	Hors d'œuvre
Légumes	Vegetables	Poisson	Fish
Viande froide	Cold meat	Deux Plats de viande	Meat (Two courses)
		Légumes	Vegetables
		Entremets	Entremets

DESSERT / DESSERT

CAFÉ OU THÉ SIMPLE	1 fr.
COFFEE OR TEA.	
CAFÉ, PAIN ET BEURRE	2 fr.
COFFEE, BREAD AND BUTTER	

OBJETS DIVERS DE CONSOMMATION
MISCELLANEOUS

		fr. c.
PAIN	BREAD	.15
BEURRE	BUTTER	.50
CONSOMME	SOUP	1 25
ŒUFS	EGGS	1 25
OMELETTE	OMELET	1 25
RUMSTEACK	RUMPSTEAK	2 50
¼ POULET	¼ of CHICKEN	3 .
½ POULET	½	6 .
VIANDE FROIDE	COLD MEAT	2 50
PATÉS DE FOIE GRAS ou autres	PATÉS of FOIE GRAS or GAME	3 50
POMMES DE TERRE	POTATOES	1 .
LÉGUMES DE SAISON	VEGETABLES	1 50
FROMAGE	CHEESE	1 .

		fr. c.
PALE ALE	la ½ bouteille	1 25
BIÈRE DE STRASBOURG	la bouteille	1 25
SELTZER WATER et LIMONADE	la ½ bouteille	1 25
CAFÉ NOIR	la tasse	.50

VINS — WINES

		fr. c.
BORDEAUX 1er Choix	la ½ bouteille	2 .
Supérieur	la ¼ bouteille	1 .
	la bouteille	6 .
MARGAUX	la ½ bouteille	8 .
GRAVES Supérieur	la ½ bouteille	4 .
PORTO	la ½ bouteille	4 .
	le ½	1 .
SHERRY	le ½	4 .
	la ¼	1 50

CHAMPAGNES

MOET et CHANDON	la ½ bouteille	7 .
G. H. MUMM	la bouteille	14 .
	la ½ bouteille	7 50
Vve CLICQUOT	la bouteille	14 .
	la ½ bouteille	7 50

LIQUEURS

COGNAC	le verre	.50
FINE CHAMPAGNE 1867		1 .
Gde FINE CHAMPAGNE 1808		2 .
ABSINTHE (Avec Gomme)		.75
VERMOUTH		.75
BENEDICTINE		1 .
CHARTREUSE		1 .

Paris. — Imp. L. GRIM et BRIARD, 104, rue Saint-Martin.

Guide Continental Officiel

de la Comp.¹e Internationale des Wagons-Lits & des Grands Express Européens

ORIENT-EXPRESS

Méditerranée-Express

SUD EXPRESS

PENINSULAR-EXPRESS

Direction Générale — 46. Rue des Mathurins, PARIS

Le **Guide Continental officiel** est déposé dans toutes les voitures, sleeping-cars, voitures-salons et restaurants, agences et succursales de la Compagnie des Wagons-Lits et des Grands Express Européens.
Il est adressé chaque mois aux principaux hôtels, clubs, sociétés, kursaals et grands établissements publics du continent.
Il est mis à la disposition des voyageurs dans les agences et sur les bateaux des grandes Compagnies de navigation.

Publicité : à l'Office Général de Publicité des Voyages, 25, Rue de la Paix, Paris

CHEMINS de FER du NORD FRANÇAIS
du LONDON CHATHAM & DOVER et du SOUTH EASTERN

Cie INT^{le} des WAGONS-LITS
ET DES
GRANDS EXPRESS
EUROPÉENS

CLUB-TRAIN PARIS-LONDRES

CLUB TRAIN
✳
PARIS-LONDRES
ET VICE-VERSA

TRAIN DE LUXE LIMITÉ. SALONS ET RESTAURANT
BATEAU SPÉCIAL

Départ de Paris (Gare du Nord) tous les jours, à	3.15 SOIR
Arrivée à Londres (Victoria, Charing ✠ ou Holborn Viaduct) à ...	10.46 SOIR
Départ de Londres, tous les jours, à	3. » SOIR
Arrivée à Paris (Gare du Nord) à	10.47 SOIR

Traversée moyenne en 70 minutes
SUPPLÉMENTS

	Simple	Aller et Retour		Simple	Aller et Retour
Paris à Calais.	6'25	10' »	Douvres à Londres	6'25	10' »
Calais à Douvres	6 25	10 »	Paris à Londres	18 75	30 »

SE RENSEIGNER ET RETENIR SES PLACES:
A PARIS: 3, Place de l'Opéra;
A LONDRES: 122, Pall Mall et 3, 4 et 5, Gracechurch Street.

A partir du 15 Mars, les voyageurs de 1re Classe seront admis sans paiement de Supplément entre Paris et Calais, dans la voiture de 1re classe qui entrera dans la composition du "CLUB-TRAIN".

CHAMPENOIS & Cie 66 BOUL^d St MICHEL PARIS

The newly designed system from the USA was mounted and had been devised by George Westinghouse. It soon became widespread worldwide, as well as the hooking and unhooking system allowing vehicles to be effortlessly joined to the locomotive of any European network with a normal gauge.

It took two years of great effort and negotiation before the first vehicles were constructed and the necessary authorizations from the various European companies were obtained, in order to make possible the hooking of the new cars to their trains. Nagelmackers began the service from Ostend to Köln and Berlin, and then on the Berlin to Paris line. Success was immediate, but the business initially had huge financial difficulties due mainly to the elevated expenses necessary for the construction of the special cars, expenses initially not met by revenue from the service. After various vicissitudes the company was merged with Mann's Railway Carriage. Nagelmackers managed to regain control, and in 1876 he founded the CIWL, an acronym for "Compagnie Internationale des Wagons Lits." In 1883 this denomination was extended to include the phrase "et des Grandes Express Europeens" (and of Large European Express Trains).

96 TRAVELING FROM PARIS TO LONDON ON THE CIWL CARRIAGES MEANT BEING PART OF AN EXCLUSIVE CLUB: AS IS CLEARLY EVOKED BY THIS POSTER WHICH WAS DESIGNED FOR THE FRENCH AND ENGLISH RAILWAY COMPANIES OF THOSE DAYS.

97 TOP THE FAMOUS FRENCH PHOTOGRAPHER, NADAR, TOOK THE PHOTO OF GEORGE NAGELMACKERS IN 1898; THE BELGIAN BUSINESSMAN, IN 1876, CREATED THE CIWL AND CONCEIVED THE IDEA OF THE FAMOUS INTERNATIONAL TRAIN: ORIENT EXPRESS.

97 BOTTOM THIS 1925 POSTER ADVERTISED THE CIWL'S "GOLDEN ARROW" EXPRESS, WHICH CONNECTED LONDON TO PARIS, VIA CALAIS. IT IMMEDIATELY CREATES AN ATMOSPHERE OF LUXURY AND ENJOYMENT TYPICAL OF THAT "GREAT GATSBY" ERA.

Cie WAGONS LITS

CIE INTERNATIONALE DES WAGONS-LITS

PULLMAN CAR

The GOLDEN ARROW
ALL PULLMAN TRAIN
DAILY BETWEEN
LONDON CALAIS PARIS
Departs: LONDON 10.45 a.m. *Arrives*: PARIS 5.40 pm.
Departs: PARIS 12 noon *Arrives*: LONDON 7.15 pm.

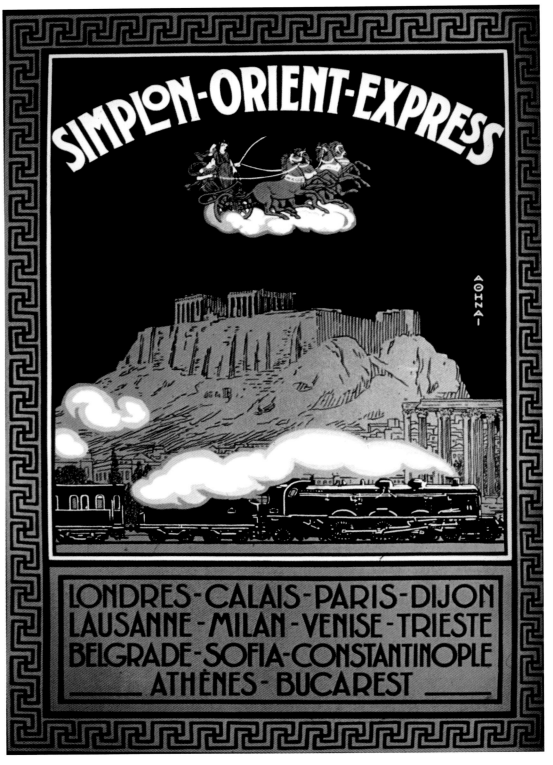

tinguish this new route, the train was baptized the Simplon Orient Express. Not until the 1930s did the Orient Express service reach its peak with three parallel connections working simultaneously: The Orient Express, The Simplon Orient Express and the Arlberg Orient Express, which went through Zurich, Innsbruck and Budapest, from where some carriages went to Bucharest and Athens.

In those years of relative peace and prosperity, before the Second World War, the train reached its highest level of comfort and luxury. Air connections were still scarce and uncomfortable so businessmen and diplomats would regularly use these trains. The CIWL soon added a connection between Paris and Calais, thus extending the service to London and Great Britain. The golden period ended when war broke out and the service was suspended in 1939. In 1945 the service began again but amidst great difficulties: Athens was no longer reachable because of the closing of the border between Yugoslavia and Greece, which lasted until 1951. In the following year, it was Istanbul's turn to remain isolated because of the dispute between Turkey and Bulgaria.

In 1962, the Orient Express, Arlberg Orient Express and Simplon Orient Express services were downsized, with fewer trains running and less destinations reached. The service was renamed the Direct Orient Express and its control was passed from CIWL to the national railways in 1971. The last journey from Paris to Istanbul was on May 19, 1977. Naturally we cannot omit to mention that since 1982 the Venice Simplon Orient Express continues to run as a private tourist service using carriages from the 1920s and 1930s, connecting Venice to London and Paris.

In the same year on October 4, the Train Express d'Orient was inaugurated, which become the Orient Express, a whole train created and managed by CIWL and pulled by different locomotives in the different countries crossed. The Orient Express connected Paris's Gare de l'Est to Istanbul. Initially, the route from Paris touched Munich and Vienna before reaching Giurgiu in Romania. Here passengers were taken by ship down the Danube to Ruse in Bulgaria where they would get on another train headed for Varna. The last segment of the journey to Constantinople (as it was still known by many) was by ferry. A first variation on the route was introduced in 1885, deviating from Vienna for Belgrade and Philippopolis (now Plovidiv, the second biggest city of Bulgaria, in the region of Thrace). The route was finally completed in 1889 with the completion of the direct line to Istanbul. In those years, the Orient Express was a daily service from Paris to Budapest, three times a week from Budapest to Belgrade and Istanbul, and weekly from Belgrade to Bucharest and Constanta, on the Black Sea. The service all the way to Istanbul ended nearly a century later, on May 19, 1977.

The history of this legendary train was varied and complex: The First World War caused a suspension of the service until the end of the hostilities in 1918. In the meantime, however, the Simplon Tunnel had been opened and the service resumed using this more southern and faster route. The new route went through Lausanne, Milan, Venice and Trieste, completely bypassing Vienna. To dis-

The CIWL naturally did not limit itself to running just the Orient Express. Its activity also extended outside of Europe. In Egypt, CIWL managed the Star of Egypt train, which connected Cairo to Luxor and other branches reaching Beirut and Teheran. Its original carriages were made out of teak wood and remained in service until 1922 when they substituted with metal ones, which are still used today. One of the teak carriages, number 2419, was chosen on November 11, 1918 to sign the armistice that ended the First World War. These were the years in which CIWL commissioned famous artists of the time to make special decorations for each single carriage. The aim was to reinforcing the exclusive nature of the service, which was to be on a par with the most luxurious hotels of the time.

Nagelmakers's Orient Express undoubtedly became synonymous with luxury and sophistication. In the same years, though, there were other famous trains, unfortunately almost completely forgotten now. Besides the already quoted Indian Suitcases, certainly a luxury train compared to the average service, but especially famous because it was part of a direct connection between London and the British colonies in the East, other trains must be mentioned.

The North Express, for example, also managed by CIWL, from 1896 ran a night service between Paris and St Petersburg. It passed through Brussels, Köln, Hanover, Berlin and what was then called Königsberg, now Kaliningrad in Poland. Travelers had to change trains at the border with Germany because the Russian tracks were wider than European ones and at the time vehicles still had not been made which could

change their gauge. As well as the North Express, the CIWL also ran the South Express from Paris to Lisbon. Thus the company was able to offer a connection between Russia and the Portuguese capital, from which big steam ships left for South America.

But the rich travelers who could afford the luxury of CIWL carriages were not merely traveling for work. In fact, at that time it was very fashionable to sojourn on the French Mediterranean beaches. Thus, in 1900, the Riviera Express was born, initially connecting central Europe, Amsterdam, Hamburg and Berlin to Nice. The posters of the time depict this and other trains in wonderful Mediterranean landscapes, among palm trees and the beaches of Cannes, Nice and Monte Carlo. The attractive colored labels which were stuck on passenger's luggage also came from then. These travelers certainly didn't move around with small suitcases or rucksacks but with dozens of large cases.

100 THESE TWO SPLENDID ADVERTISING POSTERS BY A.M. CASSANDRE WERE CREATED IN 1927 TO ADVERTISE THE ETOILE DU NORD PARIS-AMSTERDAM AND THE NORD-EXPRESS WHICH CONNECTED LONDON AND PARIS TO WARSAW AND RIGA VIA BERLIN.

101 THIS ADVERTISING POSTER WAS CREATED BY DU NORD, CIWL AND PLM COMPANIES, TO PROMOTE THE CONNECTION BETWEEN LONDON AND VICHY. THE COMPARTMENT OF THE PULLMAN CARRIAGE IS DESIGNED AS A LOUNGE.

OTHER EUROPEAN LUXURY TRAINS

In Great Britain, in the meantime, the numerous railway companies competed more in terms of speed than the comfort of their carriages. One of the most famous trains was the Flying Scotsman, which ran the 390 miles (630 km) from Kings Cross station in London to Edinburgh's Waverley Station. It ran along the East Coast Main Line, which wasn't built as a single line but developed in conjunction between three railway companies. North British Railway built the first part in 1846, from Edinburgh to Berwick, followed in 1853 by the Great Northern Railway, which opened to traffic the section between London and Doncaster. It wasn't until 1876, though, that the line was completed, when the North Eastern Railway connected Doncaster to Berwick. It certainly wasn't thought of as a rapid connection between London and the Scottish capital. Both York and Newcastle were terminus stations in which the train would have to reverse direction, also changing locomotive.

The story of the Flying Scotsman began in 1862, (with an obviously slightly different route, seeing as part of the East Coast Main Line had not been completed yet). In that year a train service leaving at 10 in the morning from London Kings Cross for Edinburgh was established. The journey lasted about 12 hours and included a half hour break in York to eat. On timetables the train was called the Special Scotch Express. In 1888 a true and proper competition began to establish the fastest connection between London and Edinburgh. The outcome was a sort of armistice between the various companies who agreed on a new timetable that set the exact time for each train to run. That for the Special Scotch Express was set at eight and a half hours.

The service and comforts aboard also began to improve, but the real changes occurred when in 1924 the various English rail companies were reduced to the big four. The Edinburgh-London line became the dominion of the London North Eastern Railway, known as the LNER. The company emphasized the prestige of the connection and renamed the train the Flying Scotsman. To better highlight the novelty, a locomotive was also given the same name and was taken to the British Empire Exposition.

The climax of the story of this train came in the 1930s. From 1928 the London-Edinburgh route became non stop and the speed increased, reducing travel time to seven hours and 20 minutes. Some of the most beautiful English steam engines pulled that train, such as the Pacifics, designed by famous engineer Sir Nigel Gresley. One of these beautiful machines, the Mallard n. 4468, all in blue, set the world speed record for steam locomotives of 125.5 mph (200 km/h), which remains unbeaten to this day. But another Pacific of the same A4 group, n. 4472, leading the Flying Scotsman, had already reached 100 mph (160 km/h) in 1934. The train in those years was also famous for the service provided onboard: travelers could use one of the best restaurants in Great Britain, sip aperitifs in a cocktail bar carriage and even go to the hairdresser's.

Another famous English train at the turn of the century was the Cornish Riviera Express of the Great Western Railway, which from 1904 ran, non stop, from London Paddington to Plymouth. The journey lasted 4 hours and 25 minutes and at the time it was the longest non-stop service in the world.

102 A group of LNER workers are polishing the Pacific Class A1 no. 2597 "Gainsborough" appointed to haul the famous "The Flying Scotsman" train from London to Edinburgh.

103 On the 2nd of May 1932, the Flying Scotsman leaves King's Cross station in London for Edinburgh. The splendid Pacific of Class A1 no. 2750 Papyrus is hauling it. The journey used to take just seven hours and twenty minutes.

104-105 THE CORNISH RIVIERA EXPRESS WAITS FOR THE GO-AHEAD AT THE LONDON STATION OF PADDINGTON. THE TRAIN CONNECTED
THE CAPITAL CITY TO PENZANCE VIA BRISTOL AND PLYMOUTH ALONG THE SOUTHERN COAST OF DEVON AND CORNWALL.

105 THE CORNISH RIVIERA EXPRESS' ENGINE DRIVER GIVES THE FINAL RUB TO THE LOCOMOTIVE'S FRONT PLATE BEFORE ITS DEPARTURE
FROM PADDINGTON. THE LOCOMOTIVE IS THE KING GEORGE III, ONE OF THE KING'S CLASS ENGINES.

THE TRANS-SIBERIAN EPIC

n the meantime, a few thousand miles away, another exceptional project was taking shape: the Moscow-Vladivostok railway. The Trans-Siberian route, partly because of its span, 5770 miles (9285 km), partly because of the mystery surrounding Russia and Siberia, became synonymous with adventure. To this day, a journey on these tracks remains a very special experience.

In the mid-19th century, the need to connect the eastern-most lands of the Russian Empire to the European side became impelling: trips from Moscow or St Petersburg to Vladivostok could take three months. When railways began to spread in Europe, it was immediately thought that their use could solve the problem. But the distance was enormous and the technical difficulties huge.

From 1870 various studies were made and routes proposed, but only in 1875 was a final route chosen, which followed approximately the 55th parallel. Other solutions contemplated a more northern route, but this one prevailed because it was more practical for communication with Central Asia. The project was postponed, though, due to the onset of the Russian-Turkish war, and was only started again in 1882. In 1887, surveys were begun on how to navigate round the major natural obstacle of Lake Baikal.

On May 31, 1891, near Vladivostok, Czarevitch Nicholas, the yet to be Emperor Nicholas II, gave the go-ahead for the works to begin. Construction finally ended on November 3, 1901, but the services between the two terminals only began on July 14, 1903. Numerous difficulties had been overcome: marshlands with dozens and dozens of bridges having to be built, for a total length of more than 30 miles; the climate was

the harshest imaginable; and let's not forget the dozens and dozens of workers who died, including many Italians, for the sake of this huge enterprise.

Lake Baikal posed an enormous obstacle. It was impossible to cross with a bridge such as when the trans-continental railroad met the Great Salt Lake, in Utah. The solution, until they were able to lay a track south of the lake, was to use a ferry in the summer months. In winter the ice is so thick that not even special ships could break it. Once the idea of unloading passengers and goods onto sleighs was discarded, the solution found was to use the incredible strength of the ice. With an unusual and courageous choice, it was decided to put the tracks straight onto the ice. That way the service was only interrupted for a few days a year, those necessary to lay them when the ice consolidated, and the time taken to remove them in the thaw.

The railway soon became a vital artery of the Russian Empire. Between 1906 and 1913 over three million farmers, thanks to government incentives, moved to Siberia. They produced and exported large quantities of wheat. Traffic on the line grew so quickly that it had to be doubled to a two-way system, which was practically complete in 1913.

106 TOP THE JOURNEY ALONG THE TRANS-SIBERIAN RAILWAY USED TO TAKE DAYS AND THE CARRIAGES, AT LEAST THOSE OF WEALTHY TRAVELERS, WERE PROVIDED WITH ALL THE COMFORTS OF THOSE TIMES. ATTACHED TO THE TRAIN, THERE WAS ALSO A CARRIAGE WHICH HAD BEEN TRANSFORMED INTO A CHAPEL.

106 BOTTOM THE ARRIVAL OF THE TRAIN IN THOSE DISTANT LANDS WAS OFTEN AN EVENT WHICH DESERVED TO BE REMEMBERED WITH A PHOTOGRAPH. THE STATION WORKERS AND TRAIN DRIVERS POSE FOR THE PHOTOGRAPHER AT THE OB STATION AT THE START OF THE 1900S.

Nice : Vue prise de la route de Villefranche.

107 The possibility of reaching Vladivostok with the train and, from there, Japan, tickled the fantasy of European travelers. A French magazine of those times dedicated a whole edition to the new railway.

108 TOP A FREIGHT TRAIN ON THE TRANS-SIBERIAN CROSSES THE BRIDGE OVER THE KOSSUL RIVER, AT THE START OF THE 1900S. THE LINE WAS IMMEDIATELY USED FOR THE TRANSPORT OF HANDMADE ARTICLES WHICH, UP TILL THEN, WERE TRANSPORTED IN LONG CARAVANS ON RAMMED EARTH PATHS.

The Trans-Siberian played a fundamental role in both the resistance to Hitler's invasion and in the counter-offensive that the Soviet Union organized against the Germans. Whole factories in western Russia where dismantled and sent to the safer oriental territories, from where, thanks to the railroad, they could supply munitions and men quickly, thus staunching the German advance and eventually defeating it.

The passenger trains, which ran on the line, were of various kinds, with carriages divided into "hard" and "comfortable" according to the Russian custom. In 1914 CIWL obtained the concession to run a luxury train. Considering the duration of the journey, about ten days, very special services were offered.

The train had the usual sleeper and restaurant cars and many

special fittings. These included the double ventilated roof, thicker walls and double-glazed windows for the extreme coldness of the terrain traversed.

On the train, travelers had access to a library and a religious chapel. The landscape could be admired thanks to a panoramic car at the back, and in the luggage compartment there was even a photographic laboratory.

The other trains were naturally far less luxurious: boiling water was available in all the stations on the line. This was supplied on tap to all passengers who would bring teapots for the trip. The legend regarding the Trans-Siberian grew so fast that in 1904 a series of Liebig figures, made famous by the extremely rare Ferocious Saladin, portrayed the railway and the cities crossed.

In the years of the Cold War permission for a journey on the Trans-Siberian was difficult to obtain for a Western citizen. If they managed to get permission, the journey was fraught with rigid restrictions: they were not allowed to take pictures in stations and especially of bridges. They were also absolutely forbidden to get off the train in intermediate stations. Things changed later, but the trip has remained just as fascinating.

A well-known writer and journalist such as Tiziano Terzani, correspondent for 30 years in Asia for *Der Spiegel*, dedicated a whole chapter of his wonderful book *A Fortune-teller Told Me* to his journey on the Trans-Siberian, describing the melting-pot of people that crowd the train and the instant markets which throng around the train at every stop.

108-109 THE DINING CARRIAGE OF A TRANS-SIBERIAN TRAIN IN 1941: THE LINE WAS OF VITAL IMPORTANCE DURING THE RESISTANCE WHICH THE RUSSIANS MANAGED TO ORGANIZE AGAINST THE GERMAN INVASION IN THE SECOND WORLD WAR.

109 TOP THE CONSTRUCTION OF THE TRANS-SIBERIAN INVOLVED HUNDREDS OF MEN WORKING FOR YEARS IN WILD AND BARREN REGIONS. THIS IMAGE SHOWS A TEAM OF WORKERS PLACING THE WOODEN TIES UPON WHICH THE RAILS WERE FASTENED.

109 BOTTOM A GROUP OF WORKERS, AT THE START OF THE 1900S, WORKING ON THE CONSTRUCTION OF THE EMBANKMENT FOR THE TRANS-SIBERIAN'S RAILS, THE LINE WAS BUILT AS A SINGLE RAIL, BUT IT WASN'T LONG BEFORE THE TRACK WAS DOUBLED.

TWO LEGENDARY
AMERICAN TRAINS

At the beginning of the 20th century even some trains in the United States became famous. They peaked in popularity only a few decades later, though, and we cover them by talking in general about the fastest and most beautiful steam locomotives ever built.

Let's remember two trains that are both very famous but with very different stories. The first is the 20th Century Limited which the New York Central Railroad began running in 1902 between New York and Chicago.

The train quickly became so famous that it became a national institution. The 20th Century Limited traveled along the Water Level Route, and was in direct competition with the Broadway Limited managed by the rival Pennsylvania Railroad. It ran the 932 miles (1500 km) between the two cities in just 15 and a half hours, at an average speed of nearly 62 mph (100 km/h). The train was famous not only for its speed, but also for the luxury it afforded: travelers got on and off at stations on a specially made red carpet.

The inaugural trip of the 20th Century Limited took place on June 17, 1902. On that occasion the train reached Chicago Union Station in just 15 and a half hours, three minutes early. It was a huge success because until then the journey would take about 20 hours. Better by over four and a half hours, an undoubtedly exceptional event, which paradoxically disappointed reporters of the time for the ease with which it was reached.

110-111 A POWERFUL LOCOMOTIVE, "HUDSON" J1 (4-6-4) OF THE NEW YORK CENTRAL, HAULS ONE OF THE MOST FAMOUS AMERICAN TRAINS, THE "TWENTIETH CENTURY LIMITED," ON THE LINE WHICH, FLANKING THE HUDSON RIVER, GOES TO NEW YORK.

111 THIS 1902 IMAGE SHOWS THE "TWENTIETH CENTURY LIMITED" AS IT WAS, SOON AFTER THE INAUGURATION OF THE LINE ON JUNE 17TH. THE TRAIN CONNECTED NEW YORK TO CHICAGO IN JUST 15 HOURS AND A HALF, INSTEAD OF THE USUAL 20 HOURS.

112-113 THE ENGINE DRIVER CASEY JONES IS PICTURED AT THE CONTROLS OF THE LOCOMOTIVE NO. 638 OF THE ILLINOIS CENTRAL RAILROAD, WITH FIREMAN BULL MCKINNIE STANDING ON THE STEPLADDER. THE STORY OF CASEY JONES BECAME A FAMOUS POPULAR AMERICAN BALLAD.

112 BOTTOM A DAILY NEWSPAPER OF THOSE TIMES RECOUNTS THE INCIDENT IN WHICH CASEY JONES DIED AND WHICH TRANSFORMED HIM INTO A LEGEND. THE TITLE IS DRAMATIC: "DIED UNDER HIS CABIN – THE SAD END OF THE ENGINE DRIVER CASEY JONES."

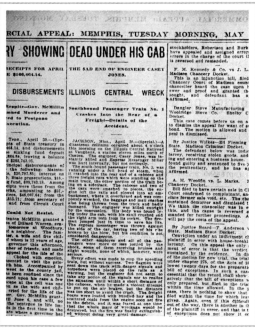

Another train that was just as famous and still runs in the States is the Cannon Ball Express. Its story is quite different and it has become a part of American music and folklore. The story tells of its driver, Casey Jones, and the accident in which he was killed on the night between April 29 and 30, 1900, whilst driving the Cannon Ball Express on the Illinois Central Railroad, between Memphis and Canton.

The events of that night became a legend over the years, and are remembered in many American songs. Casey Jones was in truth called John Lutther Jones and at the age of 17 he moved to the city of Cayce where he was employed as a telegraph operator. The nickname "Casey" was given to him because he came from that city. In 1888 he was hired by the Illinois Central Railroad as a stoker, then becoming a driver in just two years. He soon became famous with the railway personnel because he would boast that he was always on time thanks to his particular use

*The ballad of Casey Jones"
is nowadays an essential part
of popular American culture.*

the meantime, local train n.26 from Canton was arriving, also being accommodated into a side track. But when the two goods trains started moving again to free the main line, a problem with the brakes blocked goods train n.72, its tail remaining on the main exchange north of the station. The express emerged out of a bend at full speed and only then did Casey Jones see that the line was blocked. He immediately understood that a crash was unavoidable but tried everything to stop the train, remaining in the cabin after having thrown stoker Sim Webb off the train, thus saving his life. The impact was extremely violent and destroyed the luggage compartment and several goods carriages. But Casey Jones's sacrifice in not jumping out of the cabin saved other lives.

Even though the official inquiry blamed him, for not having paid attention to the yellow warning flags on the line, thanks to his sacrifice he was immediately deemed by all to be a hero. The story would have certainly been forgotten over the years if a railway mate of Jones's, probably Jordan Fulton, a black workman in the Canton works, had not written a ballad in his memory. It was such a beautiful and sad song that it inspired many other artists over the years to come.

Another little known aspect of the story is to do with the name of the train. In fact, on that night, there was no Cannon Ball Express, but just Express n.1. In the company documents and timetables of the time, there is not trace of a train by such a name. Nor did the articles written in the following days and weeks ever mention it. It wasn't until 1903 that a newspaper, telling the story, titled "The Illinois Central Cannon Ball Derails Close to the City." So where did the name come from? In those years people generally called all express trains "Cannon Ball" for their truly amazing speed at the time. It is reasonable to suppose, then, that over the years, as the story becoming more legendary that Cannon Ball Express became the name attributed to the tragic train. Only years later did ICRR's Express n.1 leaving at 11.15 pm get an official name, but it was The City of New Orleans.

of the locomotive's whistle, modulated at first, then louder and louder. On the evening of April 29 Casey Jones was asked to replace a sick colleague at the helm of express number 1, from Memphis to Canton, departing at 11.15 pm. The convoy was composed of locomotive 382 and six carriages. In the cabin were stoker was Sim Webb and on the train conductor J.C. Turner. Because of a series of inconveniences, the train left 50 minutes after midnight, about and an hour and a half late. Casey Jones was set on recuperating the delay as much as possible, and he drove the train at maximum speed on a difficult line, with many bends, and where many accidents had taken place.

Whilst the locomotive was running south, the circumstances leading up to the forthcoming tragedy were set. In the Vaughan station, two goods trains, n.72 and n.83 were maneuvering into side tracks, but they were both too long to fit in and some cars were still on the main line. In

THE RECORD-BREAKING TRAINS
1900 - 1930

MAN TAMES
THE HORSE
OF STEEL

116 TOP STEAM LOCOMOTIVES IN CHINA HAVE BEEN FOR MANY YEARS SYMBOLS OF PROGRESS AND DEVELOPMENT. BECAUSE OF THIS THEY ARE OFTEN DECORATED WITH SLOGANS, SUCH AS THIS ONE WHICH SYAYS: "STUDYING THE TEACHINGS OF MAO TSE-TUNG."

116-117 TWO CLASS QJ STEAM LOCOMOTIVES OF THE CHINESE RAILWAYS ARE WAITING FOR THE GO AHEAD AT THE STOPOVER AT HARBIN IN THE PROVINCE OF HEILUNGKIANG. THE ONE ON THE LEFT HAS A PLATE IN HONOUR OF GENERAL ZHUDE.

117 THIS CHINESE LOCOMOTIVE OF CLASS SY (WITH A MIKADO WHEEL ARRANGEMENT OF 2-8-2) IS STILL ON SERVICE AT THE COAL MINES OF TANGSHAN. THE PLATE READS: "PRODUCING WITH SAFETY."

The first decades of the 20th century were the golden years of steam locomotion throughout the world. Technical developments continued until electric propulsion and then diesel took over.

Steam locomotives were still in regular service in many countries for decades even after the advent of diesel. Some still run to this day, you may see them in some remote areas of the world.

There are a few hundred machines either kept for historical purposes or for pulling old trains. But the charm of "real service" is another thing altogether. China, probably for just a few years more, is the paradise for steam train lovers from the whole world.

They go there to photograph the last passenger and freight trains still regularly hauled by steam engines, nearly all big QJs with five loaded axles. But alas, even China has recently stopped making them.

Three Chinese locomotives of the class QJ, wheel arrangement 2-10-2, await their turn for service in the locomotive yard of Changchun in the province of Kirin. These locomotives have been used especially for the freights services.

To understand what a great railway network entirely run on steam means, you just have to go back to 1985, for example, when the locomotive depot of Harbin, in Northern China had 100 steam engines in regular service.

These were very big machines by European standards. They would wait in line for their turn to fill up with coal under a huge wooden hopper and then on to fill the tender with water.

A little further on, the machines at the end of their tour of duty, after having cleaned their furnaces and checked the lubrication of bearings and wheels, would mount on a huge rotating platform which would direct them to one of the free stalls in the huge circular depot. Images and practices which in Europe and the United States had disappeared almost 40 years earlier.

A depot of steam locomotives, due to all the care and attention these machines need, pulsates with a life unknown in the sheds of diesel or electric locomotives, which are little more than simple parking areas between one run and the next.

118 BOTTOM A RM CLASS CHINESE PACIFIC (WHEEL ARRANGEMENT 4-6-2), AWAITS TO RESUME ITS SERVICE. THE SLOGAN ON THE RECTANGULAR PLATE READS: "SERVING THE PEOPLE," WHILE AROUND THE BOILR ARE THE FOUR OBJECTIVES OF THE COMMUNIST PARTY PLAN.

118-119 TWO CHINESE STEAM LOCOMOTIVES OF THE SY CLASS MOVE THE COAL CARTS IN THE MINE'S LARGE SQUARE RAILWAY OF TANGSHAN. CHINA CONTINUED TO BUILD STEAM LOCOMOTIVES UP TO A FEW YEARS AGO.

120-121 This spectacular image of double traction involves two QJ class locomotives of the Chinese railways hauling a freight train on the Jitong line, which in 2004 was the last great connection in the world made entirely by steam.

121 A small narrow-gauge steam locomotive hauls a load of trunks on the forest railway of Anshan, in the district of Liaoning in China. Up to a few years ago, forest railways stretched for thousands of miles.

Steam traction has always required complex plants and many people working on them around the clock. A steam engine was never allowed to arrest completely between runs, but would merely rest at a lower boiler pressure. The caretaker, almost like a groom with a thoroughbred, would watch over the machine, checking that the stationing fire, much smaller than the normal one, would not get too weak and that the water in the boiler should not drop below minimum levels. Before resting, the machines would have their water replenished in the tender, their furnaces cleaned of any debris and ashes emptied from under the furnace. Then all the washers, ball bearings and wheels had to be checked and lubrication oil topped up.

Often some maintenance job had to be carried out, a bolt tightened, the compressed air pump had to be checked, or the water injectors in the boiler. At regular intervals one also had to open the smoke chamber on the front of the locomotive, that part of the boiler where discharge fumes from the cylinder went before being expelled into the atmosphere creating the suction which favored combustion in the furnace. The draught from the furnace also brought much ash with it, creating a deposit on the bottom of the smoke chamber itself which had to be periodically removed.

el after shovel. Just think that on a 691 locomotive, the Italian Pacifics which drew the most important trains along the Milan-Venice route, it was necessary to provide a team of two stokers, because one couldn't handle the whole trip on his own, however trained and robust. Not that drivers had a much better time. In Italy, for example, locomotives except for a few machines of American build, were driven standing up. Often they had to hold their heads outside to better see the line and signals. In open cabs the heat was unbearable in front of the furnace and terribly cold just two steps back: a torture in any case preferable to what drivers were subjected to at the beginning of the century, in

Other operations had to be carried out before returning to service: the pressure in the boiler had to be brought back up to the standard level, from 170 lbs/square inch up, according to the locomotive. It was also necessary to check the security valves, fill the sandbox, and check lubrication again. Activity would never stop around a working locomotive, and this meant having a complex and expensive organization which railway companies were quite happy to eliminate as soon as possible.

The work of the stokers and drivers was vital. Working conditions improved for them, too, with the evolution of locomotives. In the early years cabins were little more than a tin roof, and the work itself was extremely harsh. The stoker during a journey would have to shovel tons of coal, also making sure that it was stacked properly in the furnace. To get the best effect, it was necessary that the fire was prepared in a particular manner. This depended naturally on the dimensions of the furnace, the kind of locomotive, and the coal available. In other words the stoker soon learnt not only to shovel mountains of coal, but how to become a real furnace artist, using other equipment such as mandrels and pokers, to remove debris and better dispose the burning coal.

Where the construction of steam locomotives went on for longer and where more powerful machines were made, they soon realized the limits of human strength and found other devices to help operations. The main one was certainly the stocker, an automatic loader which directly placed the coal from the tender into the furnace. Other locomotives adopted fuel oil, which was nebulized in the furnace with special injectors. But in countries where the evolution of the steam locomotive stopped earlier, these devices were never adopted and stokers kept perspiring, shov-

the tight, closed cabins of FS group 470 locomotives. The heat was such that the machines were soon nicknamed "crematories."

There were extreme situations which now seem impossible but were once common in daily life. The older drivers still remember the terrible conditions that they endured when they entered a long gallery, say uphill, driving a particularly heavy train. The machines, under stress, would erupt steam and smoke, which soon filled the gallery and obviously the cab too. At that point, often, the driver and stoker, once they had set their equipment, would lie on the floor of the cabin covering their faces with wet cotton, waiting for the locomotive to take them out of the tunnel by itself.

Notwithstanding this, with few exceptions, they all deeply loved their work and sometimes gave maniacal attention to their locomotives. To travel nowadays in a steam engine cab is still a unique experience, especially if accompanied by a driver who explains the complex operations which are necessary to get the most out of these machines. One may say that the difference between driving a steam engine and a diesel or electric one is comparable to the difference between riding a horse and driving a car – both reach their destination, but the experience of the journey is radically different.

122 THE FIREMAN OF A LOCOMOTIVE OF THE WESTERN MARYLAND RAILROAD, STILL IN SERVICE FOR HISTORICAL TRAINS, PLACES COAL ON THE TENDER BEFORE STARTING THE JOURNEY IN THE ALLEGHENY MOUNTAINS TOWARDS FROSTBURG.

122-123 A FIREMAN HURLS SHOVELFULS OF COAL INTO THE LOCOMOTIVE'S FIREBOX. THIS IS AN OPERATION THAT THE FIREMAN HAS TO CARRY OUT WHILE MAINTAINING HIS BALANCE ON THE MOVING PLATFORM CONNECTING THE CABIN TO THE TENDER.

THE DEVELOPMENT OF STEAM LOCOMOTIVES

Nearly every railway administration that developed steam locomotives has its own "school." This means that, in contrast to what happens with modern rolling stock, which is rather similar everywhere, with a little experience it is easy to distinguish at first glance a German locomotive from an Italian one, or say, an English or American one.

Naturally basic technical progress followed the same tracks: to improve the performance of locomotives it was necessary to increase their weight and, at the same time, get more power. These objectives were reached over time by building bigger and bigger boilers, increasing the number of axles, powered and not. The restrictions were binding: on the one hand the axial weight could not be too excessive for the rails, on the other hand, the dimensions were not to exceed the size limit set for circulation. If the first limit became less rigid over time, with the introduction of more and more robust rails, for the second the only way was to make locomotives longer. From the 20 ft (6 m), tender included, of the Rocket, the American "Big Boys" built for Union Pacific reached 130 ft (40 m) in length.

Longer locomotives, though, meant more difficulties on bends, a problem which was solved with various technical tricks. The elimination of the flanges from the central wheels, the possibility of sideways movement for the axles at the extremities, and finally, true and proper articulations of the engine apparatus, such as the locomotives designed by Anatole Mallet.

Among other technical innovations, the main one was surely the adoption of superheated vapor. If passed through an appropriate element, it can reach temperatures well above boiling point of 100 degrees Celsius and with lower humidity. This leads to the practical result of significantly increasing its expansion capacity. Also of interest is the use of compound expansion. This system uses the residual expansion capacity of vapor already used, making it work inside another cylinder operating at a lower pressure. Other important devices were the water pre-heaters inside boilers such as the Nielebock-Knorr or Franco Crosti models.

UNION PACIFIC

AMERICA SAYS "keep 'em flying." But to keep 'em flying we must keep 'em rolling—on the rails. Materials, thousands of carloads, for planes, tanks and guns must be rushed to production and assembly plants. Completed armament also must be transported.

Union Pacific is powered to do the job. Twenty "Big Boys," largest steam locomotives ever built, have recently been added to the large fleet of other super-powered rail giants placed in service during the past five years.

Millions of dollars also have been invested in freight cars, new rails and property improvements. For defense as well as industry's normal needs, Union Pacific—the Strategic Middle Route connecting East with West—supplies the demand for dependable transportation.

The Progressive
UNION PACIFIC RAILROAD
The Strategic Middle Route

Let "Big Boy" speed your freight

A gigantic, rolling power-house . . . the 600-ton locomotive "Big Boy" speeds the heaviest freight loads. Equipment designed to handle any freight shipment . . . large or small . . . backed by modern facilities and men who know their jobs are assurance of dependable performance.

Union Pacific traffic experts are located in metropolitan cities from coast to coast. They offer you complete cooperation in handling any traffic problem.

UNION PACIFIC RAILROAD

BE SPECIFIC: *Ship* **UNION PACIFIC**

RAILWAY MASTERPIECES OF THE TIME

THE COUPE VENT – It is almost impossible to describe all the kinds of steam locomotives made over the years, just as it is extremely difficult to draw a chart in terms of their importance or technical specifications adopted. We have therefore decided to choose a route of our own through the hundreds of different locomotives, dweling a little on the ones that seemed more interesting to us.

At the beginning of the century, among the most famous steam locomotives in Europe there were those of the PLM (Paris Lyon Mediterraneé) C Series, nicknamed, due to their particular shape, "Coupe-vent" (wind cutters). They were used to pull among the most prestigious

Les Locomotives

Collection F. FLEURY

Locomotive P. L. M. pour Train rapide, série C
ae 61 à 180, pesant 52,000 kilogs
vitesse de 150 à l'heure

trains of the Belle Époque to the French Riviera. One hundred and twenty were made, starting in 1898. The Coupe-vent had a 4-4-0 wheel arrangement and a double expansion engine which allowed it to reach 70 mph (112 km/h). For the first time ever, pressure in the steel boilers reached 213 pounds per square inch. The two big driving wheels had a diameter of six and a half feet (1.9 m). What made them more attractive, even to the public at large, was undoubtedly the aerodynamic profile of its smoke-box and the fairing which jointed the chimney to the dome.

THE COW – In those same years, the Italian locomotives of group 500 of the Rete Adriatica and the FS's 670s were just as innovative. The model was nicknamed "The Cow," not so much for the shape or demeanor, but with reference to the rich fees which accompanying technicians "milked" in the various tests and exhibitions. The machine was sent to the Universal Expo of Paris, where it raised much interest for the technical solutions it had adopted. The main one was the position of the furnace, above the front carriage so as to be bigger and produce more vapor.

The boiler was therefore mounted in the opposite direction to the usual, with the cabin in front and the chimney behind. The coal was stashed in a container between the boiler and the cabin, whilst the water was taken from a cistern carriage with three axles on the tail. Another significant novelty was the adoption of a Plancher engine with compound expansion but with asymmetrical cylinders. 43 models were built up until 1906, partly by Borsig in Berlin and partly by Breda of Milan. The Cow used a 4-6-0 wheel arrangement, with two loaded wheels of six feet and four inches (1.9 m) in diameter, reaching a top speed of 68 mph (110 km/h).

THE T3 – This was a small but very efficient and versatile engine. This three-axle locotender (a locotender carries its own water and coal, rather than in a separate tender) was built from 1878. Some 1300

models were made, proving its noteworthy technical success. It was the classic engine for local trains, with a top speed of only 25 to 30 mph (40 to 48 km/h). On the other hand, it could go practically everywhere, having an axial weight of only 11 tons. Until the Second World War it was especially used in Germany and many dozens were exported abroad. Many have survived to today and are used to tug historical trains.

THE ATLANTIC NORD – The first of these splendid locomotives of a classic 4-4-2 wheel arrangement was presented by the Compagnie du Nord at the Universal Exposition of Paris in 1900. For the time, the machine was very advanced and incorporated all the most recent technical innovations.

People also liked its chocolate color with yellow lines. It was not a casual choice, because the machine was used on the main express trains on the Southern France line, until it was substituted with the fabulous Pacific in the 1930s. It easily reached 75 mph (120 km/h), with peaks of 85 mph (140 km/h) with fast trains. There were 185 built for various companies, and not just French ones. One model is kept in the French railway Museum of Mulhouse.

THE GREAT WESTERN RAILWAY'S CITY CLASS 4-4-0 – This group of 27 English locomotives would not be particularly significant if it weren't that one of them, n.3440, nicknamed "City of Truro," is held to be the first machine in Europe to break the 100 mph (160 km/h) barrier. For this reason it is very well known among British enthusiasts. The City of Truro broke this symbolic speed barrier in 1904. At the end of its career, in 1931, a model was placed in the York Museum. Put back on the rails in 1957, especially for fans, it was finally retired for good in 1961.

A few years ago it was newly restored and brought to pressure to celebrate the 100th anniversary of the speed record. From a technical point of view, as we said, the machine was certainly not ground-breaking. It was the last machine with a 4-4-0 wheel arrangement and external chassis built by Great Western Railway.

THE PRUSSIAN P8 – This group of locomotives, which included 4000 models in various versions, was one of the most characteristic of the German railway. It was a simple and sturdy locomotive, which had two simple expansion cylinders moved by overheated vapor. It was intended to pull light passenger trains. The "P" stands for *personenzug*, in German, passenger train. In truth, though, it was an extremely versatile locomotive also used for goods. The top speed was set at 68 mph (109 km/h). Its construction in 1906 was entrusted practically to all the most important German locomotive factories. They formed group 38 of the DR, the Reich's railway, and after the First World War many were given as reimbursement to the various railway administrations of Europe.

THE SWISS RAILWAYS' A 3/5 – Built from 1907 onwards, these attractive locomotives with a 4-6-0 wheel arrangement were very useful for the difficult climbs of the Gottardo, which could be as steep as 2.6% in some cases.

They had saturated simple expansion steam engines which

made them particularly appropriate, and could be used both on the steep mountain ramps and flatter runs, usually leading important passenger trains.

From 1913 on, the machines were endowed with a steam superheater, increasing performance. The A 3/5 is undoubtedly one of the best-known Swiss steam locomotives also thanks to the classic and clean design of the body.

128-129 THE A3/5 IS ONE OF THE MOST BEAUTIFUL SWISS STEAM LOCOMOTIVES, AND IT WAS BUILT, STARTING FROM 1907, IN TWO DIFFERENT SERIES PRODUCED BY SLM AND MAFFEI IN 51 MODELS. THE 705, PRESERVED BY THE SWISS RAILWAYS, WAS BUILT BY SLM.

129 TOP LEFT THE LOCOMOTIVE NO. 3440, CITY OF TRURO, WAS BUILT IN 1903 FROM A DESIGN BY ENGINEER WILLIAM DEAN FOR THE GREAT WESTERN RAILWAY. IT IS FAMOUS FOR BEING THE FIRST LOCOMOTIVE TO HAVE SURPASSED 100 MILES PER HOUR.

129 TOP RIGHT THE PRUSSIAN P8 LOCOMOTIVES, LATER BECOMING SERIES 38 OF THE DEUTSCHE REICHSBAHN, WERE A GROUP OF MACHINES WHICH WERE QUITE WIDESPREAD IN GERMANY AND, LATER, THROUGHOUT EUROPE. STARTING FROM 1906, 4000 SPECIMEN WERE BUILT.

THE ITALIAN FERROVIE DELLO STATO'S GRUPPO 640 – These locomotives were the first example of that "Italian school," which were developed thanks to the engineers of the Florence Ufficio Studi, first for the Rete Adriatica, then, from 1905 for the Ferrovie dello Stato. They are light machines, slender but powerful, based on simple but modern technical ideas. For example, the 640 did away with compound expansion, in favor of the simple variety, thanks to more efficient superheaters. The power lost with simple expansion was thus amply compensated by the superheated vapor, without useless construction complications. But the real jewel in the crown of this locomotive was the front tender, invented by Giuseppe Zara.

Also known as the "Italian bogie," it associated the movements of the front loaded axle with those of the first engine axle, whose sideways movement was allowed by universal joints in the relative sockets. The system proved very effective at high speed too, entering bends better than the traditional loaded boogie and using the weight of the locomotive to the best advantage.

All the Italian locomotives built after 1907 mounted this front bogie with the sole exception of the GR 690, which then became 691. The 640, with a top speed of about 60 mph (95 km/h), was in service until the 1970s. The same criteria and the same overall design was used a few years later for locomotives of group 625, one of the reference points of Italian steam locomotives, with 341 models built. Compared to the 640, these locomotives mounted two cylinders of a slightly smaller diameter and lower wheels, 4 feet and 11 inches (1.5 m) instead of six feet and one inch (1.8 m). Their speed was therefore a little lower, whilst power (800 HP) was substantially the same.

GROUP 740 OF THE FS: THE ITALIAN STANDARD CLASS – This is the most numerous group of Italian steam locomotives, with 470 models. Many of them, conserved and restored, are still in service with trains for tourists and enthusiasts. Essentially conceived as a freight train engine, in the course of their career they were especially used on mountain and secondary lines, also for local passenger trains.

The 740 machines, also with a 2-8-0 arrangement, were developed out of the decision to abandon compound expansion in favor of the simple kind, as soon as superheated steam allowed for similar results to be achieved. The structure of the 740 is similar to the 730 constructed in 1906.

These, instead, were ordered from 1911 on, with a simple expansion engine, external cylinders and superheated steam. The power was certainly not exorbitant, 980 HP at 28 mph (45 km/h: the top speed was 40 mph/65 km/h), but on the other hand these were extremely reliable machines.

On the same design, with the same carriage, engine and boilers, the FS from 1922 also made 41 tender locomotives 940s with a 2-8-2 arrangement for passenger and goods trains on mountain lines. One mustn't forget that many 740s were fitted from the 1950s (some in 1941) onwards with the Franco Crosti pre-heater. The device was mounted on or under the boiler and divided into two elements on the side. The 741 and 743 machines took on an unmistakable appearance, with the chimney stack very close to the cabin.

THE 685, QUEEN OF ITALIAN LOCOMOTIVES – Only one is still in service, 685 n.196, used on the most prestigious historical trains. Its elegance earned it the title "Queen of Locomotives" from Italian enthusiasts. In fact, these 2-6-2, whose construction began in 1912, may be considered the best product of the Ferrovie dello Stato's Ufficio Studi. The FS chose for the 685 the same solution as for the 640 and 740: compound expansion was abandoned for the 680 group. The machine developed soon proved very appropriate: it used a four-cylinder simple expansion engine with vapor superheater. Naturaly, it had the famous Italian bogie which allowed it to easily reach 75 mph (120 km/h), combining speed with fair power (1250 hp).

From an aesthetic point of view, the result was more remarkable, thanks to the aerodynamic cabin and big powered wheels, six feet and one inch (1.8 m) in diameter. There were 271 models built, and another 121 were obtained from the conversion of the 680. These locomotives were practically entrusted with all the most important passenger trains on non-electrified lines.

The last prestigious model in service was the Adria Express from Ferrara to Rimini until 1967.

GREAT WESTERN RAILWAY'S CASTLE CLASS – The Castle class locomotives, with a 4-6-0 wheel arrangement, are among the best known of the Great Western Railway. There were an evolution of the Star class and 165 of them were built from 1923 to 1950. The locomotives in this class distinguished themselves for their special performance in driving the Cheltenam Flyer express.

On June 6, 1932, the Tregenna Castle locomotive (n. 5006) pulled the express the 77 miles from Swindon to Paddington at the impressive average speed of 81 mph (130 km/h). The Castle model used a simple expansion engine, with four cylinders, softer than the two cylinder, and superheated vapor.

They remained in regular service until the 1960s, but many have been conserved and kept for historical trains.

DRG 44 Series – This imposing locomotive for freight trains, with a 2-10-0 arrangement, was made from 1926 and nearly 2000 models were produced until 1949. It is the first German locomotive unified for goods. Not many European locomotives have five coupled axles, a technical solution which, on the one hand allowed more powerful machines but on the other hand had problems guaranteeing perfect bend insertion with a rigid step, i.e. with a number of axles coupled together using connecting rods. In Great Britain, the first locomotive with five coupled axles wasn't made until 1943, whilst in Germany the first experiments

134-135 The 7029 locomotive "Clun Castle" of the Great Central Railway, hauls, at full steam, a special excursion train in June of 1993. These machines, first built in 1923, were able to travel at 100 mph (160 km/h).

135 The locomotives of the G12 Group were the first with the wheel arrangement 2-10-0 to be mass produced in Germany since 1917. This example was registered as Class 36 by the JZ, the Yugoslav railways.

date back as far as 1912. In 1917 the first important 2-10-0 group appeared, the Prussian G12, with some1350 models built. When the German state pre-unitary networks were built, in 1921 the group G12 locomotives became part of the DRG (Deutsche Reichsbahn Gesellschaft), forming group 58. Their perfect functioning induced the engineers of the German railways to put a 2-10-0 in the "Locomotive Standardization Plan." In those years, the DRG had inherited 284 different kinds of locomotives from pre-unification, and it was necessary to bring order to a situation which was also creating financial loss and running problems. So, in a short time they decided to reduce the stock to 29 groups of standard locomotives.

The machines in group 44 had three cylinder engines, simple expansion and superheated steam. Together with a modern boiler (the same which was later used for the fast Pacific) allowed 2000 ton trains to be pulled at 35 mph (56 km/h).

Following the division of Germany after the Second World War, locomotives were shared among the DB, West Germany's state railway, and the DR, East Germany's.

Those that went to the DR stopped being used in 1967, whilst on this side of the wall they were still used until 1976. Most memorable in those years were goods trains of over 3000 tons with double traction running through the Mosel Valley.

THE PACIFIC, ELEGANCE AND SPEED ON RAILS – Pacific locomotives are synonymous in the whole world of elegance and speed: the name that distinguishes them is applied to machines using the 4-6-2 arrangement in the United States. This arrangement, with a two-axle front trolley as a guide, three big loaded wheels and a loaded back trolley under the furnace, was appropriate for developing more powerful and faster machines. After that, the need for more power and the dimension of the boilers led to an additional axle, giving a 2-8-2 configuration also known as a Mikado, which led to construction of beautiful and impressive locomotives, less elegant, though, than the smaller Pacifics.

Practically all the European and US railway networks used Pacifics in the golden years of steam power. Described here are the most attractive and famous ones running on the railways of that time.

One of the very first Pacifics circulating in Europe was the Baden IVF, a unique machine of particular elegance built by Maffei of Munich in 1907 for the State of Baden. It had a 4-cylinder engine, simple expansion and superheated steam, with wheels of five feet and eleven inches (1.8 m) in diameter.

The top speed, 75 mph (120 km/h), allowed it to pull the fastest trains of the time. One of the test runs was held on the Mannheim-Offemburg-Basel line, where the locomotive pulled a train of 460 tons, rather heavy for the time, at an average speed of 60 mph (95 km/h) with no particular problem.

It was only a year later that the Bavarian S3/6 saw the light. Generally considered one of the most beautiful locomotives of the time. It had a 4-cylinder engine with compound expansion, innovative for the time, fed with superheated steam. It was a hugely successful machine, with a 159 of them made in Maffei's Munich works. In the 1930s it was reclassified into group 18 of the DRG and used to drive the most prestigious German trains from Rheingold in the tract between Emmerich and Mannheim. The Bavarian S3/6 had great power, 1750 HP at 45 mph (72 km/h) and a top speed of 80 mph (130 km/h).

In France, naturally, they didn't just stand and watch, and in 1909 the PLM (Paris-Lyon-Mediterraneé) started using its first Pacifics, simply called 231. Up to 1934, in various versions, 460 were built. Initially, they used simple expansion until moving on to compound starting with the C series in 1912. They were very fortunate machines, blessed with continuous improvements (the last series built, the G series of 1934, had an impressive horse power of 2800) and were in service for a long time.

Just as successful were the K series Pacifics in the US of Pennsylvania Railroad, which represented perhaps some of the most beautiful American locomotives of those years. The K4s were used to lead the famous Detroit Arrow and Broadway Limited. In 1936, among other developments, n.3768 was given a fairing by the famous architect and designer Raymond Loewy.

The K4s locomotives were designed by J.T. Wallis of the Pennsylvania Railroad Traction Office, using the boiler and other mechanical parts from the L1s 2-8-2 Mikado and inspired by the experience on the Pacific K29s built in 1911 by Alco. At the time, the American company was one of the most important in the world and had decided to build its own locomotives to have the best possible rolling stock. The K4s were undoubtedly very well turned out machines; notwithstanding they were rather traditional in conception. "Penn" as the US company was known, then experimented with all kinds of innovations, but without departing from the basic concept which guaranteed them a career of over 30 years.

They had a power of about 3000 HP, a top speed of 95 mph (150 km/h) and they could easily cruise at 75 mph (120 km/h). They had a simple expansion engine, fed with superheated steam and wheels of six feet and seven inches (1.9 m). As we will see, in the United States, the Pacifics were soon replaced by bigger and more powerful machines in the 1930s and 1940s.

138 THE WONDERFUL 387043 PACIFIC OF THE CSD (THE RAILWAYS OF CZECHOSLOVAKIA BEFORE THE SEPARATION) STOPS AT THE BRNO YARD AMONGST OTHER HISTORICAL LOCOMOTIVES. BUILT IN 1925, IT REACHED THE REMARKABLE SPEED OF 80 MPH (130 KM/H).

138-139 THE 01-1100 PACIFIC OF THE DB IS ONE OF THE MOST FAMOUS GERMAN HISTORICAL LOCOMOTIVES, AND IS OFTEN USED TO PULL SPECIAL TRAINS. A CHARACTERISTIC OF THIS LOCOMOTIVE IS THAT IT IS FUELLED BY DIESEL OIL INSTEAD OF COAL.

Back in Europe, a few years later, in 1925, Czechoslovakia put a splendid Pacific in service, the 387, built by Skoda (in total 43 were built). The Geman School inspired the machine, three cylinders on superheated steam and simple expansion. It could reach a top speed of 80 mph (130 km/h). Its career lasted until the mid-1960s, until the electrification of the main Czechoslovak lines. A year later, in Germany, the Borsig made the first Br 01, one of the most famous and attractive European Pacifics of all times. In various versions, 231 of them were built. It would take too long here to list all the modifications these locomotives saw over the years, from the change in boiler to the change in fuel to oil. They remained in service until the 1970s in both East and West Germany. From a mechanical point of view, they used a two-cylinder superheated simple expansion steam engine reaching 80 mph (130 km/h).

Much less fortunate was the career of the only Italian Pacific, the 691 made in 1929 from the reconstruction of the 690 of 1911. There were 33 built and they were used on the main lines of the Val Padana, which were the only lines equipped with rails that could withstand their weight. In the reconstruction of the 690 a bigger boiler was made, the rear loaded axles was substituted with a Bissel trolley and a Knorr pre-heater added. The power thus grew to 1750 HP (at 55 mph) and the top speed was 80 mph. In 1939 the 691.026 was subjected to a curious experiment, where it was loaded with a heavy fairing, making it very similar to a tank. The mantle, besides being a useless weight to transport, got in the way of maintenance and was soon removed. The 691s stayed in service until the 1960s. The only one to have survived the scrapyard, n.022, is kept in the Museo della Scienza e della Tecnica of Milan.

Equally famous in those years were the Pacific Nord Chapelons, which were used to drive the fast Fleche d'Or Paris-Calais train, at 87 mph (140 km/h). These machines were the product of the genius of Andrè Chapelon, considered to be one of the most talented railway engineers of all time.

He thought it possible to improve the performance of the already excellent steam locomotives of the time by changing the shape of the steam collectors, the discharge system through the chimney and the temperature.

The idea was therefore not to build new machines, but to change the already existing ones. When Chapelon managed to apply his theories, transforming a locomotive of the Parigi-Orleans (PO) company, the results proved him absolutely right: power went from 2000 to 3000 HP

140 This image was taken in London in 1947 and shows the luxurious Pullman carriages of the Fleche d'Or/Golden Arrow London-Paris Express. The convoy was hauled by the best steam locomotives of the days.

140-141 This image of 1929 shows the 231.E34 Pacific in Paris waiting for the go ahead, at the head of the Fleche d'Or express for Calais and London. It was one of the most prestigious services of that period.

with a saving in the consumption of fuel of a good third. PO thus had some locomotives modified and so did Compagnie du Nord, asking Chapelon to transform a batch of its Pacifics. So, as of 1934, the 48 locomotives of the Nord 3.1100 series were reclassified upon the birth of the SNCF, the French State railways, as the 231E series, number 1 to 48. These superb locomotives used compound expansion and superheated steam and were capable of delivering a steady power of an impressive 2700 HP at 87 mph (140 km/h).

Besides their undoubted technical qualities, their fame can also be attributed to their livery, one of the most attractive in the history of European railways – chocolate with fine yellow lines highlighting the fine proportions of the machine.

Fortunately, one of these locomotives, the E22, was saved from destruction and can be seen in all its elegance in the Mulhouse French Railway Museum.

Until now, in our excursion among the most famous Pacifics, we have not spoken about English machines, and there's a good reason for this. British companies in fact developed in the same years the splendid 4-6-0 locomotives easily equaling the performance of the continental Pacifics. In Great Britain, therefore, Pacifics appeared relatively late, but they were still unforgettable machines. We are naturally talking of LNER (London & North Eastern Railway) class A4 locomotives and, in particular, locomotive n.4468, a.k.a. The Mallard, which in 1938 established the world speed record for a steam engine, a record which still stands today at 126 mph (202 km/h).

The A4s were designed in 1935 by famous engineer Sir Nigel Gresley to haul a new train, the Silver Jubilee, between the stations of London King's Cross and Newcastle. The name was a homage to the 25 years of the reign of King George V. Gresley began from the already excellent class A3 Pacific, giving it more power by increasing boiler pressure (249 pounds per square inch) and the size of the furnace. These modifications contributed to increasing the production of steam and simultaneously reducing the consumption of both coal and water. Gresley also decided to give the locomotives a fairing which not only had an aesthetic purpose, but also created a flow of air which stopped the steam and vapor from going into the cab, which so hindered drivers' sight. It seems like a detail, but the problem had afflicted the A3s and in any case at 100 mph it was absolutely necessary for the view from the cab to be perfect. The A4s had large wheels of six feet and eight inches (2 m) in diameter powered by a three-cylinder engine, with simple expansion and superheated steam.

" *The Mallard still retains
the world speed record for steam.* "

MALLARD

The speed record was set during a special test organized for July 3, 1938: the 4468 Mallard locomotive was chosen also because it was the first with a KylChap exhaust, which further improved its performance (and which was then mounted on the other locomotives too). The locomotive hauled a convoy of six carriages and a dynamometric car thanks to which it was possible to certify a top speed of 126 mph (202 km/h). The Mallard is now at the York Railway Museum but there are six of the class still in existence out of a total of 35 built.

If the A4s were the queens of the LNER, the Duchess Class (their precise definition is Princess Coronation Class) were the most attractive of LMS's Pacifics (London, Midland & Scottish Railway). They were designed by another famous English engineer of the time, William Stainer who was head of traction for LMS, especially to respond to the performance of the competing LNER locomotives.

LMS decided to challenge the rival company on traffic to Scotland, introducing a new train from London Euston to Glasgow with a single stop in Carlisle. The convoy was dubbed Coronation Scot. The problem was that the Princess Royal Class Pacific locomotives were not considered as good as the new prestigious train. Stainer therefore designed a new family of Pacifics, starting from the Princess Royal project: he increased the diameter of the boiler, introducing new superheating elements and mounted bigger wheels. He also simplified distribution and opted, like Gresley, for a full fairing. The first five locomotives left the Crewe works in June 1937: they were painted, like the train Prussian blue with thin white lines. Another five, also faired, were painted brown instead, with white bands for use with the traditional LMS carriages of the same color. Overall, 38 were made, many of which with only partial or no fairing. Unlike the LNER A4, the Duchess Class Pacifics were 4-cylinder machines, simple expansion, also with superheated steam. The top speed was set at 100 mph (160 km/h), and they were capable of hauling convoys of 600 tons at over 100 mph (160 km/h). Three of these locomotives are preserved in good running order.

The third famous English Pacific was designed by engineer Oliver Bulleid, head of the Southern Railway. We are naturally speaking of the

144-145 A Pacific locomotive of the Duchess Class passes through the station's exit switchers at the head of a historic train. These engines were built (the first in 1939) for the British railway company, LMS.

145 top The "Pacific" no. 35028 "Clan Line" is owned today by the Merchant Navy Locomotive Preservation Society, which after five years of laborious restoration got it back into working order in November 2006.

145 bottom The Pacific 46229 "Duchess of Hamilton" awaits its turn for service in the Marylebone yard. Some of these locomotives received a fairing and were used at the head of the Coronation Scot Express.

Merchant Navy Class made from 1941 to haul trains from the London Victoria to the ports for connections to the Continent. There were 30 of these engines built. Bulleid devised a machine that had certain innovative aspects: a chain in an enclosed oil bath commanded valve distribution. Many commands had vapor powered servos – among these the door to the furnace – and the design was also rather unusual with an oval smoke box door and a body which was not a true and proper fairing but rather an aesthetic artifice for the locomotive to go with the carriages on the network. They used a 3-cylinder engine, with simple expansion and superheated steam, allowing a top speed of 80 mph (128 km/h). After that, Southern Railway built a simplified version of the Merchant Navy, which formed the West Country Class, also known as Battle of Britain or Bulleid Light Pacifics, of which 110 models were built. These locomotives were entrusted with the Golden Arrow train that ran from London to Dover, the British section of the London-Paris route, and which on the Continent was called the Fleche d'Or.

146 top and 146-147
The funeral train of King George VI, which arrived in London on the 12th of February 1952 from Sandringham, was hauled by the Brttania locomotive which, from then onwards, kept the roof of its cabin painted white, in memory of the event.

147 The Pacific Brittania, before the 55 models of the Class 7, was one of the last steam locomotives with this wheel arrangement built in Great Britain, in 1951. The Class 7 were very good locomotives, but the steam era had now come to an end.

The last English Pacifics, built as late as the 1950s, were the Britannia Class a.k.a. British Railway standard class 7. They made 55 of them and they pulled the main, prestigious British trains until the advent of diesel. It was certainly a technically well turned out machine, capable of noteworthy performance to the point that BR were thinking of making a second generation, from which the n.71.000 Duke of Gloucester prototype emerged. But, the era of steam power, at least in Europe, was ending and nothing came of it. There is a curious fact regarding the first locomotive in the group, called Britannia. The machine hauled the funeral train of King George VI from Norfolk to London in February 1952. From then and for many years, to commemorate the event, the locomotive kept the cab roof painted white.

We could stop at this point but we would like to remember two Pacifics, which were far apart, but equally important. The first represents the swan song of European locomotives for fast trains, the second the last group of Pacifics in regular service in the world.

The DB's Br 10 is in reality made up of two Pacifics, dressed and built between 1956 and 1957 by Krupp. In those years, the German reconstruction had already begun and the DB already had excellent electric and diesel locomotives. Perhaps the idea with these two machines was to see how and whether the big pre-war Pacifics still had a future. In those years, in fact, the Br 23s were made for light trains. They had 3-cylinder, simple expansion and superheated steam engines and reached 100 mph (160 km/h). Notwithstanding their excellent performance, they were dumped a few years later.

Six thousand miles further east, however, the RM series Pacifics of the Chinese railways kept hauling passengers until at least 1990. The RM class is the last steam locomotive project for this kind of traffic of the Chi-

nese railways. Built between 1957 and 1961, they were based on the design of the SL6 whose chassis and wheel arrangement they kept and 258 were made. The boiler followed the Russian technical customs, and was similar to that mounted on the Mikado of the JS group with which they share many other parts in an evident effort for standardization.

They were not particularly powerful locomotives and their limits became evident when in the 1970s the length and weight of trains increased considerably.

Many of them ended their career in secondary services and, from the data available (in those years China was not as easy to visit as today, especially in some areas) we know that many were concentrated in the Xi'an area. The last services were certainly run in Manchuria around Shenyang, Changchun, Harbin, and Jiamusi.

With the disappearance of the Rms at the beginning of 1990 we can close the story of the Pacifics, which began nearly a century earlier. Other steam locomotives in any case deserve attention: the big articulated Mallet locomotives and American aerodynamic trains, or the giant South African Garrats, as we cannot close this chapter in history without a mention of the rack locomotives, i.e. those used for steep climbs with cogwheel which engages a special toothed rail. Nor can we disregard the curious Shay, Heisler and Climax geared locomotives, in which movement is transferred to the wheels by gears and drive shafts rather than rods.

THE GREAT AMERICAN ARTICULATED LOCOMOTIVES

The ample spaces and large distances in the United States always favored big sizes, and railroads were no exception. Freight trains lengths are measured in miles and before the Second World War giants appeared on American lines. The record goes to the very famous Big Boy of Union Pacific, a 541-ton monster (the A4 Mallard only weighed 170 tons), a mere 131 ft (40 m) long. Twenty-five of these giants were made by ALCO for Union Pacific, especially to solve the traction problem of freight trains on the 75-mile (120-km) line between Ogden in Utah and Evanston in Wyoming. The stretch included a long climb up Sherman Hill with a 1.55% inclination through the Wasatch hills. The Big Boy developed a power output of 6290 HP and was capable of hauling 3300-ton convoys at 45 mph (72 km/h), whilst on a flat stretch it could easily reach 80 mph (128 km/h). This articulated locomotive was often classified as a Mallet even if this is not completely true. Two distinct engine groups moved the Big Boy with four articulated axles on two trolleys according to a 4-8-

0 + 0-8-4 arrangement. This way the locomotive could enter bends of only 96-yard radii. The engine was 4-cylinder, simple expansion and superheated steam: this is the technical difference from the locomotives designed by Anatole Mallet which were articulated but with compound expansion, i.e. they had 2 high pressure cylinders and 2 low pressure ones for every engine. A Big Boy hauled its last train on July 21, 1959; that day regular service ended even if some were kept in working order until 1961. Six models have been saved from destruction.

148 THE SPECTACULAR ARTICULATED LOCOMOTIVE OF THE UNION PACIFIC CLASS 4000 WAS NICKNAMED BIG BOY FOR ITS GIGANTIC DIMENSIONS. IT WAS ABLE TO HAUL TRAINS WEIGHING OVER 4000 TONS AT 68 MPH (110 KM/H).

149 THE IMPOSING PROFILE OF THE BIG BOY NO. 4007 OF THE UNION PACIFIC ADVANCES ON A REVOLVING PLATFORM: THIS ARTICULATED LOCOMOTIVE WHEEL ARRANGEMENT 4-8-0+0-8-4 IS LONG, OVER 130 FT (40 M), AND WEIGHS, TENDER INCLUDED, 541 TONS.

Many other articulated locomotives of great charm ran on American lines between the two wars. Some of them had Challenger or Yellowstone wheel arrangements, i.e. 4-6-0+0-6-4 and 2-8-0+0-8-4. Among the former, 105 examples of the Union Pacific's class 3900 were made from 1936.

Notwithstanding their massive look and their 40-yard (36-m) length, they were very fast machines used for the company's main passenger trains, particularly those between Salt Lake City and Los Angeles which were made up of up to 20 carriages.

Only 72 Yellowstones were built, for four different railway compa-

nies. They were distinct projects, which only had the six of the locomotives and wheel arrangements in common.

In 1928 Northern Pacific decided to adopt some machines of this type and commissioned ALCO, then one of the main steam locomotive factories in America, to make its first Yellowstone model, with specific technical characteristics. The company wanted to use the machines on the flat stretchs of North Dakota, using the low quality coal extracted in those areas. As a consequence, the designers had to make a huge furnace, with a surface of 20 square yards, the biggest ever made at the time. ALCO celebrated the even by serving a dinner for

twelve people sitting inside! Apart from some vaporization hitches which limited power to "only" 5000 HP, Northern Pacific decided, in 1930, to order another 11 from Baldwin, creating class Z-5 and numbering them from 5000 (the ALCO prototype) to 5111.

Southern Pacific's Yellowstone instead made up class AC-9. Twelve models were made in 1939 by Lima and were employed along the southern lines of the network. Initially built for coal, they were then converted to fuel oil.

They served alongside the famous Cab Fowards of the Southern Pacific with articulated locomotives with the Mallet system in which the

boiler was turned 180 degrees from the usual position. The cab and the furnace were therefore in a frontal position, easing the task of drivers on the Sierra climbs rich in curves and galleries. They used fuel oil, brought to the furnace from the tender with a special conduit, avoiding the problems caused by coal for other locomotives with this configuration.

There were 256 Cab Forwards, divided into various groups and with different configurations and they lasted 46 years in service – testament to a truly successful design. Going back to the Yellowstone, the Duluth, Missabe & Iron Range Railroad started using them, creating the M-3 and M-4 groups. They were used to pull goods trains of 115 carriages, weighing 8750 tons, up hills of 2.2%. The first supply of eight machines (class M-3) was made by Baldwin in 1941 and gave excellent results, leading the company to order another 10 in 1943 (class M-4).

Both groups were used for heavy trains carrying minerals from the Duluth area.

The biggest Yellowstone group was the EM-1 of Baltimore &Ohio, and 30 of these were made between 1944 and 1945 by Baldwin. In truth the company didn't really want them, having already decided to switch completely over to diesel. But they were forced to restrict themselves by the War Production Board. These machines were used for heavy coal and goods express trains on the line from Cumberland to Grafton and when it was dieselized, they served in the Pittsburgh area. They started being decommissioned in 1957 and the last one was removed from service in 1960.

AERODYNAMIC TRAINS BETWEEN THE TWO WARS

Another characteristic aspect of the American railways in the years between the two wars, was undoubtedly that of the large express trains drawn by faired locomotives. These were very fast and luxurious trains with which railway companies responded to the growing competition of air and road transport. One of the most famous is the legendary Hiawatha on the Chicago, Milwaukee, St. Paul and Pacific Railroad in 1935. It ran two trains a day, morning and afternoon, connecting Chicago with the "Twin Cities" of Minneapolis and St. Paul, already forming a single urban area. The convoy was a spectacular train with a fairing colored red and white, hauled in the first years by splendid Atlantics. In 1937 they were substituted by the Hudson class F7, six locomotives with a 4-6-4 wheel arrangement especially designed for this service. They were very powerful machines capable of hauling the Hiawatha, 12 carriages weighting about 550 tons at a speed of 120 mph (190 km/h). Just as famous was the Crusader of Raeding Railroad, which from February 1938 connected Jersey City to Philadelphia. The train's carriages were stainless steel just like the elegant aerodynamic fairing covering the two G-1sa Pacifics, n.117 and n.118 destined for this service. The company logo sat on the front of the locomotive and fine blue lines made the appearance all the more spectacular. On the Western coast ran the Coast Daylight of Southern Pacific hauled by the splendid GS. Starting from 1937, various versions of this locomotive were made, with a 4-8-4 wheel arrangement capable of traveling at 87 mph, and the series from GS-2 to GS-5 were completely faired and painted orange red and black for use with the Coast Daylight which connected the two main Californian cities, Los Angeles and San Francisco. Only in 1955 did they give way to diesel engines. Even the 20th Century Limited, the express train of the New York Cen-

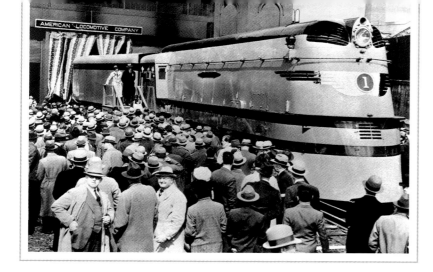 

tral Railroad, which from 1902 connected New York to Chicago and was considered a kind of national institution, was changed into an aerodynamic train in 1939. The company ordered it from famous designer Henry Dreyfuss. The result was a very luxurious train in art deco style. It was composed of a luggage car, six sleeper carriages with different arrangements, five compartment carriages and a salon, two restaurant cars, a bar, and at the back a panoramic carriage. Even the NYC class J-3a locomotives were endowed with beautiful fairings. The service on board was the best imaginable at the time, but NYC wished to add a detail which was to become synonymous with exclusive service and luxury. When the train arrived, a red carpet would be unrolled for the wealthy passengers, leading them to the station hall. Since then, wherever in the world a famous person is to be received, a read carpet is lain.

We cannot forget, though, in this short review of aerodynamic trains

(in those years there were over 100 of them with varying lengths of service and success), the incredible aerodynamic locomotive of Pennsylvania RR built in 1939 by renowned designer Raymond Loewy. It was a prototype, called 6100 or Class S1, which saw no further production. But when it was presented at the New York 1939 Expo, it was a huge success. Its profile similar to a missile and the unusual axle arrangement of 3-2-2-3 struck observers. In other words, it had two trolleys with three axles at the ends and two groups of loaded axles in the centre, but it wasn't an articulated locomotive. It had 4 simple expansion cylinders running on superheated steam and could haul 100-ton trains at a 100 mph (160 km/h). Unfortunately it was too heavy for the rails of many lines and required complex maintenance. It was abandoned only ten years later, but remains an interesting example of the design and technological developments of the American railroads at that time.

The Century in the Highlands of the Hudson

NEW YORK CENTRAL SYSTEM

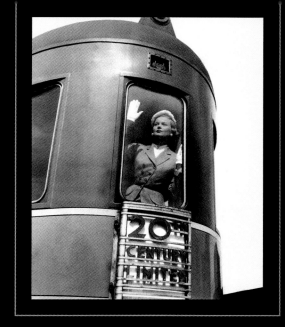

154 THIS POSTER, DESIGNED BY LESLIE RAGAN FOR THE RAILWAY COMPANY NEW YORK CENTRAL, GLORIFIES THE JOURNEY ON THE NEW AERODYNAMIC LUXURY TRAIN, WHICH REACHED CHICAGO ALONG THE RIVER HUDSON.

155 THESE TWO IMAGES OF THE MOST FAMOUS AMERICAN CAREENED TRAIN, THE 20TH CENTURY LIMITED, SHOW THE LOCOMOTIVE J-3A READY TO HAUL AND THE OBSERVATORY CAR AT THE REAR, BOTH CREATED BY THE DESIGNER HENRY DREYFUSS.

> *The 20th Century Limited was known in the 1960s as the fastest train in the world.*

THE GIGANTIC GARRATS

156 DIVIDED INTO SEGMENTS AND SIMILAR TO AN ALLIGATOR, THIS GARRAT STANDS IN THE SETTING SUN AT THE YARD. THESE ARTICULATED LOCOMOTIVES TAKE THEIR NAME FROM THEIR CREATOR, THE ENGINEER HERBERT WILLIAM GARRAT, WHO DESIGNED THE FIRST OF THEM IN 1909.

The story of these locomotives began in 1909 when engineer Herbert William Garrat found a new solution to build powerful articulated locomotives. In practice, these machines are made up of two groups of independent engines articulated with a central chassis holding the boiler and cab. The water and coal reserves are placed on motor carriages, contributing with their weight to increasing the adherence of powered wheels. The first model had a 0-4-0+0-4-0 wheel arrangement, but in the course of the years the machines got bigger until they needed 4-8-2+2-8-4 configurations.

The most recent were built in the 1950s for the South African and Zimbabwe railways where many are still working and are used to pull tourist trains. One of the best known is the Garrat GMAM of South Africa Railways: notwithstanding the narrow gauge (three and half foot) of the South African network, they are big machines, nearly 132 ft (40 m) long, without the cistern car for water which often goes with it. They reach the respectable speed of 60 mph (95 km/h). Thirty-five were made and they were mainly used for heavy goods trains of over 2000 ton. The South African lines have particularly tight bends and the extreme articulation of the Garrat design guarantees easy movement. Long and massive, but also agile on exchanges, they recall the sliding movement of alligators.

157 A GARRAT GMAM OF THE SAR (SOUTH AFRICAN RAILWAYS) HAULS, WITH EFFORT, A SPECIAL TRAIN FOR ENTHUSIASTS. THE CURVES ON THE SOUTH AFRICAN NETWORK ARE VERY NARROW AND THE ARTICULATION OF THE GARRAT FACILITATES ITS CORNERING.

COG LOCOMOTIVES

Lines with rack and pinion or cogs are used when the line is too steep for the natural adherence of locomotives to pull a train. One therefore resorts to a pinion and cogwheel also known as a rack system. Locomotives are thus equipped with an extra cogwheel, which by engaging into the rack hauls the train forward. There are various systems, which we are not going to analyze in detail. The racks used on mountain lines create a whole series of problems, especially on very steep climbs. These problems also extend to the construction of the steam locomotives, whose boiler must be mounted in a horizontal position so that the water covers the fire tubes and the furnace dome. Some steam driven rack railways are still working, for tourist purposes, in various parts of the world. Here, we would like to remember two lines that were an integral part of their national networks.

The first is the Austrian Erzbergbahn, with a normal gauge, connecting the iron mines works of Erzberg to the steel factories of Donawitz. Until 1978 the heavy mineral trains were hauled by symmetrical double traction (a locomotive leading and one behind) by Group 97 rack tender locomotives, wheel arrangement 0-6-2T. The machines were equipped with an Abt rack which allowed them to overcome the most difficult passage from Vordemberg to Eisenerz with inclinations reaching 14% (with natural adherence it is not possible to go above slopes of 3.5 to 3.8 %). Group 97 locomotives, built from 1890 onwards in the Floridsdorf works, have been operating consistently for more than 80 years, and were the oldest in service of the OBB. Of the 18 built, 14 of them survived dieselization, guaranteeing practically all services. The locomotive display that they were offering on the Stiria Hills was truly incomparable and in the last years of service it attracted enthusiasts form all over the world.

Further south, in Italy, a regular service with rack steam locomotives survived until 1981 on the Paola-Cosenza line. It was carried out with tender locomotives of Group 981, which the FS had ordered from Breda in 1922. The old Paola-Cosenza line was replaced by a new route, much of which ran under galleries, on August 2, 1915 to connect Paola, a station on the Tyrrhenian line, to Cosenza, the provincial capital further in-

land. The FS decided to build it as a complementary railway and the route was studied as a consequence. Only 17 miles (27 km) long, it had tracts with gradients of 7.5% (or better, in railway terminology, 75/1000) and it became necessary to equip it with a Strub-type rack.

The original engines of the line consisted of eight Group 980 tender locomotives made by the Swiss SLM of Winterthur. Their performance wasn't totally satisfying and in 1922 the FS asked Breda for the eight 981s. One must say that traffic wasn't very intense and that most passenger services, from 1937, were carried out with diesel railcars also having rack and pinion. Italian 981s were merely average, of low power (only 530 HP) but sufficient for the work they had to undertake. They had a compound expansion and superheated steam engine which had a particular characteristic: on the natural adherence tracts, where the cogwheel mechanism was useless, the locomotive worked on simple expansion, which in the racked parts the steam from the cylinders was sent through a device called a receiver to the low pressure cylinders which transmitted the movement to just the cogwheel. Their more prestigious service allowed them to continue to 1981: they in fact pulled the Rome-Cosenza carriage, which was unhooked at the small station of Paola from the express which continued to Reggio Calabria. A small train, made up of the 981, a braking car with cogwheel, and the carriage to Cosenza.

The journey took a long time due to the very low top speed of 25 mph (40 km/h) on the natural adherence tracts and barely 10 mph (16 km/h) on the rack, but also for the necessary maneuvers, where the artificial adherence tract began, taking the locomotive to the back of the train. For security, in fact, due to its better braking system, the locomotive in the rack section was always put "below" the carriages. This service, very picturesque and fascinating for lovers of steam locomotion, was decidedly anachronistic for its times and ended with the closure of the direct Rome-Cosenza connection.

There has been talk of reactivating the line and its steam locomotives for tourism purposes but the costs and bureaucratic difficulties have halted all projects until now.

---

158 THIS IMAGE SHOWS THE COMPLEX DOUBLE MECHANISM MOTOR OF THE 981 LOCOMOTIVES OF THE ITALIAN RAILWAYS. THE RACK-AND-PINION WHEEL WAS MOVED BY LOW PRESSURE CYLINDERS, WHILE THE DRIVING GEAR WAS MOVED BY HIGH-PRESSURE ONES.

159 AN AUSTRIAN RACK LOCOTENDER CLASS 97 (WITH A WHEEL ARRANGEMENT OF 0-3-1T) IN SERVICE ON THE ERZBERG RAILWAY, HAULS A TRAIN OF EMPTY CARRIAGES. THESE LOCOMOTIVES WERE FIRST BUILT IN 1890.

GEARED FOREST RAILWAY LOCOMOTIVES

Before finally closing the great book on steam traction we must dwell on a kind of locomotive which developed at the beginning of the 20th century, especially in the United States. The American mountains are in fact traversed by thousands of miles of forest railways whose aim was to take the wood that had been cut down into the valleys. These lines were often little more than rested on the ground, with very tight bends, conditions in which normal locomotives could certainly not work regularly. Thus locomotives were moved by two or three two-axle motor bogies, which imparted movement from the engine pistons via a drive shaft. The movement was then transmitted to the other axles either with gears or small connecting rods. Three main families were developed; the most famous are the Shay type, with vertical cylinders and the drive shaft on one side of the locomotive. In these machines, the movement was then transferred to the other axles through gears. Climax locomotives instead had their cylinders normally oriented and transferred movement to a blind axle. This, through gears, moved the central drive shaft, which in turn moved the carriages. Sometimes, to simplify the mechanics, only one axle on each car was driven through gears, whilst the other was moved by a coupled connecting rod. The third system was that of the Heisler in which the drive shaft was directly moved by the pistons of the steam engine, positioned in a V shape. The movement was then transmitted to the wheels with the usual system of gears and coupling rods.

Notwithstanding the mechanics, which may seem very complicated, these locomotives worked very well and are venerated, especially by American enthusiasts. Many survive, both in working order and in static displays.

160 A GROUP OF WORKERS WORKING ON A FOREST RAILWAY IN NORTH AMERICA, POSE NEXT TO A SHAY STEAM LOCOMOTIVE.

160-161 A SHAY GEARED STEAM LOCOMOTIVE IS READY TO LEAVE AT THE HEAD OF A TRAIN OF 47 CARRIAGES LOADED WITH NEWLY CUT LOGS. THIS IMAGE WAS TAKEN IN 1904 IN THE LOADING AREA OF THE CUMMER LUMBER COMPANY OF MICHIGAN.

161 TOP IN THIS PHOTOGRAPH, TAKEN IN CADILLAC, MICHIGAN, AROUND 1904, THE VERTICAL CYLINDERS AND THE GEARED TRANSMISSION OF THIS SHAY TYPE LOCOMOTIVE ARE VERY CLEAR, A LOCOMOTIVE WHICH WAS USED ON THE FOREST AND MINES RAILWAYS.

ELECTRIC AND DIESEL TRACTION ARE BORN

In both Europe and the United States the golden years of steam traction occurred at the very same time that electric and diesel traction were being developed, and were destined to revolutionize railways within a few years. The first experiments applying electricity to railways began at the end of the 19th century.

In 1879 German engineer Werner von Siemens presented at the Berlin Expo a sort of miniature train on a little narrow gauge railway, fed by a central rail. It was little more than a toy, but it could pull 30 people for 295 yards (270 m). It was the first example of electrical energy being applied to a train.

A few years later, in 1881 in England, Magnus Volk, an electrical engineer built a short line of a two-foot gauge through the Brighton forest. The line, singularly considered the first electrical railway in the world, was fed with 110 volts by a third rail. To see a true application, however, we have to go to the United States, where, in 1895 Baltimore

& Ohio made three electric locomotives with DC to substitute steam traction in an over a mile-long gallery of a steep gradient in Howard Street. Its construction was ordered by General Electric, which made machines composed of two perfectly identical semi-units articulated together. Each of these two parts rested on two axles, each moved by an electric engine, without gears through a system of rubber bumpers. The three locomotives were fed with 675 v DC through a sliding shoe making contact with a special side rail. They remained in successful operation until 1912.

A second fundamental chapter in the development of electric traction goes back to 1901, in Germany, when Siemens and AEG technicians experimented with two different electric railcars on the 14-mile (22-km) railway between Merienfel and Zossen near Berlin. The line was equipped with an aerial power system (three-phase alternating current at 10,000 v, 50 Hz) made up of three wires on the side of the

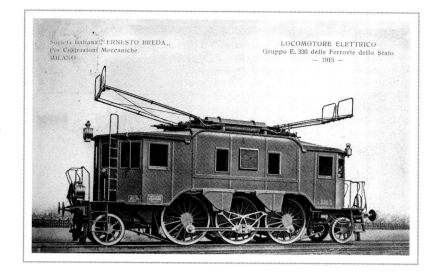

162-163 A historic photograph: the visitors of the Berlin Fair of 1879 travel among the pavilions on a toy train hauled by the first electric locomotive designed by Werner Siemens. It's little more than a toy, but the way ahead is clear.

163 top The E330 electric locomotive of the State Railways represents a milestone in the development of the electric traction in Italy. Sixteen were built and used in particular for the most important passenger trains.

164-165 This fascinating image shows us a GG1 electric locomotive of the Pennsylvania Railroad, stabled at Broad Street station in Philadelphia in 1936. It's regarded as the most beautiful American electric engine.

line, one above the other, on which three tram-like bows made contact, horizontally one above the other. Incredibly, notwithstanding the precarious installation and a disastrous accident which led to the partial reconstruction of the line, the two railcars reacted well, proving the validity of electric railways. In October 1901, the speed of 100 mph (160 km/h) had already been beaten, and two years later, in a new cycle of tests, the Siemens engine reached 128 mph (205 km/h) and the AEG one 130 mph (210 km/h), amazing engineers watching. From then on electric traction was to rapidly spread throughout the world, and this time Italy was to be in the forefront.

The first tramlines used direct current (DC) engines at relatively low tensions of 500-600 volts. At the beginning of the century, the industry was able to supply AC at far higher voltages and at frequencies of around 50 or 60 Hz: characteristics that posed a challenge in the designing of engines. Initially, they preferred to transform the current in-

to DC for the engines, until they were capable of using AC in the reduced frequency of 16 and 2/3 Hz. Another possibility was instead given by the use of three-phase AC at circa. 3000 v and 15 Hz, which forced one to use a much more complex aerial conduction line especially in correspondence of crossroads. This led to the birth of two schools of thought: those favoring high tension single phase alternating current (15.000 v), which became rapidly widespread in Switzerland with the electrification of the Berne-Loetschberg-Simplon line in 1913 and then spread to Germany and Austria; and the three-phase system which was successfully adopted in Italy.

Let's begin with the latter system and for the sake of brevity we'll only hint at the numerous experiments with other electrification systems that Italy had begun with great pioneering spirit from 1899 onwards. Two years earlier, the Public Works Ministry had nominated a commission of specialists with the task of choosing the best electrical traction system possible.

The commission decided to hold a series of experiments in the field. A system of accumulators on the Milan-Monza and the Bologna-San Felice sul Panaro lines, a third 650 v high tension rail on the Milan-Varese, and a 3000 v low frequency (15 Hz) three-phase system to be tested on the Valtellina lines, Lecco-Colico-Sondrio and Colico-Chiavenna. It would have been very interesting to recount the three trials in detail, but it would take a whole volume. Let's say that the Valtellina experiment notwithstanding great difficulties due to the complicated procedure for setting up the aerial lines, proved to be the safest. In June 1906 a regular service began with Italian electric locomotives through the Simplon Tunnel between the Briga and Iselle stations.

That date was an epic one for the development of electric traction in Europe and deserves a few lines of further analysis. In the previous years, the experiment in Valtellina had developed so that the electric railcars for passenger transport and electric freight locomotives of group 340 RA, then E430 of the FS were no longer able to support the increase in traffic. Thus the Ufficio Studi di Firenze in collaboration with Ganz planned three new locomotives with decidedly more powerful 1-C-1 wheel arrangement (for electric locomotives the number of loaded axles is indicated by a letter of the alphabet A=1 B=2 C= 3 axles, and so on) and are classified E.360.

In the meantime in Switzerland concern was increasing for the Simplon Tunnel services, which was about to be terminated, on how to guarantee the safety in the 12-mile (20-km) tunnel, when it was a common experience that personnel and passengers risked suffocation due to engine exhausts in much shorter tunnels.

The Italian authorities took the initiative and offered the Swiss electric traction with the "Valtellina System" for the Domodossola-Iselle-Briga route. The offer included the use of the brand-new E.360s and the drivers trained for them. On its part, Brown Boweri proposed that the Swiss railways oversaw the electrification of the line and managed its use. After a series of surveys, the Swiss agreed and the Simplon Tunnel was electrified. The line was converted to 15,000 volts, like the rest of Switzerland, only in 1930. The success with the Simplon encouraged the Italian FS, which immediately proceeded with other electrification projects. The first was the line through the Giovi Pass, connecting the important port of Genoa with the Paduan plain. To run on this line, the renowned electric E.550 was used, dubbed the Mulo dei Giovi (Jovian Mule) by railway men. In total 186 of them were built from 1908, all in the Vado Ligure plant of Westinghouse Italy.

The locomotive had five coupled axles, with small wheels designed to increase traction at low speeds. The electric motor (fed with 3400 v AC) was connected to the axles through connecting-rods and the machine was capable of developing a top speed of 31 mph (50 km/h); at this speed, the E.550s were able to haul freight weighing 380 tons up the Giovi slopes, whilst the most powerful steam locomotives available didn't go over the 130 tons and at no more than 15 mph (24 km/h). The E.550 was the first of a breed of tri-phase electric locomotives whose last examples only lowered their pantographs in the 1970s. The success of the system was such that until the advent of DC electrification in the 1930s, the FS used it as a standard, building a network of 1120 miles (1800 km).

On the other side of the Alps, in the meantime, the difficult Lotschberg line was electrified at 15.000 v AC, with Be5/7 locomotives made by BLS. Thirteen units were built by Oerlikon, with two 933 kW engines, each connected to the five axles through connecting rods. They hauled trains of 350 tons at 30 mph (50 km/h) with no problems on slopes of 27/1000. Still in Switzerland, the Gottardo line was soon electrified too.

In 1919, after having tested three prototypes, the SBB chose the Be4/6 produced by Brown Boweri, ordering 39 of them. These machines still used the technology derived from steam traction, such as transmission with connecting rods. However, these locomotives used a rheostat brake for the first time (applying the property of all rotating electric machines – in this case the traction engines – of being reversible machines, capable of working both as engines and elec-

166 This beautiful image of the Be4/6 no. 12320, which was built in 1921 for the St. Gotthard line, shows perfectly the particular 1-B-B-1 wheel arrangement of this powerful locomotive. Thirty-nine models were built in total.

166-167 The "crocodile" of the SBB classified Ce 6/8 is one of the best-known electric locomotives thanks to its characteristic profile. It was originally used to haul freight trains on the Gotthard line.

trical energy generators. The engine brakes the convoy absorbing the mechanical power and changing it into electrical power, which is dissipated as heat in a special rheostat).

We cannot conclude this tribute to the first years of electrical traction in Switzerland without recollecting one of the most famous locomotives of all, the Ce 6/8, known to everyone as the Crocodile. It is undoubtedly one of the most attractive European electric locomotives, unmistakable for its long nose and wheel connecting rods. Thirty-three of them were made. It was an articulated machine with a 1-C+C-1 wheel arrangement moved by four engines of 550 kW each, providing a total

power output of 2200 HP, very noteworthy for the time. It was used to haul heavy goods trains on the San Gottardo line.

Italy and Switzerland were certainly in those years at the forefront of electric traction. They also both happened not to have any coal, which they had to import from abroad, whereas they did have considerable sources of hydroelectric power. This situation significantly influenced the widespread use of electrical traction in Europe. In Germany, the first plans for an extensive electrification of the network date back to the 1930s, whilst in France the Paris-Orleans (PO) company electrified its lines from 1926. Great Britain, however, remained faithful to steam traction.

168 TOP THE SUCCESS OF THE E626 LOCOMOTIVES OF THE ITALIAN RAILWAYS WAS ASSOCIATED WITH THE NETWORK USING DIRECT CURRENT 3000V AS A NATIONAL STANDARD. IN TOTAL, 448 E626S WERE BUILT.

168 BOTTOM LEFT IN THE 1930S, THE E18 ELECTRIC LOCOMOTIVE OF THE DRG, WHICH WAS CLASSIFIED 118 BY THE DB, REPRESENTED THE PINNACLE OF GERMAN RAILWAY TECHNOLOGY IN THIS AREA. IT WAS ABLE TO HAUL PASSENGER TRAINS OF 700 TONS AT 90 MPH (150 KM/H).

168 BOTTOM RIGHT THE E428-058 IS ONE OF THE FIRST SERIES OF THIS TYPE, CHARACTERIZED BY THE FRONT FACE FOR THE ELECTRICAL EQUIPMENT. THE TWO FOLLOWING SERIES ADOPTED MORE AERODYNAMIC PROFILES IN LINE WITH THE DESIGN OF THOSE YEARS.

169 THE E428 GROUP OF LOCOMOTORS WERE THE MOST REPRESENTATIVE OF ELECTRIC TRACTION IN ITALY DURING THE 1930S. CONSTRUCTED IN THREE SERIES, THEY HAULED THE MAIN PASSENGER TRAINS ALONG THE ENTIRE PENINSULA UP TO THE 1960S.

In the United States, the situation was different. The length of the lines made the cost of electrification prohibitive, with the exception of the networks connected to the big cities on the Eastern seaboard. In that area, the smaller distances and the more intense traffic convinced the railway companies of the benefit of electric traction. The most memorable image of this electrification is certainly the splendid GG1 locomotive built for Pennsylvania RR from 1934 and of which 139 were made. Towards the end of the 1920s, the company had an enormous amount of traffic, over 800 trains a day. It served the main connections in the country, New York-Philadelphia-Washington. It was the very increase in the number of trains on this line, besides the increase in their size and weight, which persuaded Pennsylvania RR to choose alternating current electrification at 15,000 v and 25 Hz. The locomotive the company chose had a 2-C+C-2 wheel arrangement, i.e. with two groups of three engine axles fitted on the chassis, better distributing the 216 ton weight and improving the ride, especially in bends. The GG1 was powered by 12 305 kW engines, each having a continuous power of 3680 kW (reaching a peak of 6000 kW), which allowed it to easily haul trains of 20 1600 ton carriages at 100 mph (160 km/h). This performance would be quite respectable even today. Also contributing to the locomotive's success was the bodywork designed by architect Raymond Loevy, who had already successfully applied his talents to the fairings of many steam locomotives.

Returning to Europe, we must remember two German electric locomotives of those years: the E44 and the E18 of the DRG. The first, of which nearly 190 were made, were the heart of the first great German electrification project, that of the Stuttgart-Ulm-Munich line. They used a BB wheel arrangement (two two-axle trolleys) powered by four 550 kW engines.

They were not particularly fast, only reaching 55 mph (88 km/h). After the war, this speed limit relegated them to goods services. The E18 in contrast was explicitly designed to haul fast and heavy trains on the main lines of the network, and the speed sought was 93 mph (150 km/h). The designers adopted a 1Do1 wheel arrangement, which was quite unusual for the time.

It was powered by four 760 kW engines. Even though not relying on the famous designers the DRG chose a very pleasant and snazzy body, which contributed to the fame of the E18a even after the war when they continued in service with the DB.

The nation that between the two wars bet most on electric traction was Italy. The Ferrovie dello Stato not only decided to electrify the main lines of the network, but, with great courage, they staked everything on the evolution of electric locomotives, thus giving up, from 1929, on the construction of steam locomotives (the last order was that for the 50 Gruppo 744 for the South Italy lines).

The FS also gave up on three-phase AC traction and invested in 3000V DC traction. The choice wasn't easy, but the FS convinced themselves that three-phase traction, even with its successes, would not have been able to develop further technical advances: the objective limitations of the system (speed of locomotives, technical complexity of the aerial line) seemed to prejudice the growth of a modern network. In the meantime, the introduction of mercury arc rectifiers made the production of high voltage DC electricity much more economical and simple. The FS, after having studied some systems in the USA, decided to electrify to 3000 v DC the Benevento-Foggia to test the validity of the system, which relied on a single aerial conductor supply. The route chosen, a mountain one, was ideal ground for a comparison with the performance of three-phase locomotives. They decided to order, from various companies, 14 prototype locomotives all based on the same design: a BoBoBo wheel arrangement, i.e. with three engine trolleys with two axles articulated with each other via spherical joints on which a single rigid frame rested. Initially numbered E625, the locomotives then became the E626s and their success was such that the FS had 448 units built. The superiority of both the system and the locomotive induced the Italian railways to choose DC traction as standard. The Study Office thus produced numerous groups of electric locomotives in a few years, among which, of particular importance, was the E428. In a short time Italian engineers accumulated a noteworthy experience in the field, which they made exemplary use of in the production of the ETR 200 in the 1930s.

The 16 trains built from 1936 (in total 18 were commissioned, but two were destroyed by bombing in the war before going into service) made the most of the technological innovations available at the time. The new steels allowed for robust but light structure, and the traction engines had reached an excellent efficiency. Engineers of the Material and Traction Service of the FS thus thought of a light and fast train for the new electrified lines. The success of the first model built by Breda, which immediately reached 108 mph (170 km/h), attracted the attention of the Fascist regime. The train (which was to originally have first- and second-class seating) thus became a luxury train capable of traveling at exceptional speed for the time, therefore constituting a propaganda gloss for Fascism. But besides this historical and political aspect, the ETR 200 was a really exceptional train from both an aesthetic and technical point of view. It was designed by two renowned architects, Giuseppe Pagano and Giò Ponti, and the aerodynamic front, called "viper head," was tested in the wind tunnel of the Turin Polytechnic. The air resistance coefficient obtained, 0.32, was truly exceptional, as it was half the figure achieved by usual electric locomotives. The train was made up of three elements resting on four trolleys for a length of 206 ft (62 m) and over 100 tons in weight. To improve the aerodynamic performance, the three elements were connected to each other with mantles in line with the body as well as with the normal corridors. Its lower part was completely streamlined.

The ETR had air-conditioning, a real luxury for the time, and unique internal salons. It was set to reach a top speed of 100 mph (160 km/h), much less than it could have reached and maintained in regular service. World fame, however, was achieved on July 20, 1939, when the ETR 212 between Pontenure and Piacenza established the world speed record on rails, touching 126 mph (202 km/h). On that day, the 196 miles (315 km) between Milan and Florence were covered in just 1 hour and 55 minutes at the incredible average speed of 102.5 mph (165 km/h). For the sake of history, it is right to remember that the record was established with some adjustments: the voltage of the line was increased and the exchanges on the line had been blocked, but the train was a standard one. The ETR 200s may be considered the first high-speed trains in history, precursors of the famous Japanese Shinkansen of 1964 and the French TGV of 1978.

RAILWAY AND THE WAR
1930 - 1945

THE ROLE OF THE RAILWAYS
DURING THE SECOND WORLD WAR
PAGE 174

THE ROLE OF
THE RAILWAYS DURING
THE SECOND WORLD WAR

174 TOP THE REALITY OF WAR IS ALWAYS DIFFERENT TO THE IMAGE PORTRAYED IN ENROLMENT POSTERS. A LONG TRAIN OF BRITISH SOLDIERS LEAVES FOR WAR. THEY ARE TRANSPORTED IN CLOSED CARRIAGES AND NOT IN PASSENGER CARRIAGES.

On Friday September 1, 1939, the Germans invaded Poland. It was the first act of the Second World War, even though in the weeks following the event, few knew what was going to occur from that point on. The European railroads quickly found themselves directly involved in the tragic events of those years.

The importance of rail transportation for military purposes had been thoroughly established during the First World War. For example, the Austro-Hungarian Empire and Italy extensively utilized their network for the movement of soldiers, ammunition, and provisions to the front, as well as for hospital-trains. Along the Italian coasts, the armed trains defended the coastline from raids from Austrian ships. The areas directly behind the front of the Austrian-Hungarian positions in the Regions of Trentino, Veneto, and Friuli-Venezia-Giulia, were supplied by a "Feldbahn," a field railroad, leading almost right up to the front line and which could be quickly disassembled and moved.

174 BOTTOM IN THIS PHOTOGRAPH GERMAN TROOPS PREPARE TO FIRE A 28-CM HOWITZER MOUNTED ON A TRAIN DURING THE FIRST WORLD WAR. RAILWAYS HAVE ALWAYS BEEN USED FOR WARFARE AND NOT JUST LOGISTIC SUPPORT.

175 "A QUICKER END TO THE WAR DEPENDS, MORE THAN ANYTHING ELSE, ON THE SUPPORT THAT THE UNITED STATES GIVES TO THE ALLIES." THIS POSTER CREATED IN 1917 REMINDS THE RAILWAYMEN OF THEIR RESPONSIBILITY TO DO THEIR PART.

A SPEEDY TERMINATION OF THE WAR

This depends more than anything else on the support the United States gives the Allies. Our country cannot do justice to the job, unless railroad men get busy and do their part.... Are you awake to your responsibility?

THE NATION IS COUNTING ON YOU

ERNEST·HAMLIN·BAKER

CANTEEN SERVICE, SAVANNAH CHAPTER, AMERICAN RED CROSS AT-WORK.

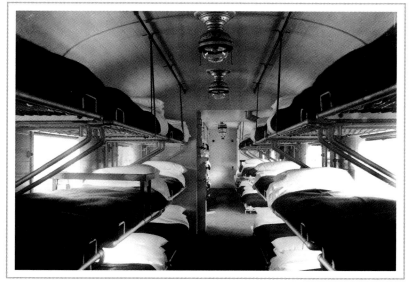

176-177 AN INTERESTING IMAGE, DATING FROM AROUND 1917, SHOWS THE INTERIOR OF AN AMERICAN HOSPITAL CARRIAGE. IN THE FOREGROUND IS THE MEDICAL OFFICERS OFFICE, WHICH IS SEPARATE FROM WHERE THE HOSPITALIZED SOLDIERS ARE TREATED.

177 TOP THE RED CROSS' TRAINS AND THE HOSPITAL TRAINS HAVE SAVED THE LIVES OF MANY INJURED SOLDIERS, ALLOWING FOR A RAPID EVACUATION FROM THE BATTLE GROUND. THIS PROPAGANDA-STYLE PHOTO SHOWS AMERICAN RED CROSS NURSES AT WORK.

177 BOTTOM THIS PHOTOGRAPH OF A BRITISH ARMY HOSPITAL CARRIAGE, WHICH WAS USED IN EUROPE, CLEARLY SHOWS HOW THE SOLDIERS' BERTHS WERE STACKED IN TIERS OF THREE.

In Germany, the State Railways (Reichsbahn) were directly dependent upon the Ministry of Transportation, guided by Julius Dorpmuller, who remained continuously in office from 1937 to 1945. From the outbreak of the war, the Nazi war machine had already identified the perfectly functioning railways as an essential part of their war effort. In addition to logistical functions, the generals turned to the railways as an essential part of their military capability. Since 1934, the Krupp steel mills produced a significant quantity of large caliber artillery mounted on special railcars. These were part of the first two German artillery development plans called "The Long-Term Plan" launched in 1932, and the 1936 "Emergency plan," ordered directly by Hitler. We won't describe the various types of gun carriages mounted on the cars over the years, but instead limit ourselves to the 380 mm naval pieces, baptized "Sigfrid," mounted on apposite 8-axle railcars (with a total weight of 294 tons), which shelled the beach at Dunkirk in May 1940 from over 25 miles away. The vehicle that epitomized the enormous effort that the German railways bore during the war years was without a doubt the steam engine Br 52, nicknamed "Kriegslokomotiv" (war locomotive). The first one was presented to the Nazi authorities in September 1942; it was a lighter and simplified version of the excellent Br 50 locomotives, 2-10-0 of the DRG. It met two vital objectives: reduction in the length of time it took to build; and a locomotive able to run on the tracks of the occupied countries, which were often much less robust than the German lines. The production began at full speed in the plants of the major German companies: Esslingen, Henschel & Sohn, Jung Krauss Maffei, MBA, Schicau, Schwartzkopff and Florisdorf. Just three years later, at the end of the conflict, 6,239 had been constructed and their career in the years following the war continued on the railroads of half of Europe.

The Allies also boasted great war locomotives of their own, though not in such numbers. In 1942 the American army founded the US Army Transportation Corps (USATC), which was tasked with coordinating and organizing ground transportation, particularly trains. It was more than obvious that it would not have been possible to use American locomotives, for reasons of size and axle weight, as well as for the number of machines required. Baldwin and ALCO had already in the past produced excellent 2-8-0 engines for the Italian and British railroads. Starting from this experience, the US military ordered over 1800 locomotives with a 2-8-0 wheel arrangement, originally classified as G.I. 4-16-0 that were sent on freight ships, first to Europe and then North Africa. They were initially used to assist the English machines in preparation of the Normandy landing, and they then supported the troops as they advanced, using the French network. In the south, they landed in Italy after the liberation of Sicily and traveled up the peninsula with the Allied armies.

Another American locomotive that was built explicitly for the war was the W.D 4-16-4, nicknamed "MacArthur" from the name of the famous General. It was initially created for the Middle East and North African lines and some 200 were produced from 1942 onwards. It was developed on the design of a similar machine developed in 1924 for the Wyoming & Southern. Originally used in Egypt and Iran, they were brought to Turkey, Italy, and Germany.

In the UK, the government created the Railway Executive Committee (REC) in 1939, with the goal of coordinating the activities of all the private railroad companies. After having analyzed the available machines, the REC favored a locomotive with a 2-8-0 wheel arrangement that was already used by the LMS (London Midland Scottish) and classified as 8F. Fifty-one machines were immediately requested from the LMS, while approximately another 600 were ordered from North British Locomotive Company, Vulcan, and Beyer Peacock. The first ones were available in August 1940 and were classified WD 300-899 and then WD 70300-70899.

Foreseeing use outside of the UK, the REC stipulated some modifications to the LMS machines, the main one being the implementation of a compressed air brake, not present on English machines who normally used a vacuum brake system.

In 1943 the REC decided to order more machines, very similar but as simplified as possible in order to be able to be built quickly and with the materials available. As such a group of 935 2-8-0 wheel arrangement locomotives designated the "Austerity class" were manufactured by North British Locomotive Company (545 machines) and Vulcan (390 machines). They were classified WD 70800-70879 and WD 77000-79312 with non-consecutive enumeration. A version heavier than the Austerity was also made, with an extra motor axle and a 2-10-0 wheel arrangement, as of December 1943. The 150 machines built were classified WD 73650-73799. Naturally, in addition to these main locomotives, other smaller locomotives were also produced.

180-181 Thousands of the Group 52 locomotives, baptized "Krieglokomotiven" (war locomotive), were constructed. Here, two of them, registered by OBB (Austrian Railways), are waiting to go into service in the North Vienna depot.

In this brief review, some mention must be made of the integral role the railroads played in the Nazis' extermination programs. The majority of the millions of Jews from all over Europe sent to extermination camps reached their final destinations on a train, in livestock cars, in groups up of 80 to 100 people and almost always without food or water. Between 5 & 10% of them died during the trip.

The transportation of the Jews was handled directly by Adolf Eichmann, who in 1937 was already sinisterly known in this role and operated at the Reich Security Main Office (Reichssicherheitshauptamt, RSHA).

From his office, or better still from the relevant department, the

Amt IV B4 (Gestapo Police – main executioners of the Holocaust), a request to the Reich's railroads went out and was then sent to the traffic and tariff division. From there, once the urgency and cost of the transport were established, the papers were passed to the operating division who materially took care of the train formation and of the drawing up of the train schedules, which were always classified as extra trains. The German railroads requested payment for these mass transports and regardless of the fact that the people were crammed into livestock cars, they applied the tariffs for a one-way third class trip, 4 pfennig per kilometer.

If the overall number of deported on the train exceeded 400 people, and this was almost always the case seeing as each train transported between 2000 and 2500 people, the "group tariff" was applied, 2 pfennig per kilometer.

The tickets and the invoices were issued not to those transported, and not even directly to the Reich, but rather to a state office called the "Central Europe Travel Agency," which, in spite of its innocent name, organized the mass deportation of the Jews. Payment was collected from the money confiscated from the Jews. The death trains continued to run until the fall of the Third Reich when, between January and May 1945, the Russian and Allied armies began liberating the extermination camps.

The DB (Deutsch Bahn), aware of the responsibility the German railroads played in those years (historians agree that without the logistic

support of the railroads murder on that scale would have been impossible), decided in 1998 to establish a special memorial in Berlin on track 17 of the Grunewald Station. The heart of the monument is made up of 186 steel stems in chronological order, and each one of these stems, on the edge of the sidewalk is the deportation date, the number of people deported, the departure point from Berlin and the destination.

The vegetation over the years has grown between the rails of track 17 and it has been left as such to symbolically highlight that – on that track and from that platform – no train will ever depart again with a similar destination.

182 German officers supervise the deportation of a group of Polish Jews in the sorting yard of Warsaw between 1943 and 1944. The people are transported in extremely over-packed cattle wagons.

182-183 This terrible image, taken in Auschwitz-Birkenau, documents the arrival of a train full of Hungarian Jews to the Nazi's extermination camp.

183 top A tragic page in the railways' recent history: the Nazi extermination camp of Auschwitz-Birkenau in Poland – final destination of hundreds of trains packed with deportees, most of them from the Jewish communities.

At the end of the war, most of Europe's cities were heaps of rubble. This was particularly so for Germany and its allies where massive Allied bombing raids attempted to destroy the industrial infrastructure and to demoralize the civilian poplulations. The vital logistical functions of the railroads meant that every track, station, and bridge had been a target of primary importance. Overall, the European network was devastated. At the end of 1945 there wasn't one important station in Germany or Northern Italy that had not been bombed. The following statistics give an idea of the level of destruction that Germany suffered during the war: 1,234,767 tons of bombs were dropped, 60% between July 1944 and April 1945; the Allied bombs reduced the production of fuel by 90% from December 1944; and in the five months until September 1944, bombing reduced by 75% the amount of freight transported by the railroads. In addition to this damage was the sabotage carried out by partisans and resistance movements, above all in France, Italy, the Netherlands, and the Balkans.

As the German forces were beaten back following the Normandy landings, they meticulously devastated every railroad facility to prevent its use by the Allies.

184-185 Most of Germany, and Berlin in particular, was severely damaged during the Second World War. The railway infrastructure was heavily targeted by the relentless bombing raids: this was what was left of Berlin station.

185 bottom Although Britain did not suffer as badly as many European countries, the German V1 and V2 rockets caused a lot of damage in London. This is St. Pancras station after a night raid on August 26, 1942.

Besides blowing up bridges and tunnels with TNT, the Wermacht came up with the idea of a sort of railroad "harrow" which, towed behind a locomotive, would cut through the wooded sleepers with a kind of hook, making the tracks unusable. Such devices where mostly used in Italy when the German troops had to abandon first the Gustav Line, between Gaeta and the mouth of the Sangro river, and then the Gothic Line, retreating towards the Val Padana and the Brenner pass. To give an idea about the pressure that the railways had to endure during the war, let us remember, for example, the repeated Allied aerial attacks on the Palazzolo sull'Oglio bridge, one of the main architecural works of art of the Milan-Venice line.

Between July 23, 1944 and April 27, 1945 the bridge was bombed 32 times. Built in 1857, it was 883 ft (269 m) long, with nine arches at a height of approximately 130 ft (40 m). Destroying it meant blocking or severely hampering the movement of German troops and materiel on the

main railroad on the Paduan Plain. Yet however many times it was bombed, the damage inflicted to the structure was not sufficient to stop the German engineers from mending it after each attack. The pillars and arches may be blown in half but they would be restored in a few days with wood structures and steel beams on which the tracks were laid. This work went on with the constant risk of attack by Allied fighters, who ruthlessly hit every train that dared to travel by day. Many Italian railroad workers were victims of these attacks, and around 2104 were killed during air attacks and from the explosion of mines, and 404 from partisan actions.

186 THE SECOND WORLD WAR IS FINALLY OVER AND THE SOLDIERS, FREED FROM THE PRISON CAMPS, CAN FINALLY RETURN TO THEIR HOMES. IN 1945, TWO TRAINS OF VETERAN SOLDIERS ARE

WELCOMED WITH MILITARY HONORS AT THE ANNEMASSE STATION IN HAUTE-SAVOIE, WHILE THE CROWD PREPARES TO EMBRACE THEIR LOVED ONES.

A mention should be made, if only briefly, of the often heroic actions by many of the ordinary workers on the railroads in disrupting and sabotaging the German transport network. In particular, the efforts of French railroad workers became famous after the war when they inspired many celebrated movies.

After the war, the panorama was distressing. In 1940 the Italian rail network was 10,000 miles long, of which 3,200 miles were electrified and 2,800 on double-tracks. To this we must add a good 3,000 miles of private concessionary railroads, of which 1,200 miles electrified. The fleet of carriages amounted to 4,177 locomotives, 1,602 electric locomotives, 130,000 freight cars and approximately 13,200 between passenger and baggage cars. Just as numerous was the railroad fleet in concession, which was made up of over 600 steam locomotives, 383 electric and electric motor locomotives, nearly 8,000 cars and over 2,000 carriages. Five years later the numbers highlighted the level of disaster: 4,350 miles of tracks, practically the entire electrified network, 3,106 of the 3,215 miles in use, almost 50,000 miles of telephone lines, essential for circulation, over 4,700 between stations, crossing boxes and depots. It wasn't any better for the carriage material: only 1,803 steam locomotives and barely 546 electric locomotives were still in use, in practice unusable, however, due to the destruction by the aerial line and nearly 40,000 cars and 1,200 carriages.

Similarly, the French railroads had lost half of the locomotives and freight cars and over 1,988 miles of tracks were destroyed and 1,965 bridges. In Holland the situation was even worse with a destruction reaching 60% of tracks, 84% of locomotives, and 90% of cars and carriages.

Railroad workers everywhere rolled up their sleeves in order to get the service back into some operational shape. But the difficulties were enormous and for the first months after the end of the war, especially in Northern Italy, traffic was more or less nonexistent. Naturally, precedence

was given to the main connections, which were essential for the restarting the country's economic life. As early as October 1945, some lines were once again in operation, even though in a precarious way. To give an idea of the situation, in 1938 the trip from Milan to Rome lasted approximately 6 hours, in October 1946 it took – if everything went well – nearly 33 hours. Due to the lack of usable carriages, passenger services used uncovered freight cars, equipped with spartan wooden benches. Other cars became provisional shelters for many who had lost their homes from the bombings. Italians who had been deported to the prison or work camps in Germany began to return home via train, just as the skeletal soldiers from the Eastern front arrived at the Central Station in Milan.

Some months earlier, due to the completely precarious traffic conditions in Southern Italy, in the area already liberated by the Allied troops, one of the worst railroad disasters in all European history occurred, a tragedy, which, at the time, no one knew about and had practically been forgotten until just a few years ago. We will tell the story because it is symbolic of the living conditions at the time and to remember, even though belatedly, the civilian victims of that event.

It was the evening of March 2, 1944. Train n.8017 left Salerno for Potenza. It was not a passenger train, but a special freight train, made up mostly of empty cars. The investigation which ensued after the tragedy states that it was formed of 47 cars, 20 of which were uncovered. Hundreds of people had illegally found their way onboard, all heading for Potenza. They were people who were seeking food for their families, people going inland to barter the goods obtained from the American troops in the area for meat, eggs and others types of necessary staples. They were no other means of transport available unless one wanted to face the dusty roads on foot or on a bicycle. Little by little, as the train made its way, people got on, taking advantage of the frequent stops and regardless of the intervention of the American Military Police in

Battipaglia who tried to make some of them get off. When it reached Eboli, there were at least 600 people crammed onto the train. It was already night and at Rovagnano, only 27 miles (43 km) from Potenza, a second engine, a 476 of Austrian-Hungarian origin, was added to the main locomotive of the train, a large 480. This was necessary to make the climb of the last part of the line. At 11:40 pm the train departed from Rovagnano and traveled in double traction the three and half miles that separated it from the Balvano station, where it stopped awaiting a further signal to depart. The train preceding it had had problems and the tracks were not yet clear. At 12:50 am the Balvano station head gave the all clear to depart and the two locomotives, with the boilers at maximum pressure, departed to face the Arms Tunnel, all uphill, which preceded the Bella-Muro station, only five miles away. The train slowly slipped into the tunnel, a bit over 1600 ft (490 m) long, but when it was already inside something began to go wrong. The weight was excessive, the tracks were wet and the locomotive began to slide even though the train drivers employed the sanders. Then the train stopped. Meanwhile smoke filled the tunnel. The people on board covered their faces as if waiting would allow the train to depart once again. The train drivers tried many times to move the train, but probably the racket of the situation, the dark, the bad quality of the coal used, full of sulfur and the combustion produced a lot of carbon dioxide, causing a fatal confusion and no one did the only thing that should have been done: quickly back out of the tunnel. Thus nearly 400 people died from asphyxiation, the exact number was never known even though the tombstone outside of the tunnel states 509 victims – whereas approximately 200 people miraculously

escaped death. The tragedy was discovered hours later because the telegraphic connections between the stations were extremely precarious and at around 2:40 am the two station heads realized that something serious had occurred. The train drivers died at the controls of the locomotives: the front machine was found without its brakes on and with the reverse lever inserted; the second car had the brake inserted with the forward lever inserted. The confusion of the afterwar period and the military censorship meant that a veil was drawn over the tragedy and only on the 6th and 7th of March did the newspapers mention a disaster in a railroad tunnel in Southern Italy. Then for many years the tragedy seemed to be just forgotten.

These were the travel conditions of that time, very hard, just as daily living conditions were, but the joy in the months following the end of the war, and the hopes of a better future, far outweighed any feelings of fatigue and despair. The Allies, in summing up the situation of the Italian railroads at the end of the war, calculated that it would take at least 15 years to return to the situation of the 1940s. Instead, it took just five years for services to returned to pre-war levels. Even in Germany, where the destruction of the network had been even more extensive, reconstruction began as soon as possible. Both countries farsightedly took the opportunity to focus on crucial modernization of their railroad systems and were not just satisfied in simply making things work again. A new era had begun.

187 In July 1946, a group of former Belgian deportees and members of the Resistance, arrive in Paris by train for a celebration. Many of the railways in the countries occupied by the Germans actively cooperate with the Resistance.

FROM RECONSTRUCTION TO THE NEW EUROPEAN NETWORK 1945 - 1980

THE WAR IS OVER
BUT THE DAMAGES
REMAIN

190 TOP THIS IMAGE SHOWS A PHASE IN THE RECONSTRUCTION OF THE BRIDGE OVER THE TICINO IN TURBIGO, NEAR MILAN, WHICH HAD BEEN DAMAGED DURING THE SECOND WORLD WAR.

190 BOTTOM IN AUGUST 1944 THE WAR IS NOT YET OVER, BUT AROUND BREST RECONSTRUCTION OF THE RAILWAYS HAS BEGUN.

191 THESE FRENCH WORKERS, BUSILY REBUILDING THE SOULLAC VIADUCT ON THE TOULOUSE-TULLE LINE, IN THE REGION OF MONTAUBAN, MUST POSSESS NOTABLE ACROBATIC SKILLS TO BE ABLE TO FINISH THEIR WORK.

As we have seen, at the end of the Second World War the situation of the railroad networks was very delicate. In Europe most of the rolling stock was destroyed or useless. In the United States and Great Britain, although their networks were not directly affected by the war (apart from some damage caused by the German V1s and V2s in southern England), the railways were exhausted from the military effort. The railroad companies in the United States, for example, besides their normal traffic transported about a million soldiers a month, whilst the British network organized 25,000 new trains just to prepare for the D-Day operation.

But there was no going back to the days before the war. It soon became apparent during the extensive reconstruction work that economic and technological changes meant that the transportation of goods and people was entering a whole new era of radical change.

Cars were becoming ever cheaper, more comfortable and reliable, and with their spread came the construction of new huge new road networks. Ever larger trucks carried goods to any destination, even the most remote areas, with an increasing ease and flexibility unknown to the railway world. Whilst for longer journeys air transport was rapidly developing, becoming safer and far more comfortable.

The railroads faced fierce competition. Public opinion and practically all governments saw mass motorization as the key to economic progress and an assertion of individual freedom. Gasoline was very cheap, engines were becoming ever more efficient with diesel ones for trucks getting more and more powerful. Although undoubtedly, at the time, motorization was a revolution in personal freedom and mobility, 60 years on it has paradoxically become a kind of slavery and the open road is for most people a thing of the past. Too many cars and trucks crowd the roads, and now we realize that effective alternatives have not been developed. We have become over-reliant

on the internal combustion engine. The European Community has at last taken steps and has passed a plan to redress the transportation balance and move away from our obsession with the car. However, the objective, in realistic terms, is not to completely reverse the tendency of transport on rubber to predominate over any other kind of transport, but only to prevent any future increase of traffic on the roads. Of course, policies that have favored road transport for the last 50 years – with rare exceptions – cannot be replaced and rolled back in just a few years.

Take Switzerland as an example. This country had always been one of the European nations that took great care of its railways and which were not even damaged during the war. In spite of this, in the 15 years from 1950 to 1965 the percentage of passengers carried by the SBB dropped from 52% of the total to 19.6%. Goods followed on the same trend, dropping from 20% to 15%. In the same 15 years, the number of miles driven by private cars increased five-fold, and the tons of goods carried on roads tripled.

The railways tried to respond to this explosion of road transport but found themselves unable to carry out effective national and international strategies, hampered not least by the often vastly differing situations in each country.

On the one hand the heavy costs of reconstruction weighed on them, on the other the loss of traffic had a negative effect on the balance sheets, whether state or privately owned, such as in the United Kingdom. Furthermore, the railways had taken on a social role in guaranteeing the transport of people and goods, which wasn't easy to change but was proving to be uneconomical in the face of the fierce competition from the road networks.

The obligation to guarantee a transport service, even in totally unprofitable situations, clashed with the need to adjust the companies to a new economic environment. To this day the railways continue to struggle with these problems and have been unable to resolve these issues satisfactorily.

THE 1950s AND
THE RECONSTRUCTION

The massive reconstruction that was needed after the war was an obvious opportunity to make some profound and far-reaching changes. Electric traction had, even before the war, demonstrated its great advantages and that it had further potential, for example, in the application of thermal motors. Italy had already developed in the fascist era some excellent railcars powered by fuel oil, capable of providing both passenger services and short local connections with management costs below those of steam locomotives and traditional carriages.

Electric and diesel locomotives had far lower running costs than steam locomotives: requiring

TRAINS OF OUR TIMES

Three types of motive power in use on British Railways and four of the new standard locomotive and rolling stock liveries are exemplified in this scene near Bushey in the London Midland Region, at the point where water-troughs are provided on the up and down main lines. On the left is a Class 5 4-6-0 mixed traffic steam locomotive, finished black, lined in red cream and grey. In the centre is the twin diesel-electric locomotive unit Nos. 10000-10001 in black and silver hauling a main line train of carmine and cream coaches, and on the right is a suburban electric train in the malachite green livery.

less personnel and far simpler to maintain, they can be used continuously over 24 hours, and all that is needed is just a change of crew. So the same number of engines could run more trains at lower costs. Electric traction requires an aerial power line and so a costly infrastructure investment, and is therefore suitable for high traffic lines that can generate the income to justify the set-up costs. Diesel traction, however, is ideal on secondary lines, where no costly modifications are necessary, except the installation of a pump for filling up.

Italy tried to reinstate its already vast 3000 v DC network, which it had already chosen as its national standard. Part of the lines with triphase AC that had been damaged were immediately converted. Others, such as the Modane-Turin-Genoa, the Genoa-Ventimiglia, the Genoa-Voghera, and the Bolzano-Brenner lines were converted from the beginning of the 1960s. They remained fed with the two cable triphase system until the mid 1970s. These are the secondary lines in lower Piedmont.

France, had in 1946 already electrified to 1500 v DC the Paris-Lyons line and in the following years extended this system to many lines in the south of the country. Simultaneously, the SNCF began experiments with mono-phase AC at 25 kV and 50Hz, experimentally electrifying in 1951 the 48 miles (78 km) between Aix les Bains and La Roche sur Foron. The trial proved a considerable success and soon they extended this system to the Dunkerque-Thionville line. The French railways thus extended the 25 kV electrification northwards, while the southern lines continued for many years to use the 1500 v DC system.

In Great Britain, however, the use of steam traction continued for a few more years. Electrification was concentrated mainly in the southern area of the country, around big cities. British Railways, which was created in 1947 from the nationalization of the large private companies, decided in 1951 to build new and more modern steam engines. The country had such large and readily accessible coal deposits that on balance electrification was somewhat uneconomical. The modernization plan of 1955, however, aimed on the substitution of steam locomotives in favor of diesel locomotives. British Railways was the only network in Europe to follow this path, which in the United States had been developed from the 1940s.

Germany maintained steam locomotives in service during reconstruction and recommenced electrification in single-phase AC at 15kV and 16 2/3 Hz. Many difficulties ensued due to the country being divided into West and East Germany. In West Germany, the DB (Deutsche Bundesbahn) was born, whilst in the east the DR (Deutsche Reichsbahn) was created. It survived until 1990 when it joined the DB following the fall of the Berlin Wall and the reunification of the Germany.

Before the division of the German railways, the network was centralized around Berlin. The DB therefore found that they had to reorganize their network on north-south lines rather than east-west, which involved reviewing the importance of and facilities for lines. A great deal of support was received from the Marshall Plan, which the United States set up between 1948 and 1951 and contributed more than 13 billion dollars (over 80 billion euros in today's money) in order to help rebuild the 18 European nations that had united in the Organization for European Economic Co-operation (OEEC).

The New MIDLAND

First Class de luxe travel — Supple

8.50 am	Manchester Central ↑	9.21 pm	Mondays	12.45 p
9.04 am ↓	Cheadle Heath	9.07 pm	to Fridays from	
12.03 pm ↓	St. Pancras ↑	6.10 pm	4th July	2.10 p

The last word in rail comfort. Limited accommoda

PULLMAN

ntary fares

St. Pancras	**4.00 pm**
Leicester	
London Road	**2.33 pm**

book in advance   LONDON MIDLAND

194-195 A British Rail poster advertises the new diesel luxury Midland Pullman train, which comprised eight carriages, was powered by two 1000 HP electric-diesel engines and carried a total of 228 passengers.

195 top The Train Bleu's Dining Car, in 1952, is brimming with travelers. There are relatively few cars, the road network is still being developed and the train is still the most comfortable means of travel for medium and long distances.

195 center Comfort and luxury are evident in this promotional picture of the Train Bleu in 1952.

195 bottom A group of girls of the Smith College, during a deportment lesson, learn the proper handling of luggage.

196 In the 1950s the DB put into service the automotor diesel VT08 to haul express trains. Some of these engines were used for the TEE services while waiting for the delivery of the VT11.

196-197 Steam locomotive design did try to combat the rise of electric and diesel engines. This Pacific 01 0137 of the DR (East German Railways) continued in service hauling the main express trains.

THE POST-WAR CRISIS

s we saw earlier, reconstruction in every country presented serious financial problems. The increase in salaries made management costs rise, and railway companies had enormous staffs, from important junction station masters to manual workers at small country stations. Typically, railway companies were often the biggest employers in their country, An obvious way, therefore, to reduce costs was through automation, but the financial benefits clashed with the "social purpose" that the states attributed to the railroad companies. If closing an uneconomical line was difficult, it was practically impossible to reduce personnel in any significant way. This unsatisfactory situation, with variations according to the times and political inclinations of the governments in power, lasted from after the war to the 1980s and practically throughout the whole of Europe. Of course, faced with growing debt, cuts were made, but no government knew how to really tackle effectively the issue of the efficiency and competitiveness of rail transport.

Mostly they limited themselves to cutting services and those lines with little traffic, the so-called dead branches. But this really was only addressing the edges of the problem and did nothing to tackle the fundamental issues. It is fair to say, though, that probably the historical context of the time did not allow for different approaches.

We shall only briefly deal with some of these conversion plans, as they are really more suitable for an economic study than a book of this nature. British Railways were the first to experiment with a reconstruction plan. In 1963 the British government became very alarmed when, notwithstanding the modernization plan of 1955, the aim of balancing the books set by the White Paper of 1956 was not achieved. Leading the company at the time was Richard Beeching (then made a Lord), who was a highly esteemed engineer.

At least he was esteemed before his reorganization of the railways, as his policies did not make him popular with the British public and to this day his name is associated with the decimation of the network. Dr. Beeching, as he was then called, developed a radical plan, which dealt with some of the structural problems of the railway organization. He asserted that the railways could not carry out the same role of the 19th century and run trains with one practically empty carriage on secondary lines, nor could they guarantee just one car to a remote country station. The amount of trains had to be proportional to the services offered. One couldn't keep hundreds of inactive carriages for months just to cover the peaks in traffic in the holiday season.

The car cycle, i.e. the time it takes for a freight car to be available

again for a new load, had to be drastically reduced (it was calculated at around 12 days). It is quite astonishing to read this analysis and think that it dates back to 1963: the themes and problems are in fact very similar to those faced nowadays, though in the context of a radically different scenario, by many European railway companies. Was Beeching an extraordinary anticipator, capable of seeing the future of railways in terms of the problems that have stayed to this day or not? Why have these problems not been solved?

In any case, between 1963 and 1968, the British network underwent a radical restructuring. The network was reduced from 47,543 miles (76,513 km) to 33,976 miles (54,679 km). Goods depots were reduced from 5162 to 912, freight cars from 862,000 to 437,000, whilst carriages dropped from 33,821 to 19,540. Even the personnel was drastically reduced from 476,545 to just 296,274 employees. But many years later it was clear that notwithstanding the drastic diet, the deficit remained.

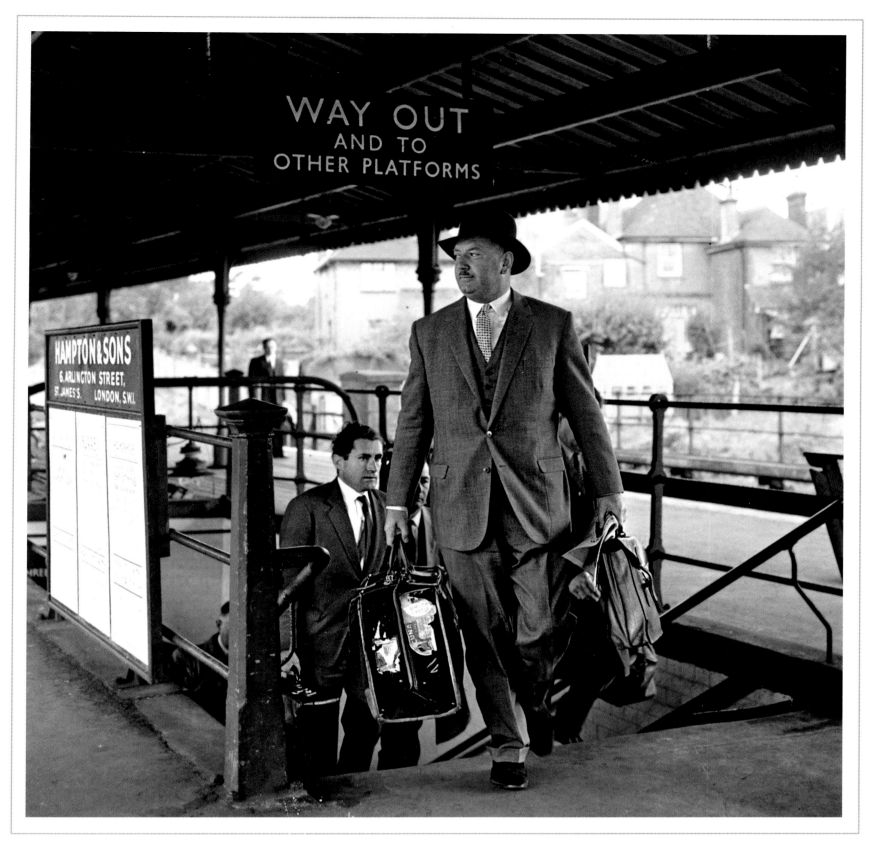

198 A CROWD OF TRAVELERS WAITING TO GET ON BOARD THE
FLYING SCOTSMAN IN KING'S CROSS STATION, LONDON, DURING
ONE OF THE NATIONAL RAIL STRIKES AGAINST THE BEECHING PLAN
WHICH ANTICIPATED STRONG FINANCIAL CUTS TO THE RAILROAD
SYSTEM.

199 TOP DR. RICHARD BEECHING ARRIVES AT A STATION IN
OCTOBER 1962 CARRYING IN HIS CASE A COPY OF HIS
CONTROVERSIAL RECONSTRUCTION PLAN FOR BRITISH RAIL, WHICH
INVOLVED MASSIVE CUTS TO THE NETWORK.

199 BOTTOM BRITISH RAIL WORKERS PREPARE THE INSTALLATION
OF THE SWITCHES THAT WILL MODIFY ACCESS TO CANNON STREET
STATION IN LONDON. BRITISH RAIL WAS CONTINUALLY IN NEED OF
NEW INFRASTRUCTURE.

Things went differently in the other European countries where something similar was tried. In 1968 even Germany, with the "Leber Plan," envisaged losing about 3150 miles (5000 km) of apparently unproductive lines, but the opposition of regional governments effectively blocked the plan. In truth the project didn't just want to close secondary lines, but it also aimed at increasing heavy goods transport, like coal and steel, forbidding their transportation by road. Naturally, the road transporters lobbied against the measures and they were severely watered down.

The DB themselves in 1975 proposed that the government should limit their operation to cover just the basic network where 90% of the traffic was concentrated. However, the government still considered the public service role of the railways was too important to be scaled back and the idea was vetoed. The same happened in Italy in 1985 when, faced with the deficit of the FS, the then minister of transport, socialist Claudio Signorile, had a list made of "lines not included in the national interest" to be closed in a matter of months. In reality, only a few miles of lines were taken out of service and it is clear today that such extensive cuts would have been a serious mistake. In those years, even Belgium and Norway studied similar solutions and also reached almost identical conclusions. However, many secondary lines were closed across Europe, as well as lines that were not directly run by state companies, tramways, and little mountain railways, except in Switzerland and partly Austria.

The number of small trunk lines fell inexorably and now what has been lost is a possible alternative to road transport. Two notable examples from Italy: in the Dolomites, the Calalzo-Cortina d'Ampezzo railway closed to make room for coaches to the Winter Olympics of 1956; and the Val Gardena Railway, one of the most spectacular narrow gauge mountain railways, discontinued in May 1960. We will see in the next chapter how the increasing congestion on the roads has led to a growing recognition of the importance of railway transport in avoiding further traffic problems, and how this attitude has resulted in tackling the network problems differently.

European railways

The conveyor belt of European economy

202 top One of the 75 locomotives belonging to the Conrail's SD60M group, built in 1993 by the Electro Motive Division, hauls a heavy freight train near Gary, in the state of Indiana on November 11th, 1995.

202 bottom A pair of Conrail's SD80MAC locomotives haul a long freight train composed of box cars. These locomotives, normally used in tandem, produce a massive 5000 HP each.

203 An Amtrak train travels along the route known as the "Southwest Chief," one of the most spectacular lines on the American network, which runs from Chicago to Los Angeles, passing through Missouri, Kansas, Colorado, New Mexico and Arizona.

What happened after the war to the railroads in the United States deserves particular attention. The dramatic increase of mass motorization and the development of air transport caused a drastic reduction in the profitability of railway companies, which were all privately owned. Even though the long distances favored the transportation of goods via railway, even in the goods sector suffered from the competition from road transport.

Many railroad companies simply failed, others survived thanks to a careful merger and diversification of activities. In 1970, for example, Burlington Northern was born from the merging of several companies. It ran nearly 23,000 miles (37,000 km) of track.

But things didn't always go well. In 1973, for example, the federal government, contrary to the country's passionate belief in private enterprise, had to intervene by instituting the United States Railway Association. This was given the task of managing the networks in the northeast of the country, which risked ending completely after the collapse of various railroad companies.

Two years later, the Rail Revitalization and Reform Act was issued, entrusting the Consolidated Rail Corporation – known to everyone as Conrail – to manage the bankrupt companies.

Conrail found itself managing a network of 24,000 miles. In the rest of the country things were not going much better. The railroad companies were still making money from the transport of goods, but they were progressively abandoning passenger services. Passenger traffic was handled by airplanes on long distances and by the legendary Greyhound buses on middle distances.

From the end of the war, passenger traffic dropped by more than 750 million passengers a year to about 300 million, and the number of trains from more than 2500 to about 500. In 1967 even the US Post, which was a crucial client, decided to use only trucks and planes.

This decision put many companies into severe difficulties, among them Santa Feone which decided to limit passenger trains to just some of the more important cities, such as Chicago, Los Angeles, and San Francisco. This was the straw that broke the camel's back: passenger services at this point risked disappearing all together from the American network and the public, which had until then substantially been indifferent to the railroads' fate, began to worry and ask for government intervention. Then Congress in 1970 issued the Rail Passenger Service Act, a law which aimed at financially supporting railway services on middle distances and which came into effect from May 1, 1971. A federal company was set up to directly handle the passenger network throughout the country – Amtrak was born. The name was derived from the merging of two words, American and Track.

The official name of the organization was the National Railroad Passenger Corporation. Private companies relinquished their passenger services (and the rolling stock necessary to carry them out) to Amtrak, which in May 1971 began the service with about 180 trains, half of those previously running. Amtrak continues and since then its network has extended to about 28,000 miles through 46 states, including some lines to Canada. In 2004, it carried over 25 million passengers. The private companies concentrated their activity in freight services, creating, over the years, big mergers and alliances. They also developed an efficient transport network on which the longest and heaviest goods trains in the world operated.

> *Amtrak trains cover a 22,000-mile (35,000-km) network in the United States, serving 500 localities.*

204-205 SHOWN HERE ARE TWO BIG DIESEL LOCOMOTIVES AT THE HEAD OF A PASSENGER TRAIN ON THE CHICAGO TO LOS ANGELES SERVICE, WHICH PASSES THROUGH SIX STATES.

205 TOP A COOK AT WORK IN THE DINING CAR ON THE SUNSET LIMITED TRAIN, TAKES A BREAK AS HE ADMIRES THE SUNSET, DURING THE STOP AT PHOENIX, IN ARIZONA. THE SUNSET LIMITED IS ONE OF THE MOST BEAUTIFUL AMERICAN TRAINS.

205 BOTTOM CROSSING THE UNITED STATES AND BEING ABLE TO ADMIRE THE SCENERY IN TRANQUILITY FROM A PANORAMIC CAR LIKE THIS, WHICH IS USED BY AMTRAK FOR ITS MOST PRESTIGIOUS SERVICES, IS AN UNFORGETTABLE EXPERIENCE.

FAMOUS TRAINS AND LOCOMOTIVES OF THE POST-WAR PERIOD

As we have seen, Great Britain after the Second World War continued running steam locomotives for years: among them, class 9F was certainly the most representative – the swan song of British steam traction. Significantly, when the last machine in class 9F, 92 220, emerged from the Swindon workshops in March 1960, British Railways called it the Evening Star, painting the carriage green, instead of the usual black. Class 9F was the last great unified group introduced by BR for pulling heavy goods trains: it had a 2-10-0 wheel arrangement, quite an unusual choice for the British network, with its many tight bends. This could have led to some difficulty for the five couple axles upon entering the bends. The project of the 251 class 9F locomotives had the experience of the 25 locomotives with the same wheel arrangement made during the war, as we saw in the previous chapter. From a technical point of view, they were undoubtedly a success. They were powerful and could easily reach 90 mph (145 km/h). They were used to haul heavy trains, not only freight, and on the whole network until the completion of dieselization.

In Czechoslovakia, too, they kept using steam traction after the war: the network wasn't electrified and the introduction of diesel locomotives was still new. In 1954 the CSD ordered a new series of Skoda locomotives with a 4-8-2 wheel arrangement for express passenger trains. The famous French engineer Andrè Chapelon was put in charge of the project. He applied all the construction principles that had made him famous throughout the world. From his design perhaps the most beautiful post-war steam locomotive was born. Classified by the CSD as model 498.1, it used a superheated simple expansion steam engine, with three cylinders. It could travel at a top speed of over 90 mph (145 mph) and easily maintain 75 mph (120 km/h) whilst hauling heavy passenger trains. Chapelon adopted all the innovations of the time, using steel frames, automatic coal loading, axles mounted on ball bearings and the Kylchap steam discharge system. The charm of the 15 locomotives was enhanced by the unusual color chosen by the Czech railways, dark blue with white pinstripes and red wheels.

206 The 498.1 of the CSD (Czechoslovakian railways) hauls, at full speed, an excursion train.

206-207 locomotive no.92220 "Evening Star" was the last steam engine built in Britain British Railways.

207 top "The Evening Star" is a British Rail Class 9F locomotive, designed by the engineer Riddles. The first one was built in 1954 and a total of 251 were constructed. The last in its series, it was rolled out of the Swindon workshops in March 1960.

208 top Water is often a problem for South African locomotives. The class 25s are equipped with a capacious trolley tender to which a tank car is usually attached, allowing it to greatly increase its range.

208-209 The class 26 no. 3450 locomotive, designed by engineer David Wardale, was painted in a fiery red and renamed Red Devil. It became one of the world's most famous locomotives, both for its appearance and for its innovations.

European and American industries continued producing steam engines for South American, Asian and African railways for many more years. Among these works we would like to recall the big Ma 2-10-2 model from Ansaldo, made for the Greek railways and the series 25 4-8-4 locomotives built by SAR between 1953 and 1954 by Henschel and North British.

The South African railway's class 25s were built in two versions: 50 traditional and 90 with a condensation tender which allowed journeys of hundreds of miles without having to stop for water. These were the biggest condensation locomotives ever built, an even more significant record seeing the narrow gauge of the South African railways, of only 42 inches (1 m). The condensation system consists in channeling the discharge vapor through special tubes into the tender. Here, thanks to special cooling ventilators in turns back into water. It sounds simple, but a filtering and purification system has to be used to eliminate combustion and grease residue that is invariably present, and this mechanism has always been the weak point of condensation tenders. In the course of the years, for this reason, many class 25 condensation locomotives were

209 SOUTH AFRICAN RAILWAYS TRIED TO SOLVE THE PROBLEM OF SCARCE WATER SUPPLIES BY PROVIDING A CONDENSATION TENDER TO 90 CLASS 25 LOCOMOTIVES. THE RELEASED STEAM WAS RECAPTURED, REFREEZED AND TURNED BACK INTO WATER.

transformed into traditional machines. In any case, according to the specifications of a Henschel publication of the time, a locomotive with a condensation tender could travel for nearly 700 miles (1120 km) without needing a top-up, and the saving compared to normal locomotives was about 90%.

We cannot forget the transformation that English Engineer David Wardale made together with famous Argentinean designer Livio Dante Porta using a 25 NC n.3450 in 1981. The machine was reclassified as a class 26 and only one model was made, but it became famous in the whole world both for the results it achieved due to its technical innovations and for its bright red livery, which earned it the nickname of Red Devil. Wardale's work is significant for the time in which it was made and for the choice of locomotive, one of the most modern machines in the world for its construction concept. Wardale, besides being an excellent engineer, was certainly a romantic who didn't want to resign himself to the end of steam traction.

He was convinced that applying the technology available in the 1970s he could bring "second life" to steam traction. So, after an initial series of experiments on a class 19D locomotive, his theory on the improvement of performance was realized with the Red Devil. The power was increased to over 4000 HP, simultaneously saving over 38% on costs. Notwithstanding, SAR decided to replace steam traction and Wardale's dream was over.

210 TOP THIS SMALL STEAM LOCOMOTIVE TRAVELS ALONG THE STEEP RAILROAD FROM SILIGURI TO DARJEELING IN NORTHEAST INDIA. IT IS NICKNAMED THE TOY TRAIN.

210 BOTTOM THESE TWO PAKISTAN LOCOMOTIVES PULLING A PASSENGER TRAIN WERE MADE IN BRITAIN, AND THE ORIGIN OF THEIR DESIGN GOES BACK TO THE 17TH CENTURY AND THE ADOPTION OF THE OLD WHEEL ARRANGEMENT OF 4-4-0.

210-211 A BIG, GERMAN-MADE LOCOMOTIVE, WITH A WHEEL ARRANGEMENT OF 2-10-0 AND REGISTERED BY TURKISH RAILWAYS AS GROUP 56, WAITS FOR THE GO-AHEAD SIGNAL.

211 BOTTOM LEFT A SPECTACULAR DOUBLE-TRACTION TRAIN HAULS A CHARTER TRAIN BETWEEN THE TURKISH CITIES OF MALAT AND ADANA. THE FACT THAT SO MANY STEAM LOCOMOTIVES ARE STILL IN SERVICE IN TURKEY HAS MEANT THAT THOUSANDS OF ENTHUSIASTS COME FROM ALL OVER THE WORLD TO SEE THEM.

211 BOTTOM RIGHT A GROUP 55 LOCOMOTIVE, BUILT IN GERMANY, HAULS A SHORT PASSENGER TRAIN THROUGH ISPARTA PROVINCE, TURKEY, IN THE MID-1980S.

At the end of the 1970s steam traction was rapidly disappearing from Europe. In the west it survived on secondary lines, whilst in the east it was still quite widespread due to the economic difficulties in those countries. Turkey was a kind of living museum, with dozens of locomotives of the most disparate origins still in service. In India and Pakistan steam was still the norm.

In Pakistan, British locomotives made in 1880 were still in service! Although steam was disappearing in Europe, paradoxically the nostalgia for it grew, firstly in Great Britain and Germany then elsewhere where special railway museums were constructed.

Many associations of amateur enthusiasts were established and thanks to them many important locomotives were saved from destruction. It wasn't long before many of these restored engines were back in working order and being used for evocative tourist excursions, an activity that was to become extremely popular. At the same time, other enthusiasts meticulously recorded the disappearance of these dinosaurs with film and photographs, creating a historical documentation of primary importance. Among them, the most famous is certainly Englishman Colin Garrat, rightly known as the David Attenborough of steam locomotives. In over 30 years of travel around the world, he practically photographed all the steam locomotives still in service, from China to those in the sugar plantations of the Philippines.

> " *Hidden in the forests and the plantations, these locomotives are steel dinosaurs.* "

212-213 A LOCOMOTIVE REGISTERED MALLET 0-6+6-0, BUILT BY BALDWIN, HAULS A CARGO OF TEAK TRUNKS IN THE PHILIPPINES IN THE MID-1970S. THE ENGINE'S FUEL IS THE SAME TEAK, NEATLY LOADED ON THE TENDER.

213 THIS SMALL DRAGON 6 LOCOMOTIVE OF THE HAWAIIAN-PHILIPPINE COMPANY, HAULING EMPTY WAGONS THROUGH A SUGAR-CANE PLANTATION IN THE MID-1970S, IS A 1920 BALDWIN.

THE ADVENT
OF DIESEL TRACTION

214-215 THE DIESEL
MULTIPLE UNIT (DMU)
ALN 668, WITH MECHANICAL
TRANSMISSION AND MASS
PRODUCED SINCE 1956,
HAS BEEN THE MAINSTAY
OF PASSENGER TRANSPORT
ON ITALIAN SECONDARY
LINES.

The diesel engine was invented by Rudolf Diesel in 1897, but its railway application was neither simple nor fast. The biggest problem was not reliability, but the weight and dimensions of the engines themselves.

For the power needed the weight of the engines became totally prohibitive. It was only by 1930 that technology solved the problem and the interest in diesel propulsion grew. Designers soon realized that the power produced allowed for the use of mechanical traction, identical to that for trucks, with gears and a crank shaft, but only for light vehicles or ones used for maneuvering. More powerful vehicles needed a different technology. There were two alternatives: electric transmission, chosen as early as 1930 in the United States, and hydraulic transmission, successfully developed especially by the German school.

In the first case, the diesel engine is coupled to a generator or alternator that produces the

215 TOP THIS ALN 56 2037,
BEFORE IT WAS FINALLY
DECOMMISSIONED AND
WRECKED, WAS TRANSFORMED
INTO A MOBILE CONFERENCE
ROOM AND USED TO PROMOTE
THE NATIONAL CAMPAIGN
AGAINST WORK ACCIDENTS,
HENCE THE UNUSUAL LIVERY.

electrical energy necessary for the DC traction engines. In the second case, the diesel engine is coupled to a hydraulic gear mechanism that drives the axle reducers through oil under pressure. Italians were the masters of mechanical transmission, making a series of railcars with two diesel engines synchronized together. First developed before the Secon World War, initially with gasoline engines, railcars became one of the symbols of Italian progress publicized by the Fascists, who nicknamed them "littorine," an explicit reference to the symbol of the regime borrowed from ancient Rome. FIAT and Breda made the famous ALN 56 and 556 (standing for Light Diesel Railcar with 56 seats, the extra 5 indicating the possibility of coupling more units).

215 CENTER THE FIRST SUCCESSFUL AND WIDELY USED AUTOMOTORS OF THE ITALIAN NETWORK WERE THE ALN 56 AND 566, WHICH WERE PRODUCED BEFORE THE BY FIAT AND BREDA. IN TOTAL 532 WERE MANUFACTURED.

215 BOTTOM THIS ALN 990 3018 STOPS AT THE SMALL STATION OF AULLA, TUSCANY, IN THE SUMMER OF 1992. THIS LOCOMOTIVE, THE LAST OF ITS CLASS AND USED FOR TOURIST SERVICES, WAS UNFORTUNATELY DESTROYED IN A FIRE.

> *In 1932, the 'Fliegende Hamburger' covered the 177 miles (286 km) from Berlin to Hamburg at an average of 90 mph (145 km/h).*

A characteristic of these machines was the decision to mount the engine and gears straight onto the chassis. An advantage for maintenance (in case of any problems the whole thing was changed) but a problem for the vibrations and knocks directly affecting the engine. After the war the ALN 880 and 990 were born, but it was especially the ALN 772 (delivered between 1939 and 1949 by OM and FIAT) which became the workhorse of local trains on secondary Italian lines until 1956 when the ALN 668 1400 by FIAT appeared (the first series of a family of engines that the Turin company successfully sold abroad). All these railcars used mechanical transmission and even if from the ALN 880 onwards the engine was mounted under the pavement and was no longer attached to the trolleys.

Even France and Germany developed light vehicles with thermal traction but not as massively as Italy. Of significance in France were the railcars that Ettore Bugatti made in 1933 for the PLM and FIAT com-

panies. The idea was clearly derived from automobiles (they had four Bugatti Royale engines of 200 HP fed by a mix of gasoline, benzene and alcohol) with direct mechanical transmission with a hydraulic joint. Thought of as luxury trains, 76 models were built. They also gained famed due to their modern and innovative design.

In the same year the Reich's railway inaugurated the famous Fliegende Hamburger train, the "Flying Hamburger" which connected Berlin to Hamburg in only two hours and 18 minutes. The convoy was made up of two cars on three trolleys: the central one was of the Jacob type, i.e. common to both units.

The convoy was powered by two Maybach diesel engines of 410 HP each, acting as generators for the electric traction motors. Thanks to the exceptional performance for the time (a speed of around 90 mph / 145 km/h), the Flying Hamburger quickly became a legend in its time.

216 THE SVT 877 DIESEL AUTOMOTORS WERE PRODUCED IN 1933 FOR THE FLIEGENDE HAMBURGER EXPRESS SERVICE, WHICH CONNECTED BERLIN TO HAMBURG IN ONLY TWO HOURS AND 18 MINUTES. EVERY TRAIN COMPRISED TWO ELEMENTS SET UPON THREE CARRIAGES.

217 A PLM POSTER ADVERTISED THE PARIS-CLERMONT FERRANT SERVICE, WHICH USED THE FAMOUS AERODYNAMIC BUGATTI TRAINS. AMONG THE TRAIN'S UNUSUAL FEATURES IS THAT ITS FUEL CONSISTED OF A MIXTURE OF BENZOLE, ALCOHOL AND PETROL.

PARIS-VICHY
3 H.49

AUTOMOTRICE RAPIDE BUGATTI

PARIS	:	15ʰ45
VICHY	:	19ʰ34
CLERMONT-Fᴰ	:	20ʰ15

CLERMONT-Fᴰ	:	7ʰ50
VICHY	:	8ʰ28
PARIS	:	12ʰ26

SAUF DIMANCHES & FÊTES

IMP. CHAIX _ PARIS _ 5 - 35.

However, developments were occurring over the Ocean where as early as 1934 Burlington introduced a luxury passenger train with electric diesel traction, called the Burlington Zephyr. The three elements of the convoy were made of an aerodynamic stainless steel and were air-conditioned, had neon lighting, radio and reclining seats: a real luxury for the time. The train easily reached 110 mph (180 km/h) and proved the ability of diesel engines to be used on very fast trains too.

It was to take years, though, before diesel locomotives took over. The process began in 1939, thanks to the legendary F series produced by the General Motors Electro-Motive Division and of which over 7000 units were made. The general idea of the GM engineers was that of creating a modular locomotive. Each unit was set on two trolleys with two axles which each had a diesel engine of over 1700 HP and a generator for four electric motors. Each unit had its own driving cabin and could be attached to other three slave cars, remotely controlled by the first. They thus formed a set easily capable of hauling any train.

After the war, using its EMD 567 engine already used in the F series, GM developed a new locomotive with a modern idea, called GP or General Purpose. The idea was to present American companies with a universal machine, fit for any kind of job. The objective was reached, with GM selling a good 10,647 Gs in six different series. From the 1960s, GM developed a new model that adopted the CoCo wheel arrangement discarding the old BoBo. This meant that the locomotive would rest on two trolleys with three engine axles instead of two. For a locomotive of the same weight the advantage of this choice was two-fold; it had less weight on each axle and a facilitated circulation on secondary lines or armed ones with light rails, and more grip and traction. Called the SD series (Special Duty), various versions were made over the years. In 1972 the SD 40-2 was presented, mounting an advanced electronic engine command system, thousands of which were sold.

218 THIS ELEGANT SOUTHERN PACIFIC POSTER ADVERTISES THE GREAT SALT LAKE CROSSING.

219 TOP THE DIESEL-ELECTRIC BURLINGTON ZEPHYR TRAINS OFFERED A FAST AND LUXURIOUS SERVICE. EACH AERODYNAMIC TRAIN COMPRISED THREE VEHICLES. FIRST PRODUCED IN 1934, A TOTAL OF 72 WERE MADE.

219 BOTTOM TO DEMONSTRATE HOW MUCH LIGHTER THE STAINLESS-STEEL ZEPHYR TRAINS WERE COMPARED TO OTHER TRAINS, THIS TUG-OF-WAR PUBLICITY STUNT WAS ORGANIZED IN APRIL 1934, IN PHILADELPHIA.

220 TOP THIS SD60M LOCOMOTIVE OF THE UNION PACIFIC HAULS A FREIGHT TRAIN THROUGH EAST KEEN, CALIFORNIA, IN MARCH 2000. BUILT IN 1992, IT WAS RENUMBERED 2470 IN AUGUST 2001. IT PRODUCES 3800 HP AND HAS A CC WHEEL ARRANGEMENT.

220 CENTER THIS UNION PACIFIC LA-4 LOCOMOTIVE HAULS THE FAMOUS "CITY OF LOS ANGELES" TRAIN.

220 BOTTOM AND 220-221 THE F SERIES GM-EMD WERE THE FIRST DIESEL-ELECTRIC LOCOMOTIVES TO BE MASS PRODUCED IN THE UNITED STATES. SOME 7000 OF THEM WERE MANUFACTURED IN MORE THAN 20 DIFFERENT VERSIONS. IN THE PHOTOGRAPH TO THE RIGHT IS THE GROUP F7 DIESEL LOCOMOTIVE OF THE ROYAL GEORGE RAILROAD. IT IS HAULING A VINTAGE TRAIN ON A TOURIST SERVICE ALONG THE SPECTACULAR DENVER & RIO GRANDE WESTERN LINE IN COLORADO.

222 TOP THIS SD60M LOCOMOTIVE OF THE UNION PACIFIC HAULS A FREIGHT TRAIN THROUGH EAST KEEN, CALIFORNIA, IN MARCH 2000. BUILT IN 1992, IT WAS RENUMBERED 2470 IN AUGUST 2001. IT PRODUCES 3800 HP AND HAS A CC WHEEL ARRANGEMENT.

222 BOTTOM A GROUP GP9 LOCOMOTIVE, OF THE WISCONSIN & SOUTHERN, MANEUVERS AT THE HEAD OF THE CONVOY. BETWEEN 1954 AND 1963, 3436 MODELS OF THESE 4-AXEL LOCOMOTIVES WERE BUILT FOR SEVERAL AMERICAN COMPANIES.

222-223 TWO GP SERIES (GENERAL PURPOSE) GM-EMD LOCOMOTIVES IN SERVICE WITH NEW ENGLAND CENTRAL RAILROAD, TOGETHER WITH ANOTHER UNIDENTIFIED ENGINE, HAUL A HEAVY FREIGHT TRAIN. OVER 10,600 OF THESE UNITS HAVE BEEN MANUFACTURED.

In Europe the construction of diesel locomotives had been in much smaller quantities, though some of the machines built distinguished themselves for the technical solutions adopted. In Great Britain, where thermal traction has always been very important, two locomotives should be mentioned – the Deltic and the Class 47. The Deltic was designed in 1961 by the English Electric Company in collaboration with Napier. This used a diesel engine of a naval origin, with its cylinders unusually arranged in an equilateral triangle. This engine gave the same power and weighed half as much as others of the time. The Deltics, of which 23 were built, were a thorough success and ended their career in 1982. In 1963 BR introduced the Class 47, of which 528 were built, becoming the mainstay British diesel locomotive. They had two trolleys with three loaded axles and a power delivery of 2750 HP, easily reaching 90 mph (145 km/h). Even France developed a significant stock of diesel locomotives, used on the lines which hadn't yet been electrified. There they used the BB67000 family which were built from 1963 in various versions (67200, 67300 to 67600) and with a total production of 492 units. These were real all-purpose locomotives, using the Bo'Bo' wheel arrangement,

electric transmission and had power outputs raging from 830 to 1470 kW. In 1967, before the great oil crisis of 1973, the SNCF designed a high power diesel locomotive for heavy and fast trains for lines such as the Paris-Basel and the Paris-Clermond Ferrand which hadn't been electrified yet. Thus, 92 CC72000 models were built – an engine giving 2250 kW and capable of reaching 100 mph (160 km/h).

In Germany they chose to use hydraulic transmission. Among the best locomotive of this kind was the V200, whose construction began in 1953 and went on for ten years, and 136 of them were built in two series by Krauss Maffei and Mak. The first units had two Maybach 12-cylinder diesel engines of 809 kW each, and Voith hydraulic transmission (later two MTU engines of 1010 kW were adopted with Mekydro hydraulic transmission), making the machines powerful and fast. The V200 (where V stands for Verbrennung, i.e. combustion) and then the 220 and 221 DBs with the new computerized numbering, were used to haul the main German passenger trains for many years. There are still many of them both in Germany and abroad, often used as locomotives for building site trains.

The era of British diesel traction began with the famous Deltic locomotive.

THE
FLYING SCOTSMAN
1862 - 1962

226 TOP IN THE 60'S, THE FRENCH RAILWAYS HAVE DEVELOPED A STRONG FAMILY OF FACTOTUM ELECTRIC DIESEL LOCOMOTIVES. 492 SPECIMENS AND MORE VERSIONS OF BB 6700 HAVE BEEN BUILT AND OFTEN USED IN MULTIPLE TRACTION.

226-227 THE CLASS 47 LOCOMOTIVES WERE THE MULTIPURPOSE WORKHORSES OF THE BRITISH NETWORK. SOME 500 OF THEM WERE MADE AND THEY MADE UP MORE THAN HALF OF THE ENTIRE BRITISH RAIL TRAIN FLEET.

227 TOP A V200 HYDRAULIC DIESEL LOCOMOTIVE BELONGING TO THE DB. FIRST PRODUCED IN 1953, A TOTAL OF 86 WERE MADE BY KLAUS MAFFEI AND WERE USED ON GERMANY'S MAIN NON-ELECTRIFIED LINES FOR HAULING EXPRESS TRAINS AND TEE.

227 BOTTOM A BRITISH RAIL DELTIC LOCOMOTIVE HAULS A HEAVY PASSENGER TRAIN. THE SUCCESS OF THIS TRAIN, AND THE LATER CLASS 47, HAS MEANT THAT BR COULD RELY ON THERMIC TRACTION AND AVOID COSTLY ELECTRIFICATION.

THE DEVELOPMENT
OF ELECTRIC TRACTION

228 THE E646.070 LOCOMOTIVE OF THE ITALIAN RAILWAYS PULLS AN INTER-REGIONAL SHUTTLE TRAIN DESIGNED IN 1961 FOR PRESTIGIOUS SERVICES, THEY ARE STILL IN USE FOR REGIONAL AND LOCAL TRAFFIC AND FOR FREIGHT SERVICES.

229 TOP IN THE YEARS AFTER THE WAR THESE LOCOMOTIVES HAVE REALLY BEEN THE FACTOTUM MACHINES OF THE DB. TWO VERSIONS WITH ELECTRONICALLY-CONTROLLED BREAKS HAVE BEEN PRODUCED (GROUP 140 AND GROUP 139) FOR A TOTAL OF AROUND 900 SPECIMENS.

It would take a whole book to give an in-depth account of the evolution of electric traction from the end of the war to the 1970s. We will therefore limit ourselves to recall the most important events and describe the most significant locomotives. We shall naturally begin with the CC7107 of the French SNCF, which between March 28 and 29 of 1955 established the world locomotive speed record of 205 mph (329 km/h), a record which lasted a good 51 years and was only beaten on September 2, 2006 in Germany by a Siemens ES64U4 locomotive, the multi-system of the Eurosprinter family. The engine was registered by the OBB as a 1216 050 and reached 222 mph (357 km/h) between Ingolstadt and Nuremberg. The CC7100 class were the first to be built by SNCF with a Co'Co' wheel arrangement and were especially employed for the main express trains of the time for the southern lines fed with 1500V DC. Their top service was undoubtedly the "Mistral," the Paris-Lyons-Marseille route, where they replaced the 2D2 9100s. Alsthom, starting from 1952, built 58 of them. They had a power delivery of 5060 CV and a maximum speed of 90 mph (145 km/h). The last was scrapped in 2001, but naturally, the record-breaking locomotive was saved from demolition.

229 BOTTOM THE E 103, ESCPECIALLY IN THIS RED AND CREAM LIVERY, IS ONE OF THE MOST BEAUTIFUL OF ALL GERMAN TRAINS. A TOTAL OF 149 WERE BUILT AND IT WAS KEPT IN SERVICE UNTIL THE APPEARANCE OF THE ICE.

e646 070

230 A SNCF POSTER, FRENCH RAILWAYS OF THE MID 60'S, PROMISES SPEED, PUNCTUALITY AND COMFORT. THE LOCOMOTIVE IS A BRAND NEW BB 16000: 62 SPECIMEN OF THESE CARS WERE BUILT BETWEEN 1958 AND 1962.

231 A SUCCESSFUL POSTER MADE BY ALBERT BRENET, PUBLICIZES THE TEE PARIS-BRUSSELS-AMSTERDAM SERVICE PERFORMED BY THE QUADRICURRENT CC40100 WHICH ALLOWED THE ELIMINATION OF THE TRACTION CHANGE AT THE BORDER.

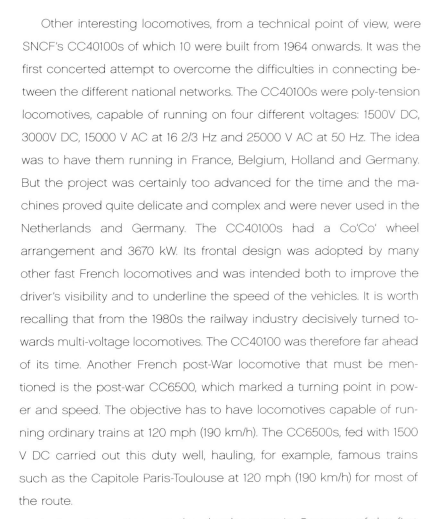

Other interesting locomotives, from a technical point of view, were SNCF's CC40100s of which 10 were built from 1964 onwards. It was the first concerted attempt to overcome the difficulties in connecting between the different national networks. The CC40100s were poly-tension locomotives, capable of running on four different voltages: 1500V DC, 3000V DC, 15000 V AC at 16 2/3 Hz and 25000 V AC at 50 Hz. The idea was to have them running in France, Belgium, Holland and Germany. But the project was certainly too advanced for the time and the machines proved quite delicate and complex and were never used in the Netherlands and Germany. The CC40100s had a Co'Co' wheel arrangement and 3670 kW. Its frontal design was adopted by many other fast French locomotives and was intended both to improve the driver's visibility and to underline the speed of the vehicles. It is worth recalling that from the 1980s the railway industry decisively turned towards multi-voltage locomotives. The CC40100 was therefore far ahead of its time. Another French post-War locomotive that must be mentioned is the post-war CC6500, which marked a turning point in power and speed. The objective has to have locomotives capable of running ordinary trains at 120 mph (190 km/h). The CC6500s, fed with 1500 V DC carried out this duty well, hauling, for example, famous trains such as the Capitole Paris-Toulouse at 120 mph (190 km/h) for most of the route.

Just as interesting was the development in Germany of the first E40 locomotives, then the 140s which were of fundamental importance in the German electrification program ran by the DB from the mid-1950s. These machines had a Bo'Bo' wheel-arrangement and were powered by 15,000 V AC at 16 2/3 Hz and had an hourly output of 3700 kW. They represented the backbone of German electric traction and around 900 of them were made.

Thanks to their extreme versatility and reliability they were practically employed for all tasks, whether passenger or goods. The queen of German electric locomotives was the E103, with a total production of 149 units by 1970. With a power of over 7000 kW the E103s were the most powerful machines of the DB and their 120 mph (190 km/h) made them the fastest too. Notwithstanding their age, in 1985 the E103.003 in an experimental run reached 176 mph (283 km/h). The DB in those years increased their power to 7440 kW. It was particularly successful because of the aerodynamic fairing. Over the years the machines were painted differently but the red and cream of the 1970s was unanimously the most popular livery.

In Italy, where electrification was at 3000 V DC, a particular school developed: the FS aimed at locomotives with six loaded axles but immediately discarded the Co'Co' wheel-arrangement because the three-axle trolleys were more aggressive towards the rails and less fit for entering the numerous bends of the Italian network. That is how the Bo'Bo'Bo' wheel-arrangement came to be chosen, three motorized trolleys with two axles, little widespread elsewhere, with a further unusual choice of having the car articulated in two identical semi-axles. It wasn't therefore necessary to allow for the lateral movement of a central truck, otherwise indispensable for entering bends as this became the pivot for the rotation of the whole car.

A solution that was maintained from 1940, with the first E 636s to the last E 656s built in 1989. All these locomotives kept the same construction model of three trolleys with 12 engines controlled electro-mechanically. During their production life they went from the 1400 kW of the E 636s to the 4800 of the E 656s. Between the two extremes of the family in 1958 they built the E 645 and in 1961 the E 646. Overall, the FS made 1223 locomotives with this design, 469 of the E 636 group, 97 of the E 645 group, 198 E 646s and finally 459 E 656s.

The only exception was the E 444, jokingly nicknamed Tartaruga, "turtle," in contrast with its speed, which used a more traditional Bo'Bo' wheel-arrangement and a normal car. Between prototypes and series models, 117 were built all together between 1967 and 1974. They could reach 120 mph (190 km/h) and were destined to haul prestigious fast trains, replacing the electric trains which were starting to show their age. The project was successful, but various problems (inadequate lines, a lack in cars capable of traveling at the speed of 120 mph / 190 km/h) prevented their widespread use.

VITESSE
EXACTITUDE
CONFORT

SOCIÉTÉ NATIONALE DES CHEMINS DE FER FRANÇAIS

S.N.C.F. 1960 - N° 50
R. C. Seine 55 B 4944

SAPHO-PARIS

PRINTED IN FRANCE FOR AND BY
THE FRENCH NATIONAL RAILWAYS

LOCOMOTIVE QUADRICOURANT CC 40100

TRANS EUROP EXPRESS
PARIS - BRUXELLES - AMSTERDAM

THE TRANS-EUROPE EXPRESS AND PRESTIGIOUS TRAINS

The Trans-Europe Express constituted the most important international rail network in post-war Europe. They were instituted in 1957 on the basis of an idea of the Dutch railways president who got the German, Italian, French and Swiss railways involved and in a second phase, also the Belgian and Luxembourg ones.

The peculiar characteristics of the TEE service were precisely established even if there were many exceptions over the years. These were: diesel traction so as not to have to change locomotive at frontiers due to a different electricity supply; blocked composition and the reversibility of trains to avoid wasting time for changes of direction in end stations, still very frequent then; being an international connection; vehicles and service of a luxury standard; a daily frequency and finally onboard customs check (at the time passengers had to get off at the frontiers for these). The

TEE services ran until 1974 when they were substituted by normal trains which also had second-class service.

Over the years some of the most beautiful European trains were used for these connections, all characterized by the red and cream livery typical of the TEE. The FS asked Breda to make a special train with two diesel railcars permanently coupled together and classed as ALN 442/448. Nine of them were made, following the much-tested philosophy for diesel railcars: two engines with an overall power of 980 HP and Wilson mechanical transmission with a hydraulic joint and a top speed of 140 mph.

The 90 seats onboard were arranged in rows of three comfy seats with ample distance between them, and a restaurant service was available with fold-away tables and air heating. From August 1957, they were used on the TEE Ligure, the Milan-Genoa-Marseilles, the Mediolanum, Milan-Verona-Munich and the Lemano Milan-Domodossola-Lausanne-Geneva. The great success soon brought attention to the few seats available and in a few years they were replaced with normal trains. In the same year the DB had also started making a diesel train originally classified VT 11.5 and then VT601, and known throughout Europe as the "big nose" due to its unmistakable profile. It was made up of 7 elements and had 122 seats in all. The disposition of the vehicles was as follows: engine, compartment carriage, salon, restaurant car with bar but no kitchen, restaurant car with kitchen and rear engine car. Each convoy was equipped with two engines delivering an overall power of 2058 kW, hydraulic transmission and it could reach 87 mph (140 km/h).

SNCF instead initially adopted 10 trains with a railcar and a trailing one already in existence, after having adapted them for TEE service. Classified as X2771-2781 (the trailing pilot railcars XRS7771-7779) they sat 39 on the driving unit which also held the small kitchen and had 42 sets on the trailing car.

The Swiss and Dutch railways began the service with already running diesel trains, classified as NS 1001-1003 with the NS and Ram 501-502 by the SBB. In 1961, though, the Swiss put a multi-voltage electric convoy in service, capable of running in Germany, identical to he Swiss one, which could run in France and Italy too. Classified Rae II 1051-1055 they became the best-known TEE trains in Europe. The standard composition was initially a pilot car with 42 seats, an engine car, a restaurant with 58 places and another 6 at the bar, a salon car with 42 seats and a pilot car with 42 seats. In the following years another intermediate car with 42 seats was added.

We cannot end this review of prestigious trains without recalling the famous ETR 301, the "Settebello" of the FS. Built in three versions from 1953, for many years it represented the apogee of elegance and luxury for railways in the whole of Europe.

Its main characteristics were that it was an electric train (the engines were therefore concentrated in engine units but distributed on trolleys throughout the train) and that the convoy was made up of seven elements in three groups (the first was made up of cars 1 and 2, the second 3, 4 and 5 and the third 6 and 7). The three groups were joined together with an automatic system. The 7-car train thus rested on 10 trolleys. The driver was cooped up in a high cab because the front of the train had a truly distinctive panoramic room with turning seats. The interior was designed by famous architects Giò Ponti and Giulio Minoletti. Together with the fairing, they strikingly expressed Italian 1950s design.

The second train not to be forgotten is the Spanish Talgo which in various versions was built between 1941 and 2000. The Talgo, an acronym for Tren Articulado Ligiero Goicoechea-Oriol, is a lowered articulated train on free axles built and sold throughout the world by the company of the same name. Its characteristics are that it is an articulated train, i.e. made up of a series of cars permanently connected, each vehicle rested on one side on just one axle, with independent

wheels, rigidly connected to the shaft as usual in the railway field. They were also connected to the vehicle behind. In practice, excluding the leading vehicles, there is always an axle corresponding between neighboring cars.

The articulation system and the independent wheels allowed the latter not to have to be always parallel to the rail even in bends, with a net improvement in the quality of the ride. The particular configuration of the axle with independent wheels, allowed for far lighter cars with a much lower floor than usual. Therefore the trains are less tall and the centre of gravity is lowered affording more stability, especially at high speeds.

Over the decades many versions of the Talgo were made, both for the Spanish large gauge and for standard gauge. Since the 1960s, variable gauge vehicles were also made, allowing for direct connections between European various cities.

Until a few years ago, the Talgos were hauled by traditional locomotives and dedicated railcars: with the XXI series, the Spanish company introduced a variable gauge convoy with full drive. A spin-off of the project was the Talgo Pendular, a passive commuter service which allowed for an increase in speed without sacrificing comfort, and the high speed Talgo 350 for the Spanish Railways also known as the AVE S-102.

234-235 THE SETTEBELLO IS THE MOST FAMOUS ITALIAN ELECTRIC TRAIN OF THE 60'S. THE HEADS OF THE TRAIN BOTH FEATURE A LOUNGE WITH SMALL MOBILE COUCHES, WHILST THE ENGINE DRIVER'S CABIN IS ELEVATED.

235 TOP THE TALGO I AND II USED PARTICULAR LOCOMOTIVES TO HAUL THE SPECIALLY HINGED CARRIAGES. THE LOCOMOTIVE TALGO II VIRGEN DE BEGOGNÁ, ALONG WITH SOME CARRIAGES, IS PRESERVED AT THE RAILWAY MUSEUM OF VILANOVA IN BARCELONA.

235 BOTTOM A 252 LOCOMOTIVE BELONGING TO SPANISH RAILWAYS HAULS A TALGO TRAIN WITH ITS CHARACTERISTIC LOW-PROFILE SHAPE. FIRST CONCEIVED IN 1941, THE TALGO HAS BEEN PRODUCED IN SEVERAL VERSIONS FOR RAILWAYS ALL OVER THE WORLD.

FROM 1980 TO TODAY
THE ADVENT
OF HIGH-SPEED TRAINS

THE REDEMPTION

238-239 FREIGHT
TRANSPORT HAS BEEN
PARTICULARLY DEVELOPED IN
THE UNITED STATES, NOT
LEAST BECAUSE OF THE GREAT
DISTANCES TO BE COVERED,
WHICH MAKE RAILROAD
TRANSPORT A FAR MORE
ECONOMIC ALTERNATIVE.
AMERICAN FREIGHT TRAINS
CAN WEIGH OVER 8000 TONS.

B etween the end of the 1960s and early 1970s many people thought that railroads had no future. Rail was perceived as an old, uncomfortable way to travel, suitable at most for transporting masses of commuters to and from the suburbs. The awareness of the advantages that rail transportation could still have came into play gradually: deaths due to highway accidents increased exponentially and traffic and parking difficulties progressively cancelled the indubitable advantages of wheel transportation. The public began to be conscious of the environmental effects on the planet due to pollution and the vast increases in consumption of non-renewable energy resources. Railroads have great advantages and still-unexpressed potential: they are responsible for only about 2.5% of greenhouse gases. To transport a ton of goods consumes half the energy used by long-distance trucks and only 1/12 of that of an airplane. Traveling by car also brings the risk of fatal accidents, which, statistically, is 37 times higher than when traveling by train. In order for these advantages to turn into concrete choices, it was necessary to profoundly renew the

239 THE MARSHALING OF
THE WAGONS INTO LARGE
FREIGHT GROUPS, READY FOR
LINKING INTO TRAINS, IS A
COMPLEX OPERATION FOR
WHICH AMERICAN RAILWAY
COMPANIES USE APPROPRIATE
DIESEL LOCOMOTIVES.

entire system, in both passenger and freight transportation. This was a path taken by all railroads, even with inevitable contradictions, that began at the end of the 1970s.

The main objectives were increased speed and comfort for passengers on long and medium distances, and its separation from city traffic; the reorganization of freight transportation; and introduction of new control and security systems.

The change, which began autonomously within individual countries, was later guided by the European Union, which, beginning in 1991, dictated the norms geared to promote and develop rail transportation. The objective, still not entirely achieved, is to gradually open railroad transportation to competition in order to stimulate increased efficiency and com-

petition within the system, as has happened in air transportation.

The impact these rules had on the railroads of Europe, is useful to remember. The first directive (91/440 in 1991) was orientated mainly toward the development and liberalization of international freight transportation, but also established some unchangeable points: the independence of the railroad companies of member states, the separation of the railroad companies, the management of the infrastructure, the right to access the network at non-discriminatory conditions for companies who carry out international freight transport. In 1991 the European Community also dictated the guidelines for the issuing of operating licenses to the railroad companies. As such, the possibility was given to private companies, and not just the traditional state railroad companies, to operate on the same networks and in direct competition. These first norms were reviewed and refined in 2001 with a series of measures known as the "First railroad package."

Italy was the first country to successfully put the Community regulations into effect thanks to the foresight of the then-Minister of Transportation Pier Luigi Bersani. In September 2001 the FNM (Milan North Railroad, a 100-year-old company controlled by the Lombardy region), symbolically broke the FS (State Railroad) monopoly with the first international freight train from Melzo to Zeebrugge in Belgium. The true turning point, however, arrived one month later when the first private railroad company, purposefully created to take advantage of the liberalization opportunities, began service on the Brennero line from Verona to Munich.

The Rail Traction Company (RTC) was created in February 2000, amid skepticism of the various personnel. Today it controls over 30% of all freight traffic on the Brennero axis, and thanks to direct competition, even the trains of the ex-monopoly State Railroad, today called Trenitalia Logistica, have very much improved their performance in terms of quality and reliability of service. The spirit of the Community norms, in this case, functioned perfectly.

In 2004 with a "Second railroad package," the EU established the terms for the complete liberalization of international freight transport (January 1, 2006) as well as that of national transport (January 1, 2007). Even more controversial due to the strong opposition of the ex-monopolized companies within each nation, was the opening to competition of passenger transportation as well. The "Third railroad package" studied by the European Commission, foresaw the liberalization of international passenger services beginning in 2010 – though the proposed date was initially 2008 – and that of national transportation beginning in 2012.

In the same package, standards were incorporated which established the conditions and procedures for the certification of train drivers. This dealt with a very important aspect, since it would permit the qualification of train drivers for every European network. In addition to the regulatory situation, the European Union engaged in supporting the integration of the national networks, overcoming the diversities of energy and signaling, and as a priority, suggesting the creation of a high-speed network which would connect the principal cities of the Continent.

While it was possible to overcome the electric current differences, thanks to manufacturers' developing carriage material for poly-tension locomotives, capable of identical travel on diverse types of tension, signaling and security systems were much more complicated. At this point, for historical and technical reasons, each administration had developed one or more national systems, completely incompatible with each other.

To assemble all devices on each locomotive would be extremely costly, and in some cases technically impossible, and would not resolve the chaos of different sets of rules each train driver should know. It was decided to develop a new signaling and control system called ERTMS (European Railway Traffic Management System), to be utilized – with priority – on the new main lines under construction and to be extended to the other lines, beginning obviously with the leading international connection lines.

240 THE RAIL TRACTION COMPANY (RTC) (THE FIRST PRIVATE ITALIAN COMPANY TO OPERATE ON THE BRENNER PASS) USES SIEMENS E189 MULTI-TENSION ELECTRIC LOCOMOTIVES IN ORDER TO OVERCOME THE CHANGE IN TRACTION BETWEEN THE ITALIAN AND AUSTRIAN NETWORKS.

240-241 TWO EU43 LOCOMOTIVES OF THE RAIL TRACTION COMPANY (RTC) ARRIVE IN A SNOWSTORM AT VALICO'S TRAIN STATION, WHICH IS SITUATED AT AN ALTITUDE OF 4265 FT (1300 M).

TOKAIDO SHINKANSEN: THE NEW RAILROAD

The history of high-speed railroads has distant roots; as we have seen in previous chapters, the search for higher speeds and quicker connections stems from the railroads themselves. High Speed as we know it today was born in Japan in 1964 with the mythical Shinkansen trains of the Tokaido Osaka line. It is useful to remember that in the West we refer to the Japanese high speed train "Shinkansen" or "Tokaido Shinkansen." In reality, *Tokaido Shinkansen* in Japanese only means "new railroad" and refers to the line and not the train. In 1958 the Japanese government authorized the construction of a ground-breaking line between Tokyo and Osaka, baptizing the project New Railroad, the Tokaido Shinkansen. In reality the trains are assigned a production number according to the model, and usually acquire a nickname. This gave birth to the first classified 0 series, the Kodama (Lightning), the 100 series Hikari (Thunderbolt) and the 300 series Nazomi (Hope). Overall, they are nicknamed Bullet Trains (Japanese *Dangan Ressha*) for the high speed and the shape of the muzzle of the 0 series trains.

At its time, the 130 miles per hour of the first Shinkansen amazed the world (we will continue to call it this according to Western usage). But if the general public was struck by the speed, sector workers were fascinated by the overall project. The novelty was to have created high speed as a specialized system, with the construction of a dedicated line, of appropriately designed means and with technological accessories aimed at services which they previously didn't have. The project was also developed for political reasons: to demonstrate to the world during the 1964 Olympics the incredible progress of a nation that had been economically and morally destroyed by the Second World War, perhaps even more than Nazi Germany. But Japanese pragmatism immediately understood that the Shinkansen could radically resolve the passenger transport problem of an old and obsolete network. The Japanese lines were traditionally at reduced gauge (42 inches/1067 mm,), winding and slow. The new train was designed for normal gauge, and put into service on dedicated lines with ample curves and numerous tunnels and bridges constructed not only to overcome valleys and rivers but also to cross the extremely dense urban areas of the country. At this point a practice model was made, with trains every five min-

242 THE 550 SERIES OF THE WEST JAPANESE RAILWAY ARE THE MOST DISTINCTIVE OF THE SHINKANSEN FAMILY, WITH A NOSE 50 FT (15 M) LONG. THE COMPANY HAS PRODUCED 16, CONSTRUCTED IN WOOD AND ABLE TO REACH 217 MPH (350 KM/H).

243 TOP THE 300 SERIES TRAINS WERE BUILT IN 1992 FOR SERVICE ON THE TOKAIDO AND SANYO SHINKANSEN LINES, REPLACING THE MUCH OLDER "HIKARI." THESE TRAINS ARE MADE UP OF 16 ELEMENTS AND CAN REACH A SPEED OF 177 MPH (285 KM/H).

utes and a punctuality which put the proverbial Swiss precision to shame. In 2004 an executive of the Japanese Central Railway publicly excused himself with passengers because the average train delay of the Shinkansen in the previous year was 12 seconds. "Only" 12 seconds, by our Western standards, "even" 12 seconds for the local rigid punctuality and efficiency standards. I don't think I am wrong in saying that we in Europe would be enthusiastic if our trains had an overall delay limited to 5 minutes let alone 12 seconds!

Over the years, the network has extended and today includes more than the Tokaido Shinkansen (Tokyo-Osaka): the Tohoku Shinkansen (Tokyo-Hachinohe), the Hokuriku Shinkansen (Takasaki-Nagano), the Joetsu Shinkansen (Omiya-Niigata) and the Sanyo Shinkansen (Osaka-Hakata), considered the main network, and three shorter branch lines from north to south, Akita, Yamagata and Kyushu, for a total of about 1,243 miles.

Originally, the network was managed by the JNR Japanese National Railway but in 1987, the year of privatization of the railroads, the Shinkansen service had accumulated a stratospheric deficit due to the costs of the traditional network, not adequately covered by the tariff. (Here we return to a discussion of the social role of railroad transportation and of the political responsibilities in these choices.) It was sub-divided into various companies, collectively called the JR Group (Japan Railway Group). They are the East Japan Railway Company, the West Japan Railway Company and the Central Japan Railway Company: each of these manages a part of the Shinkansen network and autonomously develops its own trains. The carriages are therefore quite different on each line.

Let's review some of the most significant differences: the trains from the 0 series are composed of 16 vehicles, all motorized, with a length of 1,312 feet (maximum standard length maintained even in the succeeding series) and the motors are fed 25,000 V AC, mono-phase at 50 Hz, reaching a maximum speed 130 mph; the 300X series of the Central JRC holds the Japanese speed record with 275 mph, but it usually runs at 186 mph; the 400 series of the East JRC is also known as the Mini Shinkansen because they are smaller as they have to travel on lines derived from the old narrow gauge ones: the tracks were widened from 42 inches to 56 1/2 inches but the lights in the tunnels and on bridges remained the same as before. Finally there is the E1 Max series of the East JRC, the first two-storey high-speed train in the world capable of transporting well over 1,000 people with its seven vehicles in standard composition.

243 CENTER THE 700 SERIES TRAINS ARE EASY TO RECOGNIZE FROM THE OTHER DESIGNS BY THEIR DISTINCTIVE "DUCK'S BEAK" NOSE CONE. BETWEEN 1997 AND 2004, 83 OF THESE LOCOMOTIVES WERE CONSTRUCTED; SOME WITH 8 ELEMENTS, WHILE MOST WITH 16.

243 BOTTOM THE 400 TRAINS OF THE EAST JAPANESE RAILWAY ARE ALSO KNOWN AS "MINI-SHINKANSEN" BECAUSE OF THEIR COMPACT, REDUCED SHAPE, WHICH IS ESSENTIAL FOR SERVICE ON THE OLD LINES WITH THE GAUGE EXTENDED TO 1435 MM.

THE SUPREME FRENCH: THE TGV

The success of the Shinkansen convinced even European railroad administrators to aim for high speed: the roads to cover were various and all brought interesting results. But first let's see what the advantages of high speed were for the European networks.

It is competitive with air transport for distances around 373-435 miles (and in fact the air connections between Lyon and Paris where the TGV has operated for years, have practically ceased, as is happening between Paris and Brussels); it frees capacity for traffic on the traditional railroad lines; reduces street traffic with a reduction of pollution and accidents.

As well as the direct advantages for passengers – a quicker trip means having more time to do other things – it is possible to do many activities on the train that are not possible when traveling by car or by plane. One should also calculate indirect advantages: a more rational consumption of energy, less pollution, less deaths and injuries due to car accidents, with a cost savings for the country, and consequently for all.

On the other hand, the construction of new lines is costly and can be very difficult in some countries, such as Italy which is highly populated and with difficult mountainous geography.

The French were the first in Europe to realize a high-speed network in 1978 with the construction of the TGV, acronym of Train a Gran Vitesse (High-speed train) and the opening of traffic on September 27, 1981 on the Paris-Lyon line: the studies, however, had begun in 1966 with the creation of the SNCF Research Services.

Two different design philosophies exist in the realization of a high speed network: the first adopted by the French, foresees lines dedicated completely to AV trains. No other type of train, passenger or freight, travels on them and this has two consequences: the trains all travel at the same speed making it is easier to manage traffic with frequent trains; it isn't necessary to design an infrastructure capable of taking long and heavy traditional trains, since the high-speed trains are light and potent. One can therefore design, as the SNCF did, steeper slopes, even of 35/1000, with notable savings in the construction of bridges, tunnels and embankments.

The second philosophy, adapted by the Germans and Italians, aims at having a line for high speed which can also be used by traditional or freight trains (for example, at night when passenger traffic is absent). In this case it is correct to speak of doubling, even with innovative characteristics, the existing lines. The construction costs were higher, as with the interconnections with the traditional network.

As mentioned, SNCF opted for the first solution and created a very efficient system which also extended outside of France.

Only a year and a half after the opening of the first section, the Paris-Lyon line, more than 8 million travelers had already chosen the TGV. In 1989 the Atlantique line to Brest, Rennes and Nantes to the west was opened, followed in 1990 by the connection to Bordeaux and Toulouse in the southwest.

In 1993 came the connection to the north, Lille and Calais, which was to continue with the Channel Tunnel from November 1994. Still in the same year a relationship began which joined the south east Atlantic lines and the north, passing through Charles de Gaulle international airport.

Thanks to the new section, the main French cities were now connected with short travel times (for example, Lille to Lyon is only 3 hours). A new turning point came in 2001, when 155 miles were added to the Mediterranée section between Valence, Avignon and Marseilles.

The travel times between Paris and Marseilles decreased to 3 hours for 497 miles. By comparison, Milan-Naples, similar in distance, still requires 8 hours.

At the same time, the technological evolution of the TGV continued, with travel speed from 168 to 186 mph.

The TGV, with its experimental train V150, still holds the record for the fastest wheeled train, having reached 357.1 mph (574.8 km/h) at 1:16 pm on April 3rd 2007, at kilometer point 191 of the South East line. It broke the 1990 rail record of 320.2 mph (515.3 km/h), which was also held by a TGV Atlantique. The V150 is 347 ft (106 m) long and weighs 268 tons. It was manufactured by Alstom, in collaboration with SNCF and French Rail Network. It reached its record-breaking speed in about ten minutes, releasing a power of 19.6 megawatts (over 25.000 horsepower): almost double the power produced by all the cars at the start of a F1 Grand Prix. In 1996 the TGV Duplex was also introduced, with two-level trains, each with a capacity of between 386 and 516 seats. Eurostar trains are also derived from the TGV design, connecting Paris to Brussels and to London through the Channel Tunnel. In 2000, a four-current version of the TGV baptized Thalys was born, its fleet divided among the French, Belgium and Dutch railroads, operating on the Paris-Brussels-Amsterdam-Köln line.

To provide some instructive figures, it is interesting to note that in 2005 alone, the TGV transported over 80 million passengers in France and another 20 million in Europe thanks to the 650 trains circulating every day, serving the 957 miles of lines and the 250 stations of the network.

By June 2007 the TGV Est Européen will connect Paris to nearly 30 cities east of the capital, some in Germany, Switzerland and Luxembourg, with an increase in average speeds to 200 mph.

For the future, SNCF has planned the TGV Bretagne-Pays de Loire (by 2012) and the TGV Rhin Rhone, a natural extension of the TGV Mediterranée, while the TGV South Europe Atlantique line should gain a new section between Tours and Bordeaux with another extension toward Spain and Portugal.

Technically, the train is different from Japanese electric trains whose motors are distributed on all cars.

The TGV, designed and built by Alstom, is a train with concentrated power, that is, the traction is guaranteed by two engines with a Bo'Bo' wheel arrangement at the head and tail of the train with a set number of cars in tow (8 or 10 elements).

The cars are often creating with their function in mind and therefore some of them are multi-voltage.

Some international connections, in addition, include traditional types of sections, fed with different voltages from the French 25kV AC; this is the case with connections to Switzerland and Italy where the TGV trains arrive at Milan Central Station.

HIGH SPEED IN ITALY: PENDOLINO & ETR 500

talian interest in high speed began very early: the first cross-tie laid for the 'Direttissima' Florence-Rome, the first section conceived for trains with this characteristic, was in 1970. It's a shame that the completion of only 149 miles of this line, though it lasted a good 22 years, highlighted a typical problem in the construction of all public works in Italy – the lack of respect for the necessary completion time. The first functioning section was inaugurated on February 24, 1977, 76 miles from Settebagni to the Città della Pieve, and lastly from Figline to Valdarno South, in the summer of 1992. The line was conceived for a mixture of high speed and traditional trains (in the first years of use it was common to see slow freight cars towed by the E626 built in the early 1930s). In reality the Florence-Rome replaced the old, very winding line, which had connected the two cities up until then. A true high-speed train was lacking. The FS once again took the project in hand that Fiat Railroad (today part of Alstom) had realized in 1976 for a fast tilting train, the ETR 401 Pendolino, and commissioned a train with similar characteristics. The Pendolino is one of the most extraordinary Italian railroad engineering successes in the world. It was born out of an intelligent intuition: in a country with a dated railroad network, full of curves and ups and downs, the way to rapidly increase the speed of the trains was that of intervening on the carriage material and not on the infrastructure. To improve the already good speed characteristics of the electric trains, someone thought of introducing the possibility of the inclination of the cage in a curve.

The tilting train had already been unsuccessfully experimented with in France and the UK and few engineers believed in this technology. The solution was found by the technicians of Fiat Ferroviaria who, to command the inclination system of the train, decided to use two gyroscopes assembled on the cars instead of an accelerometer assembled on the cage. In this way each vehicle began to incline at the beginning of the curve and not when it had already entered the curve, and imbalances and oscillations came across in the systems guided by the accelerometers were avoided. The system was tried and fine-tuned on a trial vehicle, the ETR Y0160, and then applied to the first real working tilting train, the ETR 401 built in 1976. The train could lean up to 10° per side in curves, allowing a 30% speed increase. The FS used this system with success in regular service on the Rome-Ancona and on the Rome-Ancona-Rimini lines, but did not continue with the experiment. Only 10 years later, faced with the obvious lack of a high-speed train project, they re-evalu-

ated the idea and commissioned from Fiat Ferroviaria a family of tilting electric trains based on the ETR 401 project. As such, the ETR 450 began service in 1988 and the name Pendolino in Italy became synonymous with High Speed. The ETR 450 traveled at 155 mph on the Rome-Florence line, at the time the only AV line of the network, and then exploited the speed characteristics allowed by the tilting on the rest of the network. It was a huge success, not so much because of the number of tilting trains made (15) but for the success of the technology: since the year 2000, besides other FS trains (ETR 460, ETR 470), Fiat Ferroviaria and Alstom sold the Pendolino all over the world; Finland has the S220, Spain, the Alaris; Portugal, the Alfa Pendular; Slovenia, the ETR 310; Germany, the VT 610; UK, the Virgin 360 for Virgin Train; and in the Czech Republic, the CDT680. In the future, trains derived from the Pendolino will also circulate in Russia and China.

In Italy the latest evolution of the family is the ETR 600. It will begin service in early 2007. The seven-element structure of the train has a completely new design with respect to the previous series. It was built entirely in aluminum to respond to the most advanced technical norms for interoperability and offers 432 seats. The order includes 26 trains – 12 for Trenitalia, classified ETR 600, bi-current (3kV DC and 25kV Alternating Current); and 14 for the Cisalpino company (an equal joint venture between Trenitalia and Swiss Railroads) classified ETR 610, 4-current and capable of circulating in Germany as well. The maximum speed is 155 mph.

The Italian railroads have another family of high speed non-tilting trains, the ETR 500, realized in 59 models beginning in 1985. They are concentrated power trains with a locomotive at the head and normally a 12-car composition. The ETR 500 is capable of reaching 186 mph and is the train used for the most important connections on the entire network. Overall, it offers 671 seats between first- and second-class. A part of the fleet is already equipped with bi-tension locomotives (the AV lines are fed 25 kV AC, whereas the historical network is run at 3kV DC). In the future all trains will be able to circulate indifferently on both networks. Just out of curiosity, let's remember that an ETR 500, the diagnostic experimental train ETRY 500-2 is the holder of the Italian speed record, established on May 25, 2006 on the Turin-Novara line hitting 219 mph.

Meanwhile, the construction of the new high speed lines and the renovation of the principle junctions of the network also continue with the construction of new, dedicated stations. The project foresees a north-south axis Turin-Milan-Bologna-Rome-Florence-Naples and a west-east Turin-Milan-Verona-Venice-Trieste, inserted in the European corridor Lisbon-Kiev at slower speed. To the opposition of environmental groups and local committees, one must add the difficulty of financial coverage of the project. At the beginning of 2006 two lines started service, the Turin-Novara (part of the Turin-Milan line) and Rome-Naples, even though their lines don't reach the center of the two cities. The Rome-Naples and the Turin-Novara are also the first railroad lines in the world to be run on a second-level ETRMS signaling and control system: the trains, which travel at 186 mph, are supervised thanks to a radio system from a control and command room which sends all necessary communication. Consequently the traditional light signals placed along the tracks have been eliminated and substituted by a continual flow of information that the train driver receives on an appropriate monitor in the locomotive. The completion of the Milan-Bologna line is expected by 2007, that of the Bologna-Florence by 2008. The segment between Novara and Milan of the line for Turin should be completed by 2009. It is more difficult to predict for the Milan-Venice-Trieste line.

250 An ETR 500 First Series of the Italian railways travels on a traditional, single rail line. With the opening of the new lines alimented by 24kV ca, the locomotives will be replaced by bi-current ones.

251 top An ETR 460P travels on the new Milan-Turin high-speed line. The Pendolino is capable of tilting and so can achieve high speeds on both the AV and traditional lines with their tighter and more numerous curves.

251 bottom A Pendolino ETR 450 in service between Venice and Rome comes out of the Catajo Tunnel, between Padova and Rovigo. The inclination of up to 10 degrees on either side of the curve allows a 30 percent increase in the allowed speed.

HIGH SPEED IN GERMANY: THE ICE

Unlike Japan and France (Italy with its delays is a separate case), the high speed saga of German railroads has a relatively young history. The first tests with the ICE (Inter City Express) go back to the mid 1980s. On November 14, 1986 the Experimental ICE for the first time reached 186 mph. But the first business service dates to 1991 when on June 2 the ICE began to circulate, connecting Hamburg to Munich. Ini-

tially, the maximum speed was set at 155 mph, and then raised to 174 mph. Soon, the white train of the DB became a reference point for the German travelers. The first lines built were the 203-mile Hanover-Wurzburg and the 62-mile Mannheim-Stuttgart. The DB put a fleet of 60 ICEs constructed by Siemens in service and then identified them as ICE1: it was a classic concentrated power train with two locomotives at

the extremities and 14 dedicated cars. It could accommodate up to 759 people and also offer restaurant and bar services.

Initially, possible frequent changes in composition were thought possible, based on the services carried out. This idea soon revealed itself to be impractical and inconvenient. Since 1997 the connections were extended to the ex-GDR (Berlin-Hanover segment) thanks to the beginning

of service for the second generation ICE, the ICE2. The main novelty of these trains is in their modularity. They are formed by a single engine, five cars and a pilot car at the other extremity, but can easily be coupled together thanks to the Scharfenberg automatic coupling system to form a train with the same capacity of the ICE 1. In this way it is possible to serve two destinations with the same train by simply separating the two trains, when necessary. The next move in 1998 was the introduction of a tilting train to increase speed on traditional lines, the ICE T (T to define tilting train). This vehicle, as with the successive ICE 3, is unlike the ICE 1 and ICE 2, an electric train, which is a train without a locomotive on the extremities but with motors distributed on all the axes. It is capable of reaching 143 mph even on rough lines and thanks also to the diesel version, has drastically decreased travel times on many classic lines, such as between Stuttgart and Switzerland, between Munich and Berlin via Leipzig and Nuremberg-Dresden. The ICE 3 was designed specifically for the Koln-Rhein/Main segment which, unlike the others, was built only for light, high-speed trains, based on the model of the TGV French network. It is made up of 16 vehicles, subdivided in two semi-trains permanently coupled together. There are two existing versions, ICE 3, mono-voltage and the ICE3M Multi-voltage, capable of traveling with four different types of energy feed. The speed of these trains is 186 mph and they are utilized for connections with Belgium and Holland and soon, with France.

Germany, though it began late, has amply caught up, creating an integrated network with capillary connections with traditional high speed trains and tilting trains unique in Europe.

252 TOP AN ICE (INTERCITY EXPRESS), THE GERMAN HIGH-SPEED TRAIN, ENTERS A STATION. THE FIRST SERVICE BEGAN IN THE SUMMER OF 1991, FROM HAMBURG TO MUNICH, AND A TRAIN ON THIS LINE HAS REACHED 155 MPH (250 KM/H).

252-253 THE ICE-T DIFFERS FROM THE ICE1 AND ICE2 IN TWO PARTICULAR WAYS: IT TILTS; AND IT IS ALSO A PROPER ELECTRIC TRAIN, MEANING THAT ITS MOTORS ARE DISTRIBUTED ALONG THE ENTIRE AXIS, AND SO THERE ARE NO LOCOMOTIVES AT EITHER END.

253 TOP LEFT THE FIRST TRAINS THAT ENTERED SERVICE, NOW CLASSIFIED ICE1, SUCH AS THE ONE IN THE PHOTOGRAPH, WERE MADE UP OF TWO VEHICLES ON EITHER END OF 14 CARRIAGES.

253 TOP RIGHT THE ICE-T HAVE BEEN BUILT IN TWO VERSIONS – ELECTRIC AND DIESEL. THANKS TO THESE TRAINS, TIMES HAVE BEEN DRASTICALLY REDUCED EVEN ON PARTICULARLY WINDING ROUTES WHICH WERE NOT DIRECTLY SERVED BY HIGH-SPEED LINES.

THE OTHER EUROPEAN EXPERIENCES

Spain has an ambitious plan to build a good 4,474 miles of lines by the end of 2010, with possible speeds of 218 mph. In the meantime, since 1992, the AVE (High Speed Spanish) trains, derived from the French TGV Reseau, offer service on the 259 miles of the new Madrid-Siviglia normal gauge line. In 2007 the opening of the Lleida-Barcelona segment of the Barcelona-Madrid-French border line is expected, as well as the Sagra-Toledo line and the Cordoba-Bobadilla line. The Spanish railroads have in the meantime supported the AVEs with S-102 trains (Talgo 350 realized by the Talgo-Bombardier consortium) and the S-103 Velaro E by Siemens derived by the German ICE3 (with the participation of Renfe, Caf and Alstom in the construction of the Spanish train).

254-255 and 255 top Spain is rapidly modernizing its rail infrastructure which has been neglected for decades. The two photographs here show the first AV trains to come into service with AVE (Alta Velocita Española) and are Spain's version of the TGV Reseau.

Look what you gain when you travel by train

Now: London to Bath, a comfortable 69 minutes

Now: London to Bristol Temple Meads, a smooth 85 minutes

Now: London to Cardiff, a relaxing 105 minutes

Now: London to Swansea, an easy 163 minutes

Pick up a free copy of the pocket timetable

Inter-City 125 makes the going easy

PUBLISHED BY BRITISH RAILWAYS BOARD 46 47/477   INDF   PRINTED BY ST. MICHAEL'S PRESS. LONDON. ENGLAND

Britain, on the other hand, has a specialized high speed line: the only important services are the Eurostar trains which travel through the Channel Tunnel connecting London to France and Belgium. They are trains derived from the French TGV and on the British network are fed with a third rail system. Naturally, we must remember the Intercity 125 and Intercity 225 trains with which many services were rendered internally: the first is a diesel train composed of Mark 3 cars encased between two class 43 diesel locomotives, the second is electric and is made up of a class 9 locomotive, Mark 4 cars and a pilot car. All these trains travel at a maximum speed of 124 mph. Recently also 14 class 80 "Adelante" diesel trains were put into use for the First Great Western company, the class 220 Voyager trains and 221 Super Voyager (these last are tilting trains) for Virgin, and those of class 220, similar to the precedent 221, for Hull Trains and Midland Mainline companies. Finally, since 2001, Virgin Train has put 53 class 390 "Pendolino" trains in service, built by Alstom, capable of reaching 140 mph.

The Belgians have three lines with standard high speed whereas the Dutch count on completing the HSL-Zuid project by 2007, a 78-mile line which joins Amsterdam to Rotterdam at the Belgian border. Some 53 miles of the line are of new construction. The Swiss, on the other hand, do not have strictly high speed lines and have opted for a carriage material upgrade, putting the ICN (InterCity Neigezeug) train in service, which adopts active tilting and connects the main cities of the confederation.

The ICN, which uses active tilting developed with Pendolino Fiat/Alstom, is a seven-element electric train with 463 seats and a cruise speed of 124 mph.

Turkey foresees the inauguration during 2007 of the first high speed line between Istanbul and Ankara, 156 miles long; the line will be electrified at 25 kV AC with a designed travel speed of 155 mph. The Spanish builders Caf provide the trains. In a second phase the line between Inönü and Gebze will be realized for an overall 133 miles.

260-261 Waterloo Station in London is the terminus for the Eurostar services that come from Paris and Brussels. The trains are based on the French TGV with adaptions for the English network.

261 The Eurostar trains, originally called Transmance Super Train, comprise two engines at either end and eight carriages. They can be powered in three different ways: 25kV ca in France; 3kV cc in Belgium; and 750V cc in Britain, and third rail.

PROJECTS
IN THE REST OF THE WORLD

The Chinese railway expected in the course of 2007 to lay 70 miles track between Beijing and Tianjin with adjustable tilt trains cruising at 185 mph. A train will run ever three minutes. There will be 60 trains carrying 600 passengers each. They will be classed CHR3, derived from the ICE3 developed by Siemens for the DB. By 2010 the construction of the new Beijing-Shanghai line is expected, 820 miles long. It will run parallel to the existing line, which is also being developed. In Taiwan, a 215-mile line will run from Taipei to Kaohsiung with 30 Japanese trains similar to the Shinkansen 700 Hikari series, built by Kavasaki Heavy Industries.

South Korea in 2004 inaugurated its high velocity network, completely separate from the traditional network and directly derived from the French TGV. The country is planning the development of its own train with better performance than the French model.

In the United State the only truly high speed service is the Acela Express managed by Amtrak, which in 2001 connected Boston and Washington. The convoy, built by the Bombardier/Alstom consortium is made up of two electric locomotives at each end of the train and six intermediate carriages also equipped with adjustable tilt allowing a 6° inclination in bends. This aspect of the train, although very similar to that of the TGV, should not lead one to think they are totally similar; the two projects are completely different. The Acela from New York to Washington takes about 2 hours and 45 minutes at a normal speed of 80 mph. Among plans under discussion for the future are developments for the San Francisco and Los Angeles area in California; the local government has created the High Speed Rail Authority for the development of the project.

Argentina is also thinking of a short connection of 190 miles between Buenos Aires and Rosario: it would be the first service of its kind in South America. Even in Mexico the government is thinking about high speed links. Other studies are also taking place in Australia, India and Portugal.

262-263 TAIWAN IS DEVELOPING A HIGH-SPEED 214-MILE (345-KM) LINE, UPON WHICH WILL RUN THESE TRAINS, DERIVING FROM THE JAPANESE SHINKANSEN 700 SERIES "HIKARI." IT IS EXPECTED THAT 30 TRAINS WILL BE BUILT BY KAWASAKI HEAVY INDUSTRIES.

263 TOP IN THE UNITED STATES, AMTRAK USES THE ACELA TRAINS ON ITS ROUTES IN THE NORTHEAST. THE TRAIN COMPRISES TWO LOCOMOTIVES AT EITHER END AND SIX CARRIAGES. THE CARRIAGES (AND ONLY THE CARRIAGES) ARE ABLE TO TILT UP TO AN ANGLE OF 6 DEGREES.

MAGNETIC LEVITATION TRAINS

Even if they are not trains in the strictest sense, we would like to cover this technology which in the last few years has seen some interesting developments. The convoys use a suspension system based on a single guide rail and magnetic propulsion. The vehicle does not move due to contact between rail and wheel, but is suspended tenths of an inch above thanks to the action of powerful magnets. Therefore the only friction hindering movement is that of air and this allows for very high speeds, great acceleration and braking without adherence problems.

The Central Japan Railway in collaboration with Kawasaki Heavy Industries is currently developing systems of the kind. It has been dubbed "Superconducting Maglev Shinkansen" by the German Transrapid consortium which includes Siemens and Tyssen-Krupp. There is only one in commercial service in the world – the Shanghai Maglev Train made by Transrapid in 2002. It connects the international airport to the city center: the line is 18 miles long and the top speed reached is 310 mph. In Japan, the Central Japan Railway Maglev has established, on a test circuit, the absolute speed record of 360 mph, but its designers are aiming for a speed of 400 mph.

The magnetic levitation system can be used for urban routes, obviously not at such high speed. In this urban Maglev or low-speed Maglev system there are two creations to remember. In March 2005 Japan inaugurated a 6-mile line, the Linimo Tobu Kyuryo Line also known as the Nagoya East Hill Line. It was used, at a top speed of only 60 mph, to reach the grounds of the 2005 Expo. In Europe from 1984 to 1995, a brief stretch of about 650 yards connected the international airport of Birmingham to the railway station. Problems of obsolescence of electronic components advised that the system be substituted with a cable railway.

The German and Japanese projects use slightly different technologies: the first uses conventional electromagnets and electromagnetic suspension of the attractive kind, the second uses superconducting magnets and electrodynamic suspension.

Studies are concentrated on three technologies: electromagnetic suspension (EMS) which uses conventional electromagnets on a special structure under the convoy which embraces the central rail; electrodynamic suspension which reaches levitation thanks to the opposite polarity of magnets on the vehicle and the windings on the rail; and

thirdly, permanent magnets, known as Inductrack which is based on the repulsive effect of permanent magnetic elements both on the vehicle. The movement is obtained thanks to a linear motor positioned either in the train or in the track. The cars have no drive and are completely screened from the electromagnetic fields which would otherwise harm passengers.

Until now, projects for new lines have come up against the high construction costs of the Maglev, but also the high environmental impact of the structure, which has to be a few yards above the ground.

In any case, there are projects for lines in Japan and China, from Shanghai to Hangzhou, in Great Britain from London to Glasgow, and in Germany between Munich airport and the central station. These developments could in some ways be hindered by the accident September 22, 2006 – still inexplicable – which involved a Transrapid on the German test circuit in Emsland where a train with dozens of passengers on board crashed into a service vehicle stationed on the line. This tragedy does not involve Maglev technology but obviously calls for an inquiry into traffic security systems.

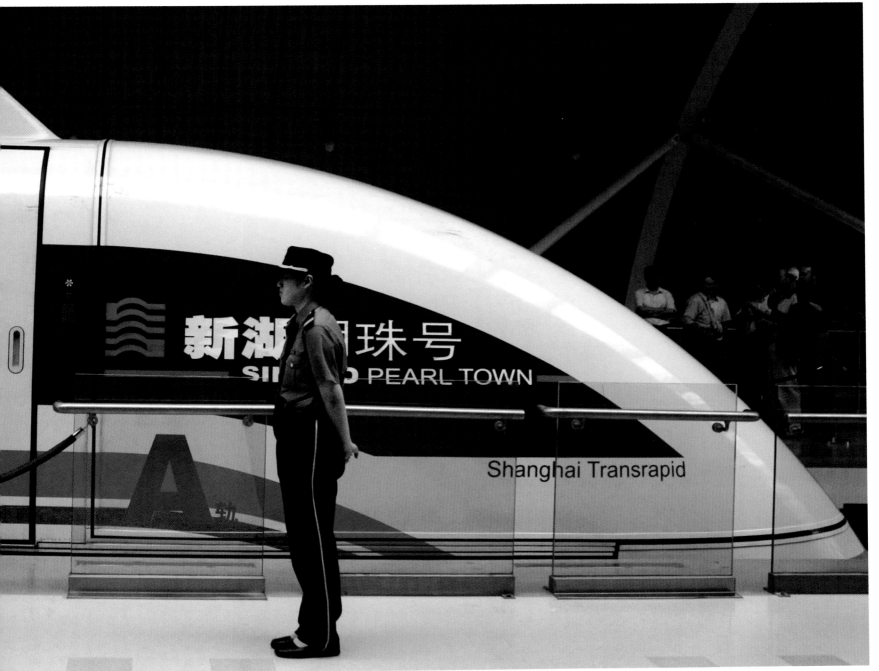

TRAVELING FOR PLEASURE AND FOR TOURISM

Whether one travels by train to go to work or to go to lessons, they have the same thing in mind: to get there in time. Traveling is a necessary evil, the price to pay to honor some commitment or to get to work or to school in time. Of course, for most of us, traveling by train means just that and little more (even though it would be nice to conduct an inquiry and find out how many love stories and simple friendships were born in the compartments of a train).

Now, as ever, it is possible to travel for pleasure alone, not just to get from one place to another but to enjoy the journey itself. It may be a luxury train with the caprice of an unusual service or an old steam train to breath forgotten aromas. Or yet again, it could be a panoramic voyage crossing dream landscapes driven by a small electric locomotive with two wooden axles which you can jump on and off from at any time. We could fill hundreds of pages with tales and descriptions of the most beautiful and curious railroads around the world but we wouldn't be doing justice to the many we'd have to leave out. One thing, however, brings together all these experiences: finally time counts no longer and the aim is no longer that of moving as fast as possible.

Over the last few years railway tourism has developed greatly and today there are solutions and itineraries catering to the most diverse interests.

The hope is that at least one of these trains, even if you are not lovers of the genre, may arouse your curiosity to the point of deciding to try it out for yourself.

270-271 THE 424.356, ONE OF THE MOST BEAUTIFUL LOCOMOTIVES OF THE HUNGARIAN RAILWAYS, HAULS THE ORIENT EXPRESS IN A CLOUD OF STEAM. THESE LOCOMOTIVES, NICKNAMED "BUFFALO" BECAUSE OF THEIR SPEED AND IMPOSING SIZE, HAVE CONTINUED THEIR SERVICE UP UNTIL 1986.

ORIENT
EXPRESS
EUROPE

The Orient Express symbolizes for many the ultimate luxury train, traveling with every comfort but also with a bit of adventure. This international line was first operated in 1883 by the Compagnie Internationale des Wagons-Lits to connect Gare de l'Est in Paris to Istanbul, but this lines does not exist anymore. It was the victim of progress and of air travel. Fortunately its appeal has been revived in the Venice Simplon Orient Express, which was created by the Orient Express Hotels, Trains & Cruises Company founded and owned by hotel tycoon James B. Sherwood

Inaugurated in 1982, this luxury tourist service includes splendid original CIWL vintage 1920s and 1930s cars and travels across various European routes. The classic one is the London to Venice, via Paris, Basel, Zurich, Innsbruck, Brenner Pass and Verona. However, periodically, this fascinating line also touches Rome, Vienna, Prague, Budapest and Istanbul, and, from 2007, also Warsaw and Cracovia.

The sight of this train, blue with CIWL golden friezes and comprising 17 cars, while it stables in Venice or Paris, or while it runs along the hairpin turns of the Brennero line, is quite stunning and always eye-catching, However, the real beauty of the Orient Express is its interiors and the service offered to the passengers. The traditional journey from London to Venice lasts two days. Although it departs and arrives in two of Europe's most fascinating cities, the real event is the experience of traveling on the train. The carriages are all vintage 1920s and 1930s models, restored rather than restructured in view of the already high standard of luxury achieved in those times. One has to admire the company's wise decision of not introducing extraneous elements, such as a shower in the sleeping cars, in order to maintain the period feel and authenticity.

A very good idea is also the booklet provided which recounts the history, often adventurous, of each car in the train. Dining car 4095 was built in Birmingham in 1927 in the "Etoile du Nord" line's style. Transferred to Europe, it was used in the Pullman services between Paris and Amsterdam, passing through Brussels, a journey of more than 350 miles (560 km). It ended its period of service with the Lusitania Express between 1961 and 1969. But other cars had a more adventurous life. Sleeping car 3309, for example, in 1929, remained stuck in a snow drift for 10 days, 60 miles (95 km) outside Istanbul, and its passengers survived only with the assistance of nearby Turkish villagers. While sleeping car 3425 was used by King Carol of Romania and others were used by German troops and also by the Allies during the war.

Nowadays, luxury is stressed everywhere on board – in private cabins, dining and bar carriages. Piano music provides a pleasant and relaxing atmosphere, while travelers enjoy their cocktails. The pleasure of dressing appropriately for every meal or appointment of the day is also one the characteristics of life on the Orient Express, which has strictly forbidden the wearing of jeans and running shoes. Dinner in formal wear is one of the trip's unforgettable experiences. The compartments of the sleeping cars during the day become luxurious private lounges, of which, the most distinctive characteristic is the elegant lampshade in front of the window. In the evening the cabin crew converts the sofa into a comfortable bed with soft sheets. Compartments can have either a single or double bed. The Orient Express tours regularly from March to November.

272 AND 272-273 THE COURTEOUS AND EFFICIENT CABIN CREW OF THE ORIENT EXPRESS IN THEIR ELEGANT UNIFORMS WITH WHITE GLOVES, WHILE THE POLISHED BRASS OF THE VINTAGE CARRIAGES SPARKLE IN THE SUN. THE KITCHEN CREW, ABOVE, INCLUDE SOME OF THE BEST CHEFS IN EUROPE.

274 AND 274-275 THE CARRIAGE INTERIORS HAVE BEEN RECONSTRUCTURED AS THEY WERE IN THE 1920S TO SUCH A HIGH STANDARD THAT THE TRAIN IS CLASSIFIED AS A HISTORICAL MONUMENT. THE DINING CAR IS IN EFFECT A LUXURY RESTAURANT ON RAILS.

THE ROYAL SCOTSMAN
SCOTLAND

276 TOP THE SPLENDID COAT OF ARMS OF THE ROYAL SCOTSMAN SUGGESTS AN ASSOCIATION WITH AN EXCLUSIVE CLUB. THIS LUXURIOUS TRAIN NEVER CARRIES MORE THAN 36 PASSENGERS ON ANY OF ITS JOURNEYS ACROSS THE SCOTTISH HIGHLANDS.

276 BOTTOM THE ROYAL SCOTSMAN'S CHEF LEANS OUT FROM THE DINING CAR AS HE WAITS FOR THE DELIVERY OF FRESH SUPPLIES FOR HIS KITCHEN. THE SUPERB SERVICE AND FOOD OF THE RESTAURANT IS ONE OF THE TRAIN'S HIGHLIGHTS.

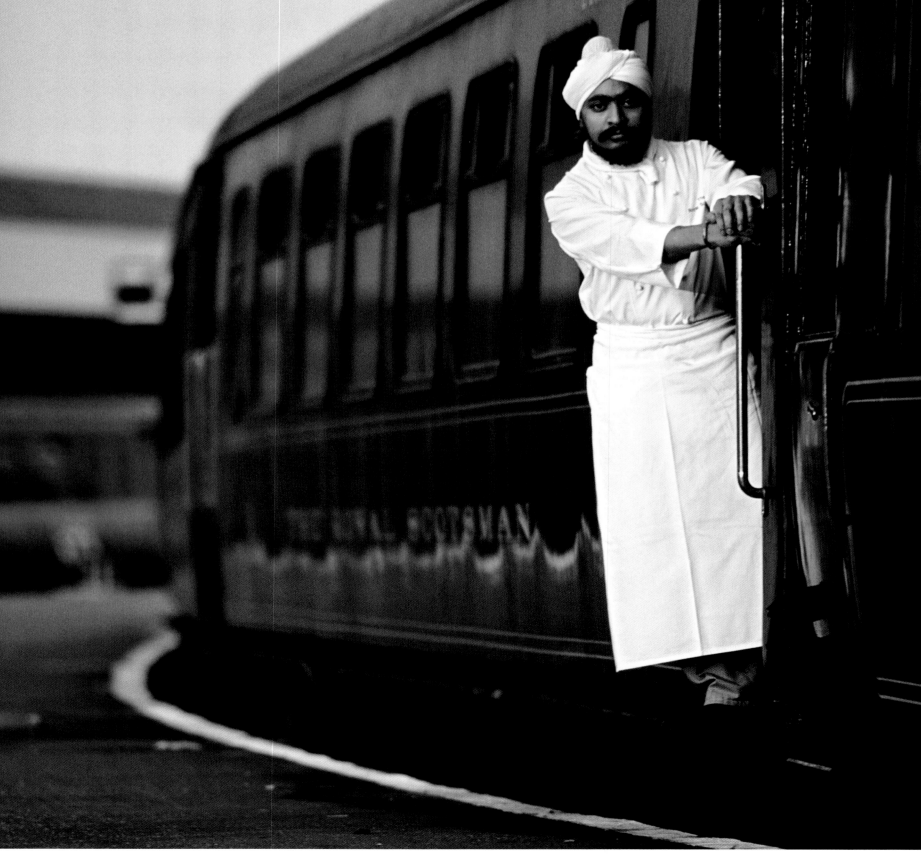

The Royal Scotsman is one of the world's most luxurious trains. Relatively new, its first journey was in 1985 and it soon earned an international fame. A fame that is quite justifiable in view of the service it offers.

A journey on this train is certainly not for everyone's pockets but it is a once-in-a-lifetime experience. The Royal Scotsman journeys every year from March to October across the Scottish Highlands. The itineraries and duration of the journeys vary from two to seven days, spent inside luxurious carriages and undertaking exclusive visits to the most characteristic of Scottish location – castles, distilleries and workshops of local products.

The train accommodates only 36 guests per journey. These are pampered and spoilt by a staff of 12 persons, two of which are chefs. Champagne and oysters are of course the order of the day. The uniqueness of this train vacation begins at the station of Edinburgh from which every tour starts. Guests are greeted with the sound of pipes played by the train's crew, all lined up along the new polished cars. The interior of every vehicle is splendid. Six of the cars are ex-Pullman carriages built by Metro-Camel in the 1960s and radically restored for this luxurious train's use. Two sleeping cars, of type MK3 (before 1997 the line used the MK1 type) are connected to these carriages, and their interiors have also been superbly improved.

The oldest vehicle of the train is dining car No. 2 built in 1945 by the LNER and baptized "Lochaber" in the 1980s. All the vehicles have been rebuilt according to the style of the Edwardian era. The train's structure is as follows: lounge with observation veranda on one side (now no. 99965 and ex 319 "SNIPE"); dining car 1 (no. 99967, ex 317 "RAVEN"); dining car 2 (no.1999 and ex LNER 1513); sleeping car 1 (no. 99961 and ex 324 "AMBER"); sleeping car 2 (no. 99962 and ex 329 PEARL"); sleeping car 3 (no. 99963 and ex 324 "TOPAZ"); sleeping car 4 (no. 99964 and ex 313 "FINCH"); sleeping car 5 (no. 99968 and ex Mk3 10541); and one crew car (no. 99969 ex Mk3 10556).

The sleeping cars all have twin and single bed cabins, with all the comfort, and more, that you would expect from the most famous hotel – private toilet and bath, wardrobe, floor-level beds. Moreover, the train does not travel during the night but stables in secondary and silent stations, thus guaranteeing a better rest for its guests. The dining car provides a wide variety of fine wines and champagnes and the menu includes salmon, shellfish specialties and also ox and lamb.

One of most beautiful lines that the The Royal Scotsman uses is, without doubt, the West Highland line, reached from Edinburgh via Glasgow. It is a difficult and tortuous track which, even today, is traveled at low speed (around 5 hours are needed to cover around 155 miles / 250 km) but it crosses one of the most wild and picturesque regions of the country.

The train tours Loch Lomond for 10 miles (16 km) and then it climbs up north and across the famous Horseshoe Viaduct, between the mountains of Beinn Odhar and Beinn Dorain. After passing the remote station of Rannoch, the train arrives at one of Britain's most fascinating sections of track which culminates in the viaduct of Glennfinnan with its 21 arches and in the nearby small station of the same name. A wonderful spectacle that the 36 guests of the Royal Scotsman can enjoy calm and relaxed in their seats.

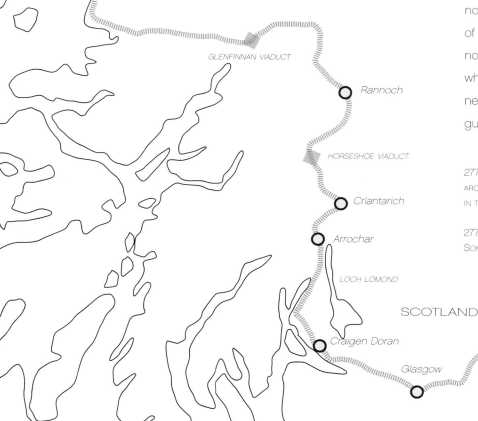

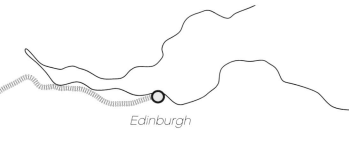

The guests of the Royal Scotsman are welcomed by the sound of bagpipes played by musicians in traditional garb.

278 top and 278-279 AFTER LUNCH, THE PASSENGERS ON THE ROYAL SCOTSMAN CAN RELAX ON THE SOFAS AND ARMCHAIRS IN THE COZY LOUNGE CAR.

279 top THE TRAIN STOPS FOR THE NIGHT IN SMALL, SECONDARY STATIONS, ALLOWING PASSENGERS TO ENJOY A TRANQUIL DINNER AND TO SPEND A PEACEFUL EVENING ENJOYING A DRINK AND CONVERSATION IN THE LOUNGE CAR.

279 bottom THE ROYAL SCOTSMAN'S SLEEPING CARS OFFER A LEVEL OF COMFORT WHICH IS ONLY MATCHED IN THE BEST HOTELS. THEY HAVE PROPER BEDS, NOT BERTHS, PRIVATE BATHROOMS AND WARDROBES BETWEEN WOODEN PANELED MIRRORS.

HARZER SCHMALSPURBAHNEN
GERMANY

The Harzer Schmalspurbahnen, Harz's railway, is the most extensive narrow gauge network of the former East Germany and today has around 80 miles (132 km) of track, running from central Germany to the south-east of Hannover. The main line is 38 miles (61 km) long and runs from Wernigerode to Nordhausen, with two other secondary lines: the first runs from Eisfelder station to Gernrode; the second, and certainly the most spectacular, goes to Brocken.

The network was established in June 1898 with the first train to run from Werigerode to Schierke. Before the unification of the two Germanys it provided a service for the local inhabitants, but it was already well known throughout the world both for the beauty of the places it passed through and also for its numerous and distinctive steam locomotives. Once the risk of shut-down and the substitution of the service for that of nondescript buses was thwarted following unification, and thanks to massive investment the line has been restored, improved and transformed in to one of the main tourist attractions of Germany. It did not, however, become part of the DB, the railways of Germany, instead it became a regional company with the support of the Sachsen-Anhelt and Thuringen provinces.

Obviously steam locomotives are still being used, though almost solely as tourist trains, whilst the routine daily service is mostly pulled by modern diesel trains. The Brocken line is an exception with regular service still entrusted, almost completely, to Group 99 steam locotenders, which are imposing machines of a 2-10-2 classification. This line rises with an almost continuous incline of 30 by thousand from the 830 ft (254 m) of Drei Annen Hohnei near Wernigerode to the

7650 ft (1142 m) of the terminal station of Brocken. An exhausting climb, interrupted about half way by a break at the Schierke's station in the heart of the woods, for water supply.

The journey on the other lines is not so difficult. Leaving Wernigerode station and having passed through the locality of Westerntor, where the offices and the main store of the railroad network are located, the line starts to rise towards Steineme, where the hardest section of the entire route starts – the 5 miles (9 km) to Drei Annen Hohne, which has 72 curves and a tunnel. The line continues to Benneckenstein station, with its characteristic wooden structure, and where there is a small railway museum, whilst another museum dedicated to mine railways is found near Netzkater station.

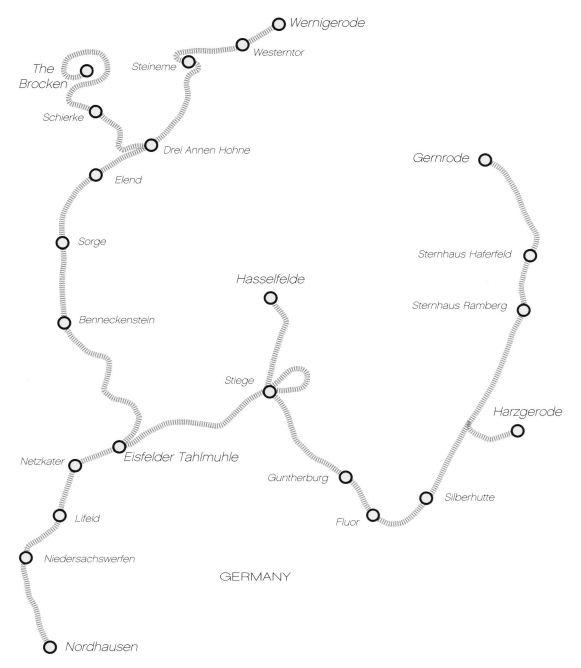

The road to Gernrode, which starts from the station of Eisfelder Tahlmuhle, is also very beautiful. After having climbed up to the locality of Stiege, the track continues through a number of charming towns, woods and fields. Harz's trains, even tourist ones, travel regularly every day and therefore it is not necessary to rely on an organized tour to visit these lines.

Some trains also include open carriages, from which you can admire even better the beauty of the countryside and the wheezing of the locomotives. Steam enthusiasts can rely on one of the numerous specialized tours which provide private trains, and organize tours to the offices and stores and allow photos and video to be taken of the train while it makes fake departures from stations, and also stops specifically to allow photographs to be taken by tourists.

281 The Harz is the most extensive narrow-gauge network of the former East Germany. It has been transformed in recent years into a magnificent tourist service with some steam locomotives.

TRAIN DES PIGNES
FRANCE

To enjoy the French province of Nice-Digne and its Train de Pignes, which arrives at Annot from the small train station of Puget Theniers, there is a special train journey. It starts from Côte d'Azur, close to the Principality of Monaco and the beaches of St. Tropez, and goes to the Alpes-de-Haute-Provence. It takes time because there are only four trains on the narrow-gauge Nice-Digne line, and they take over three hours to cover the 103 miles (166 km) of the line. The sacrifice is truly worth it because of the beauty of the trip. In the summer, it is also possible to go on a historical steam train, charmingly renamed as Train de Pignes, which covers the line between Puget Theniers and Annot. The name refers to the use of pine cones, easily found in the entire region, as fuel instead of carbon and wood during the years of poverty, even though it is quite improbable that pine

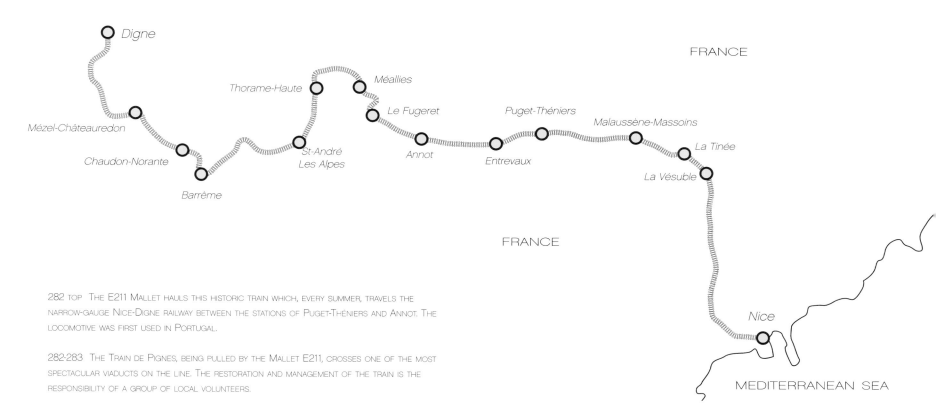

Digne

FRANCE

Méallies

Thorame-Haute

Le Fugeret

Puget-Théniers

Mézel-Châteauredon

Malaussène-Massoins

Chaudon-Norante

St-André
Les Alpes

Annot

Entrevaux

La Tinée

Barrème

La Vésuble

FRANCE

Nice

MEDITERRANEAN SEA

282 top The E211 Mallet hauls this historic train which, every summer, travels the narrow-gauge Nice-Digne railway between the stations of Puget-Théniers and Annot. The locomotive was first used in Portugal.

282-283 The Train de Pignes, being pulled by the Mallet E211, crosses one of the most spectacular viaducts on the line. The restoration and management of the train is the responsibility of a group of local volunteers.

cones have ever really been used for steam locomotives. Another version of the story states that the nickname derived from the train's slow speed, which allowed travelers to get down and stock-up on pine cones.

In 1951, the last remaining steam trains were replaced by diesel motorcars and, unfortunately, none of them survived. The historic train therefore uses two narrow-gauge, steam locomotives of different origin: the Locotender E327 of type 4-6-0T, which was built by the Fives-Lille Group in 1909 and originally used on the Bretagne lines; and a much larger Mallet, registered E211 of type 2-4-0+0-6-0T, which comes from the Portuguese Railways. This latter machine, with its quite particular wheel arrangement, was built in 1923 by the German company Henschel and, together with the other 15 of its class, was used in the Douro Valley up until a few years ago.

The train comprises five vehicles: a two-wheel truck, dating back to 1912, acting as luggage compartment; a splendid 1901 two-wheel decked carriage; the trolley car B505 built in 1892 by Desouches & David; and the two second-class trolley cars B31 and B32, which date back to 1911. The four vehicles offer in total 220 seats. Since 1981, every Sunday between May to October, the train circulates on the line with the aim of making known this otherwise neglected valley. The route covered by the train is perhaps the most spectacular part of the entire line with the two imposing stone and brick viaducts in La Done and Gros Vallon. The Train de Pignes leaves for Annot at 10:25am and arrives at noon, whereas the return trip starts off at 4:10pm and reaches Puget Theniers an hour later.

The train's restoration and management are carried out by an association of volunteers, the Groupe d'Etude pour les Chemins de fer de Provence. This group also campaigns to ensure that the Nice-Digne service is not abandoned, but rather is improved and strengthened. The regular traffic line is managed by the CFTA Company which heads the Veolia group. Together with SYMA (Syndacat Mixte Mediterraneé Alpes), the organization that regroups the region's provinces and departments and which, since 1968, has the exclusive control of Provence Railways, they have planned a vast modernization of the lines with the double objective of relaunching passenger traffic and promoting tourist use, obviously also with the steam train.

THE GLACIER EXPRESS
SWITZERLAND

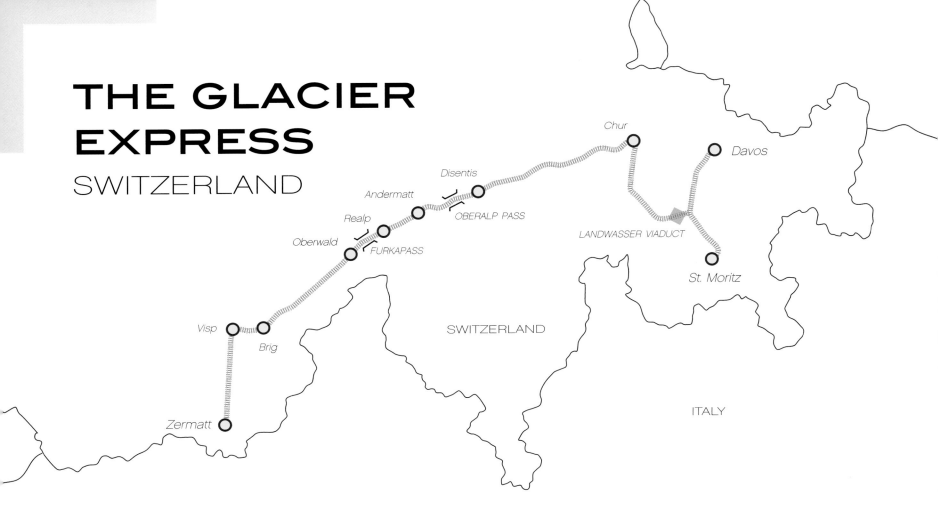

Glacier Express has to be included as one of the ten most beautiful train services in the world and it is, without a doubt, the most famous in Switzerland. The line connects Zermatt with St. Moritz, both among the most famous alpine skiing resorts in the world. The route is 180 miles (290 km) long and takes eight hours to travel through the regions of Brig and Andermatt

The narrow-gauge train, nowadays made up of modern and very comfortable panorama carriages, goes through seven valleys, 91 tunnels and crosses 291 bridges – practically one every kilometer. These statistics give a clear idea of the difficulties faced during the construction of the line, which, from its inauguration in 1931 till 1982, used to reach the edges of the Rhone glacier on top of the Furkapass. However, with the construction of the base tunnel this section of the route, very spectacular but which due to its altitude was inaccessible in winter, is no longer used by the Glacier Express.

This discarded 8-mile (13-km) section has not been totally abandoned. Thanks to the creation of a special company, it was transformed into a tourist line, the Dampfbahn Furka Bergstrecke, which operates in the summer, with original (HG 3/4) steam locomotives that were used in the 1930s. It is interesting to note that in 1947, on the electrification of the line, these locomotives were sold to Vietnam and they were recovered there while still in service during the mid-1990s.

The Glacier Express is now managed conjointly by two rail companies, Retiche Railways and Matterhorn-Gotthard Bahn (MGB). Even though it does not climb on the Furkapass anymore it still reaches a substantial height of 6,600 ft (2033 m) at the Oberalp Pass, which marks the border between the Swiss cantons of Uri and Graubunden. Along the route there are numerous sections with slopes so high that the train has to use a cog railway.

Starting from Zermatt our train descends towards Visp, where it gets onto the main line coming from Geneva and heads east towards Brig. From here the line starts to climb towards Oberwald, crosses the base tunnel under Furkapass, around 9 miles (15 km) long, passes through Realp and eventually arrives at Andermatt. This is one of the most spectacular sections of the entire line because the track, in order to achieve in a short distance the excessive climb, turns on itself with four hairpin bends, three of which are made inside tunnels. The journey continues still upwards up to Oberalp Pass and then descends towards Disentis and its large Benedictine monastery. At this station, the MOB locomotive gives up its place at head of the train to Retiche Railways, which will take the train to its final destination. Having passed Chur, the countryside becomes wilder and, immediately after the Alvenau, the Glacier Express crosses one of the most famous railroad structures in the world, the Landwasser Viaduct.

The journey is now near its end and, after traveling through the six-mile (10-km) long Albula tunnel, after passing Celerina, the Glacier Express is at last in St. Moritz. In the summer, from mid-March to mid-October, there are four daily departures of the Glacier Express. The journey is made comfortable by the modern panoramic carriages, which allow the full appreciation of the splendid countryside. Naturally, considering the duration of the journey, the train also includes a dining car and a well-provided bar car with waiters who serve you at your seat.

284 The panoramic carriages of the Glacier Express provide passengers with spectacular views of the splendid alpine scenes that the train passes through. The line is considered to be one of the top ten railway wonders of the world.

285 Whether in summer or winter, the Glacier Express travels through some of the most spectacular Swiss landscapes. The journey from Zermatt-St. Moritz-Davos is about 180 miles (290 km) long and takes eight hours.

EL TRANSCANTABRICO
SPAIN

286 THE TRANSCANTABRICO HAS A REFINED COAT OF ARMS IN KEEPING WITH ITS 1920S VINTAGE CARRIAGES. THE JOURNEY FROM LEON TO SANTIAGO DE COMPOSTELA TAKES EIGHT DAYS AND COVERS 620 MILES (1000 KM).

The journey of El Transcantabrico, the luxury train that crosses the northern part of Spain from Leon to Santiago de Compostela, lasts eight days and seven nights. It is a calm and slow-paced journey with long overnight stops in tranquil stations where the lucky passengers can sleep in the train's wonderful sleeping cars, and there are enjoyable excursions to the most interesting locations of Cantabria, Galicia and Basque Countries.

El Transcantabrico comprises eight vintage carriages – four sleeping cars and four lounge and dining cars. These carriages were built in Great Britain in the 1920s and have been completely refurbished in order to offer travelers a superbly stylish environment.

The four lounge and dining carriages are air-conditioned and are real jewels, both for their magnificent decor and their structural design. One of the carriages has a pub with a dancing floor, where obviously tango and flamenco are in the order of the day.

The decor is remniscent of a small nightclub where music and lively entertainment is provided every night until the early hours of the morning. The second lounge car includes a television and video player, and some tables where passengers can amuse themselves with numerous board games. The third lounge carriage has a second bar and the setting is luxuriously finished with couches and coffee tables where passengers can enjoy drinks served by the crew. The fourth lounge carriage is for those passengers who prefer a more relaxed and reserved journey, and it has a library which always has the main, daily European newspapers.

The four sleeping cars, each of which has four, two-bed suite cabins, are equally luxurious. All cabins feature a closet, coffee table, mini-bar, telephone and fine carpets. The private bathroom is equipped with a Jacuzzi

sauna. A large, curtained window provides wonderful views of the countryside passing by.

The cuisine is of crucial importance on the El Transcantabrico, which passes through regions where chefs believe that Spanish gastronomy reaches its zenith. During the seven-day-long journey, the team of chefs present the passengers with the most delicious and typical dishes of the local cuisine.

Some of the excursions offered in the journey's itinerary are unforgettable, starting with the Neolithic paintings of the Altamira caves, then to the medieval village of Santillana de Mar, followed by a fabulous dinner in a villa designed by Gaudi in Comillos, and finally a visit to the magnificent cathedral of Santiago de Compostela.

The 620-mile (1000-km) journey, in the distinctive blue and white cars, can either start in Santiago di Compostela or in Leon. During the tourist season, from April to October, the train alternatively leaves from one of the two terminals once a week to travel along this slow-paced and beautiful route through northern Spain.

It is also possible, moreover, to hire the entire train for groups of up to 50 people, even on different itineraries or for fewer days. The company also organizes special trips, for instance, on New Year's Day and on the occasion of the famous ceremonies celebrated during the Holy Week. El Transantabrico is managed by FEVE (Ferrocarrillas de Via Estrecha), a state-owned Spanish railway company which, for over 40 years, has been taking care of rail, passengers and freight transport on the meter-gauge network in northern Spain, the largest one in Europe.

286-287 THE TRAIN COMPRISES EIGHT, LUXURIOUSLY DECORATED VINTAGE CARRIAGES CONSTRUCTED IN GREAT BRITAIN. THERE ARE FOUR LOUNGE AND DINING CARS, WHILE THE REST ARE SLEEPING CARS.

THE TRANS-SIBERIAN

RUSSIA - CHINA

288 TOP THE GOLDEN EAGLE TRANS-SIBERIAN EXPRESS CROSSES THE STUNNING SIBERIAN LANDSCAPES ON JOURNEYS THAT TAKE BETWEEN 11 AND 21 DAYS. AT 5590 MILES (9000 KM) THE TRANS-SIBERIAN IS THE LONGEST RAILROAD IN THE WORLD.

The journey on the Trans-Siberian from Moscow to Vladivostok is still a real adventure, especially if you decide to travel the 5771 miles (9288 km) that separate the two cities on a regular service train rather than on one of the luxurious tourist charter trains, which have been covering this route for some years now. It is a memorable experience either way you choose to travel, considering that there isn't another connection in the world which is this long and which goes through such fascinating but still largely little known regions.

Officially inaugurated in 1903, the Trans-Siberian rapidly became the focal point of the traffic between St. Petersburg (at the time capital city of the Russian empire) and the eastern ports on the Pacific coast, to such a point that, after a few years, it was decided to transform it to a double track. This is an operation, moreover, that has not been totally completed as yet.

However, in 2002, the line was completely electrified with an immediate gain especially with respect to the weight of the freight trains that cross it. A regular passenger train takes about a week to complete the journey. For some time now, it has also become possible to reach China and Beijing via two branches: the first one is the Trans-Mongolian which goes through Ulanbator; while the second one is the Trans-Manchurian which arrives in Beijing by passing through Harbin first.

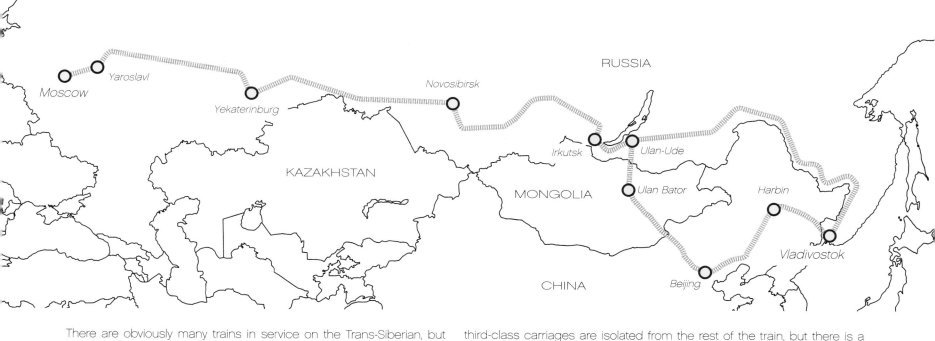

There are obviously many trains in service on the Trans-Siberian, but their formation is generally similar. Trains in Russia are divided into three classes: SV is the equivalent of our first class; Kupeyny is the equivalent of our second class; and the third category is Platskartny, which is the most popular, with open-plan cars that can be swiftly transformed into camps, instead of divided compartments.

The first class carriages have two-seater compartments with respective berths, whereas in second class, every compartment has four seats and their respective berths. There is no shower but, at least, there's the Russian samovar which provides hot water, essential for a cup of tea. The

third-class carriages are isolated from the rest of the train, but there is a dining carriage between the first and second class. In any case it is very easy to buy something to eat from the numerous kiosks available in all the stations where the train makes a stop. Oddly enough the clocks, found in each carriage of the train, remain regulated to Moscow time, thus causing an inevitable confusion after the train has gone through two or three of the seven time zones between Moscow and Vladivostock.

You can journey alone on the daily Trans-Siberian without problems if you use a travel agency for visas and hotel bookings in the cities where one wants to stop. If you prefer to undertake the long journey while being pampered and served on a luxury train, the solution is to choose the Golden Eagle Trans Siberian Express. This is a recently inaugurated "dream train" which offers an impeccable five-star service and joins the already established Siberian Tiger Trans Siberian Express. The 12 sleeping cars are each provided with a shower, under-floor heating, audio-video wiring with LCD monitor and DVD player, while the kitchen and the bar rival those of the best European restaurants. In all, the train comprises 21 carriages, the majority of which are newly built and manufactured by the Russian Zircon Service. The two trains travel from May to November with tours that last between 11 and 21 days. During the first section of their journeys, these trains are pulled by a steam locomotive, the P36 Class (the only private operated in Russia), which was renovated recently specifically for this purpose.

288-289 THE TRANS-SIBERIAN EXPRESS IS HAULED BY TWO LARGE DIESELS ON ITS JOURNEY TO VLADIVOSTOK – PASSING THROUGH UNTAMED LANDSCAPES.

289 THE CARRIAGE INTERIORS OF THE GOLDEN EAGLE ARE EXTREMELY LUXURIOUS AND REFINED, MAKING THE LONG JOURNEY ENJOYABLE AND RELAXING.

PALACE ON WHEELS
INDIA

It is possible to visit the Maharaja's India whilst travelling on a luxurious vintage train by choosing one of the classic itineraries of the Palace on Wheels, a real palace on rails now available for all travelers. The train used for this service is undoubtedly one of the most beautiful still pulling trains anywhere in the world. In any case, it is the only one able to re-create the atmosphere of India during the period of British rule.

The train is made up of 14 coaches, all air-conditioned, of course, and provided with all the possible comforts. However, the internal fixtures and fittings of these vehicles are the train's real marvel. All are different from each other, but they are united by a common theme, which is the story of India told through paintings, tapestry, inlays and silk. Each carriage is named after former Rajput states matching the aesthetics and interiors of the royal past. Each carriage also has a mini pantry to ensure the ready availability of cold beverages and, of course, the inevitable cup of tea. Dinner is served in the two dining cars "The Maharaja" and "The Maharani," which are furnished in a typically local style. Different dishes can be savored, freshly prepared by excellent chefs who are proficient in Continental, Chinese and Indian cuisine, and also typical Rajasthani cuisine is provided. In other words the train is an anthem to Indian tradition, but it does not forget the needs of the modern traveler, and is also equipped with cable radio, color televisions, DVD readers and also satellite phones. The small library present in every carriage is an elegant detail, in line with the great tradition of the English travelers of the previous century. From it one can choose a good book to read while, perhaps, sipping a drink in the bar car. The company that manages the train organizes tours with various itineraries, somewhat similar to what happens in Europe with the Orient Express, but the one-week tour with departure and arrival at New Delhi is the classic Palace on Wheels route, just like London-Venice is the classic Orient Express route. The journey starts from the Safdarjung Station in New Delhi, where passengers are welcomed on the train by the cabin crew who will take care of them during the entire tour. The train departs towards

Jaipur, which was in the past one of the most famous cities in the world. The capital of Rajasthan, nicknamed the pink city, was founded by Maharaja Swai Jai Singh II in 1727. Naturally, the tour includes a visit to the cities passed by the train in comfortable air-conditioned coaches equipped with a bar. On the third day, the Palace on Wheels stops at Jaisalmer at the centre of the Thar desert and which is famous for its fort, built entirely with sand bricks and which towers over the city.

Here it is also possible to try the excitement of a camel ride. The train continues thrugh the night towards Jodhpur, which is reached the following morning. It is the second city of Rajasthan, famous for both its refined handicrafts and for the rocky Mehrangarh Fort. In the short stop at Sawai Madhopur, there is an early morning visit to the beautiful Ranthambhor National Park, where, with a bit of luck one can still observe tigers.

The Palace on Wheels leaves for Chittaurgarh and then reaches Udaipur. The journey nears its end, but the train still goes through two important cities, Bharatpur and, perhaps most important of all, Agra, where a visit to the famous Taj Mahal, considered to be one of the Seven Wonders of the World, is a must. After an unforgettable week, the Palace on Wheels returns to New Delhi station.

290 THE PALACE ON WHEELS TAKES PASSENGERS THROUGH RAJASTHAN IN THE STYLE OF A "ONE THOUSAND AND ONE NIGHTS" STORY. THE TRAIN MAKES SEVERAL DIFFERENT JOURNEYS BUT THE CLASSIC ONE TAKES A WEEK, DEPARTING FROM AND RETURNING TO NEW DELHI.

291 FROM THE OUTSIDE THE CARRIAGES OF THE PALACE ON WHEELS APPEAR NORMAL, BUT INSIDE EACH CAR HAS A UNIQUE INTERIOR, FURNISHED WITH TAPESTRIES AND PAINTINGS, DEPICTING SCENES FROM INDIAN HISTORY.

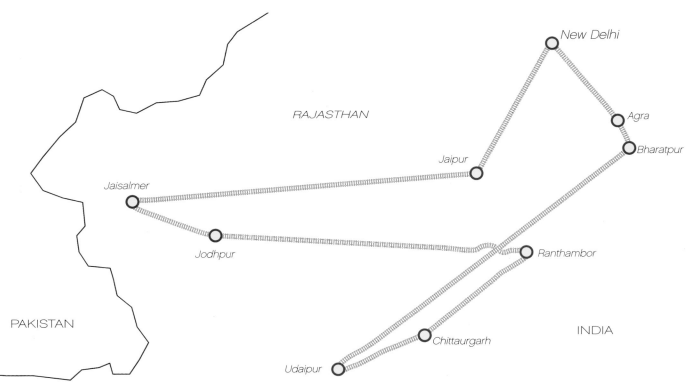

EASTERN & ORIENTAL EXPRESS

THAILAND - SINGAPORE

The bridge on the Kwai River is no longer the one made famous in the movie, but crossing it with the Eastern & Oriental Express is still a special experience. The luxurious train is the Asian twin of the legendary Venice Simplon Orient Express, and offers a range of dream journeys through Thailand, Malaysia and Singapore. From Bangkok, routes arrive to Cianhg Mai and Vientiane to the north, and Kuala Lampur and Singapore in the south.

Malaysia and Thailand have always maintained quite separate train networks, with travelers being forced to change their trains in Penang Station. The Eastern & Oriental Express is the first train which, thanks to a special agreement between the two networks, can complete the entire journey between Kuala Lumpur and Bangkok without train transfers

The train's carriages were originally built in Japan in 1971 by Mitsubishi Shoji-Kaisha and were first used by the Silver Star in New Zealand. This was a luxurious train that connected Auckand to Wellington with a night service, from 1971 to 1979, before being replaced by the Night Limited Express. The carriages were reconstructed and adapted by Gerard Gallet, the same engineer which took care of the restoration of the Venice Simplon Orient Ex-

press's carriages and also those of British Pullman. Besides undergoing a complete renovation, the vehicles were also technically modified to meet the requirements of the new service, in particular, air-conditioning, which is essential in that part of Asia, and also larger windows in the dining cars to better enjoy the surrounding scenery. All the interiors have been inspired by Oriental art and decorated using local materials as much as possible. The result is a line that takes travelers to the past and in a colonial atmosphere. The Eastern & Oriental Express offers three levels of compartments: two presidential suites, with more than 118 sq ft (11 sq m) of space, 28 state compartments, which have two beds, both at floor level, and 36 Pullman compartments, which are smaller and have one upper and one lower bed.

One of the principal attractions of the train is the observation car, which has a big covered veranda open at the sides, where you can enjoy not only the views but also the scents and the sounds of the tropical countryside. The interior is completely paneled in wood and furnished with comfortable couches and sofa. The evening can be spent in the bar car taking a drink whilst listening to piano music.

292 The Eastern & Oriental carries passengers through the mysterious atmosphere of the Far East, from Singapore north through Malaysia, into Thailand where it crosses the Thacompu Bridge.

293 The train passes through dense tropical forest in the area around Butterworth in Malaysia. To the north, in Thailand, it crosses the famous bridge on the River Kwai, though not the one made famous in the film.

The main itinerary is the three-day journey from Singapore to Bangkok. The train departs in the morning from Keppel Road station in Bangkok and travels all day until it reaches Kuala Lumpur in the evening, where it is then parked. The stop allows passengers to leave the train and admire the magnificent station built completely in a Moorish style.

On the second day the Eastern & Oriental Express arrives at Butterworth, and excursions to nearby towns are taken which take up the greater part of the day. The train then departs to Thailand and the following morning the highlight is crossing the famous bridge on the Kwai. The original wooden structure was replaced in April 1943 with a metal one 200 yards (200 m) further down river.

However, the curvy part of the bridge is a remnant of the original structure. Passengers can take pictures of the train while it slowly crosses the bridge and wait as it reverses a few minutes later to take them back on board. After a visit to the temples of the zone and to the cemetery where victims of the war are buried, the trip continues towards Bangkok where it ends its journey in the afternoon.

294-295 The train's carriages were originally used for the New Zealand luxury train, the Silver Star, and were restored by the same engineer who had recovered the CIWL vehicles for the Venice Simplon Orient Express.

295 One of the great features of the Eastern & Oriental is the open observatory carriage at the rear of the train. The Presidential Suite is equally marvelous and very spacious.

PRIDE OF AFRICA
SOUTH AFRICA

Crossing South Africa from Pretoria to Cape Town allows travelers to appreciate the diverse aspects of this beautiful country: the modern cities of Pretoria and Johannesburg and the northern grasslands; the desert area of the Great Karoo, between Kimberley and De Aar; the alpine-like mountains; and the vineyard covered hills of Cape Province.

This wonderful journey is regularly undertaken by one of the most distinguished tourist trains in the world, the Pride of Africa, and never was a name so well chosen in a nation that, in the past years, has became a symbol for its continent.

The Pride of Africa can carry up to a maximum of 72 passengers who have comfortable cabins that can accommodate two people. During its

296 top The fact that the train is hauled by Class 19D locomotives of South African Railways just adds to the appeal of the Pride of Africa. These locomotives were bought specifically for the purpose by Rovos, the company that owns the train.

990-mile (1600-km) journey it is hauled by diesel and electric locomotives, and also by some of the most famous South African steam locomotives. The train cars are vintage, even though in part restructured to improve the comfort aboard. Some even date back to 1911 and have been restored after having been left abandoned for many years in the remotest areas of the South African railroad network.

For instance, dining car No. 195 "Shangani," which was built in 1924, was found abandoned in a siding in Alberton and was completely renovated after its acquisition. Three of the magnificent teak pillars had been removed and these were faithfully crafted, restoring the Victorian atmosphere.

Apart from the sleeping cars, the train also includes two 42-seater dining cars, a lounge car and, at the rear of the train, a 32-seater observation car with an open-air balcony. Naturally, to maintain the vintage atmosphere of the train, there are no televisions or radios on the Pride of Africa. The train's journey starts from Capital Park station, which is also the headquarters of Rovos, the company that manages the train.

Capital Park is a small station annexed to a siding which, during the steam locomotives era, used to house up to 140 vehicles. The company has now restored it and aims on transforming it into a, partly working, railway museum, because the six steam locomotives which alternate at the head of Pride of Africa are based there. The oldest and smallest one is No. 439 Tiffany Class 6, built in 1893.

The other three are more modern locomotives, Class 19D, built during the 1930s and saved from scraping. They were put back into service in 1989 following extensive restoration. The two flagships of the fleet are locomotive 3483 "Marjorie" and a GMAM Garrat: the first one, a big Class 25NC locomotive, is invaluable for the crossing of the Great Karoo because, thanks to the additional tender, it can cover a

distance of 430 miles) (700 km) without the need to stop for water.

The classic route from Pretoria to Cape Town is covered by the Pride of Africa in 72 hours, with departures taking place three times a week in both directions. On the first day the appointment is at Capital Park, the private station which acts as headquarters of the train. The train departs in the afternoon and there is dinner aboard, then the following morning there is a stop in Kimberley with a visit to the "Big Hole," an open-pit ex-diamond mine at the centre of the city. "Big-Hole" is a 700-ft (215-m) "hole" believed to be the world's deepest, hand-made excavation. After a night spent crossing De Aar, the train reaches Matijiesfontein the following morning, where it stops to allow for a visit to the historic village. Departure is at around lunchtime and the final destination, Platform 24, in Cape Town's Station, is reached in the afternoon.

296 bottom The traditional route of the Pride of Africa is from Pretoria to Cape Town, but often the train reaches as far as Victoria Falls, where one can take a flight and get spectacular pictures like this one.

297 South Africa has a variety of landscapes from deserts to regions with an alpine feel and the 990-mile (1600-km) journey to Cape Town give passengers a rich appreciation of this country's beautiful scenery.

"
A trip on the Pride of Africa
gives train travelers the opportunity to
feel the atmosphere of the last century. "

298-299 THE PRIDE OF AFRICA'S DINING CAR NO. 195 "SHANGANI," DATES BACK TO 1924. IT WAS FOUND ABANDONED IN A RAILWAY SIDING IN ALBERTON AND UNDERWENT A COMPLETE AND ACCURATE RESTORATION.

299 THE CARRIAGE INTERIORS ARE STUNNING AND PERFECT DOWN TO THE SMALLEST DETAIL. THE LOUNGE CAR IS FURNISHED WITH A BAR AND COMFORTABLE COUCHES, WHILE THE SLEEPING CARS HAVE LARGE DOUBLE-BEDS – THE ROYAL SUITE EVEN HAS A BATH TUB.

THE GHAN
AUSTRALIA

The Ghan is the passenger train that crosses the entire Australian continent in 48 hours from north to south. A 1850-mile (2979-km) long journey from Adelaide to Darwin, via Alice Springs. The name of this train, which is managed by Central Australian Railway, is an abbreviated version of its previous nickname "The Afghan Express," which comes from the Afghan camel trains (the central area of Australia is desert) that trekked the same route before the coming of the railway.

The Ghan is now a comfortable and luxurious passenger train, fitted with all the comforts you could hope for. It crosses the continent predominantly as a tourist service. Commuting to work in Australia over such distances is not unknown, but is usually done by plane and often even helicopter (both of which are often used to reach isolated communities).

Turning back to our train and the transcontinental line, the current The

Ghan started its service on February 4th 2004, when the first passenger train leaving from Adelaide reached Darwin on the new standard gauge line which substituted the original narrow gauge line. It was the January 18th 1878 when work on the old tracks, in the northern part of the line, started at Port Augusta. However, it was only on August 6th 1929, with its arrival at Alice Springs, that the works were finally completed. In reality, the rails of the two tracks, the Adelaide-Alice Springs and the Alice Springs-Darwin, were not connected to each other, but the old The Ghan started the service all the same, obviously with a change in trains halfway along the track.

From the old line, only a small section from Quorn to Port August is still in use today, and for a brief distance the two lines run parallel to each other, even though at a distance. The line, named Pichi Richi Railway (the

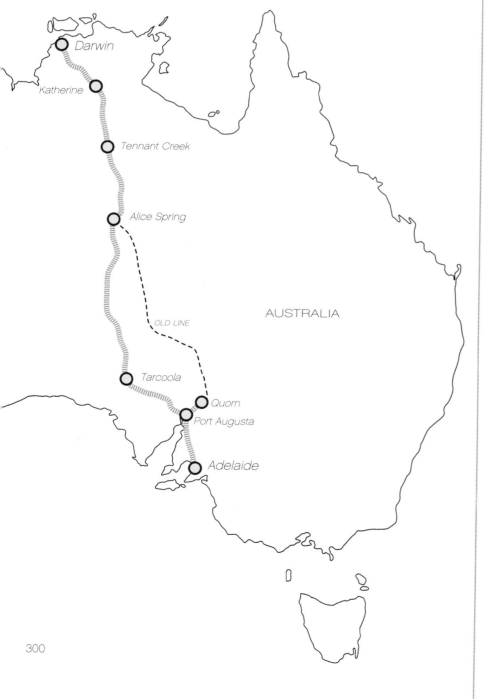

300 TOP THE NAME "THE GHAN" IS THE ABBREVIATION OF "THE AFGHAN" IN REMEMBRANCE OF THE CAMEL CARAVANS WHICH, IN THE PAST, USED TO MARCH ACROSS THE COUNTRY AND WHICH INSPIRED THE SYMBOL OF THE AUSTRALIAN TRAIN.

300-301 THE GHAN, IN ITS JOURNEY FROM NORTH TO SOUTH ACROSS AUSTRALIA, TRAVELS THROUGH THE VAST DESERT REGIONS OF AUSTRALIA.

301 TOP THE GHAN BEGINS ITS JOURNEY AT DARWIN, ON AUSTRALIA'S NORTHERN COAST, AND IT ENDS 1850 MILES (2979 KM) TO THE SOUTH IN ADELAIDE. THE SERVICE ONLY STARTED IN FEBRUARY 2004.

name derives from a local plant, the Pituri) is well known throughout Australia and, since 2002, it is also a rail museum after having restored a lot of vintage equipment, steam locomotives, cars and carriages. A journey on one of the two trains, after having crossed the continent on The Ghan, helps one to understand how difficult it was to travel in the past.

Today, The Ghan travels two times a week through the entire line with two four-hour stops in the cities of Katherine and Alice Springs, where travelers can make use of optional tourist excursions, the so-called Whistle Stop Tour. At Darwin it is possible to continue the trip on two other luxury trains, the Indian Pacific and the Overland, for Sydney and Melbourne respectively.

Like all other trains of this class, The Ghan provides its passengers with comfortable carriages, but unlike other trains it is possible to choose between two levels of service: the Gold Kangaroo Service, with proper sin-gle- or double-bed compartments; and the Red Kangaroo Service, which is more economic with transformable compartments for the night or reclining couches.

There are also two categories of on-board dining available – luxury or economy. The Ghan is also offers four special carriages which can be rented on request. The Chairman Carriage, which can accommodate up to eight people and is provided with two bedrooms, a lounge and private kitchen; the Prince of Wales Car, a lounge car built in 1919 for a royal visit from the Prince of Wales, and which has been restored back to its original condition; the Governor's Lounge, similar to the previous one, but built in 1917 for the official opening of the Trans Australian Railway; and the Sir John Forrest, a modern built car which can be used for meetings and conferences.

THE CANADIAN
CANADA

The Canadian transcontinental which connects Toronto, in the region of the Great Lakes, to Vancouver on the Pacific, is one of the most enchanting railway lines in the world. It was built between 1881 and 1885, and passes through wild and magnificent territories which still maintain the same charm of a century ago.

An itinerary which can be retraced today with The Canadian, the most prestigious train of the VIA Rail company, the Crown Corporation, that is, the state-controlled company, that from 1978, takes care of the intercity passenger traffic in Canada.

At first, the convoy was managed by the Canadian Pacific Railway, which, in the years immediately after the Second World War, following the fashion of those days, decided to substitute the traditional carriages with, at the time, very modern, aerodynamic, stainless-steel vehicles, built expressly by Budd Company of Philadelphia. The order, totaling 173 vehicles, also included observatory carriages at the end of the train, and domed observation cars in which the central part was overhead, with a completely transparent dome. The train, about 30 vehicles in all, also included sleeping cars, dining cars and lounge cars – all luxuriously furnished, apart naturally from some luggage compartments.

VIA Rai still uses these historical carriages for the Canadian, which made it famous all over the world. Obviously, interiors have been restructured to modern levels of comfort. Today, the train is aimed more towards a tourist clientele rather than business travelers and its frequency of service is limited to three days per week.

The complete journey from Union Station in Toronto to the Pacific Central Station of Vancouver, lasts three days. However, since The Canadian provides a normal passenger service and not a charter service, it is possible to purchase tickets for any intermediary stations, and also go through only some parts of the itinerary. When purchasing the ticket it is possible to choose between two service classes, the Comfort, the most economic one, (Toronto-Vancouver only costs $428), which offers reclining

302 THE CANADIAN HAS AT THE REAR AN OBSERVATORY CAR WITH A PANORAMIC DOME.

303 THE CANADIAN PASSES BY THE "SPARKLING LAKES" WITH THE CANADIAN ROCKIES AS A BACKDROP.

couches of the aeronautic type but with more room between the seats; and the Silver & Blue, which provides accommodation in the sleeping cars and meals (included in the ticket price) in the First Class Park Dining Cars

There's also the "Romance By Rail" service, especially devised for couples on holiday, which includes a two bed suite, wine and flowers and a special service. Naturally the best part of the journey is the pleasure of watching the wonderful Canadian landscape, the Canadian Rockies in particular, whilst sitting on the upper observation deck of the dome car.

Apart from the journey on The Canadian, VIA Rail also offers interesting tourist packages, which include the main destinations along the trip, but it has also catered for the "backpackers" and for the more adventurous and sporty travelers in general: the "Special Stop" service operates between Sudbury Junction and Winnipeg. It is thus possible to be left by the train at any point, in the middle of wild nature, by simply indicating in good time the exact mile marker at which you would like the train to stop. An opportunity which is very much appreciated by hikers.

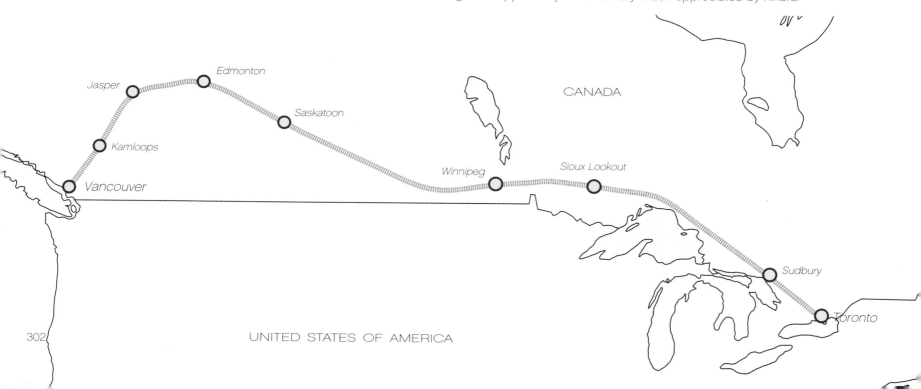

GRANDLUXE RAIL JOURNEYS
UNITED STATES OF AMERICA

The era of big North American trains is long gone, but it is still possible to enjoy them thanks to trips by GrandLuxe, the vintage train that offers various breathtaking journeys in the United States.

The GrandLuxe has three main routes: the National Parks of the West, the Great Northwest and the Rockies, and, finally, the Sierras and Napa Valley on the Pacific Ocean. This luxurious train recreates the atmosphere of the 1940s and the 1950s – the golden years of train journeys.

The train cars, painted in royal blue with golden lines, are all vintage carriages built between 1948 and 1958 and superbly restored. The company has discovered them in museums and private collections throughout America.

The sleeping carriages were once used by the Southern Pacific Rail-

road, the Nickel Plate Railroad Company, the Union Pacific, the Ohio Railroad and of the New York Central Railroad. In short, they represent a big slice of American railroad history. They have been restored while maintaining, as much as possible, their original vintage appearance but necessary services were added for a luxurious contemporary train. Travelers are welcomed in mahogany wood surroundings, with bronze finishes and splendid crystal chandeliers.

The convoy offers five different levels of cabins: Vintage Pullmans, Single Sleepers, Parlor Suites, Classic Presidential Suites and Grand Suites. Some also offer a private shower and all are equipped with air conditioning and personalized heating. The GrandLuxe's two most beautiful vehicles are, without a doubt, the observation car and the dome car, both are

the expression of the most classical of North American railroad traditions. The former was originally built for the New York Central and completely covered in mahogany panels and equipped with comfortable couches: the semicircular rear bay window, from which one can admire the scenery, is simply spectacular.

The dome car is even more beautiful. It was built in 1953 by the Budd Company for the famous Daylight of the Southern Pacific train. The carriage, which was described even at the time by the National Geographic, has 72 seats and an upper-level glass enclosure, which allows a 360-degree view of the surrounding countryside. It was considered, in the 1950s, as the apogee of train innovation. In its lower part there's a club bar, a reading lounge and a service compartment for guests.

A dining car and a 1940s era lounge car, originally used by the Union Pacific, complete the train. It also features a large bar and a piano that offers live music in the evening. The dining car offers menus linked to the cuisine of the regions being traveled through: it could be considered as a local restaurant on wheels. The GrandLuxe's journeys are about a week long and obviously include several excursions, where guests are accompanied not just by simple hosts but by experts – a sommelier if they are visiting a wine cellar, a naturalist if the excursion is in a park.

You can depart from Deven in Colorado and arrive in Oakland on the Pacific after having seen the Great Salty Lake, the mountains of Sierra Nevada and the wineries of Napa Valley in California; or alternatively visit the Great North West starting from Jackson in Wyoming to finally arrive at Seattle after having visited the National Park of Yellowstone and the Galcier National Park in Montana.

DURANGO & SILVERTON NARROW GAUGE RAILROAD
UNITED STATES OF AMERICA

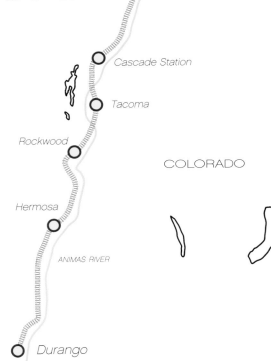

The Durango & Silverton Narrow Gauge Railroad is one of the most famous museum trains running in the United States. All this is thanks to the beauty of the sites it traverses, between the mountains of Southern Colorado, and also thanks to the restoration work which has saved the steam locomotives from being destroyed as well as original vintage cars and wagons which are still used today. The town of Durango was founded by the train company Denver & Rio Grande Railway in 1879. The railroad arrived in Durango on August 5th 1881 and construction on the line to Silverton began towards the end of that same year. By July of 1882, the tracks to Silverton were completed. As one can gather by the name Silverton, probably deriving from silver town, the purpose of this railroad was to serve the gold and silver mines of the region.

The route, around 45 miles long (around 72 km) is so spectacular that, in a few years, it became popular as a tourist attraction. In 1951, the freight service was abandoned completely in

308-309 THE DURANGO & SILVERTON RAILROAD IS ONE OF THE MOST FAMOUS NARROW-GAUGE MUSEUM RAILWAYS IN THE WORLD. IT PASSES THROUGH THE SPECTACULAR MOUNTAINS OF COLORADO ON ITS 45-MILE (72-KM) ROUTE.

309 TOP THE RAILROAD USES AUTHENTIC VINTAGE CARRIAGES AND LOCOMOTIVES, WHICH ARE MAINTAINED AS NEAR AS POSSIBLE TO THEIR ORIGINAL, PERIOD CONDITION. IT IS NOT SURPRISING THAT 18 MOVIES HAVE BEEN FILMED ON THE LINE.

favor of a passenger service. During the years, 18 movies were filmed on this railroad, amongst them *Viva Zapata* and *Around the World in Eighty Days*. In the 1960s the Durango-Silverton was registered as a National Historic Landmark, but this did not save it from a difficult period. In 1969 the Denver & Rio Grande Railway decided to terminate the service south of Durango and the line seriously risked abandonment.

Fortunately the Silverton branch was acquired by Charles Bradshow Jr who started long and costly repair works. Besides the renovation of the steam locomotives, the track was rebuilt and over 10,000 wooden ties were replaced. In 1985, the company purchased the Silverton depot, returning it to service. By the following year, already four trains a day were running to Silverton with a fifth one running to Cascade Canyon Wye.

Today, the railroad is owned by American Heritage Railways and continues its tourist service throughout the year, using steam-powered locomotives maintained in their original condition.

The coaches each feature bathroom facilities and are heated during the winter months, whilst in summer one can travel on open gondola cars. For those who want an exclusive trip it is possible to choose special coaches available in some trains, such as the two luxurious "Presidential Cars," decorated in a Victorian style. The route, which mostly follows the Animas River trail, cuts across relatively smooth wooded areas, but it also slopes up steep rocky gorges crossing the characteristic trestles so typical of North-American railroads.

The complete excursion lasts a day with a lunch break and a visit to Silverton City before the return towards Durango. If time is limited, it is also possible to return by a bus service provided by the railroad company. The number of active vehicles in the line is impressive: The Durango & Silverton Narrow Gauge Railroad has under its disposal a total of seven steam-powered locomotives, three K28 Class engines built by the American Locomotive Works in 1923 and four K36b Class ones built by Baldwin in 1925. Also included are five diesel locomotives, three of which can be traced back to the 1950s. There are more than 50 coaches, some of which date back to 1880, for example, the Almosa and the General Palmer.

310-311 An engine driver of the Durango & Silverton Railroad soaks the coal loaded on the tender before the departure, so as to prevent dust from disturbing the passengers who are looking out from the train's windows.

PERURAIL
PERU

Hiram Bingham is the name of the American explorer – he was a professor at Yale – who, at around noon of July 23rd 1911, by reaching the peak of a steep slope, was the first to discover Machu Picchu, the lost city of the Incas, at a height of about 8800 ft (2700 m) in the valley of Urubumba in Peru.

Today, Hiram Bingham is also the name of the luxury train of PeruRail, which, since August 2003, allows people to reach in comfort this fascinating place. The train departs from Poroyn station (about 20 minutes from the centre of Cuzco) at nine in the morning and returns in the late afternoon. Unlike other Peruvian lines, the railroad between Cuzco and Machu Picchu is narrow gauge and it is also the only way to reach the archaeological site. There are absolutely no roads in the area and, lately, even the use of tourist helicopter flights have been prohibited.

The railway is famous for the clever system with which it overcomes the great changes in altitude without using cog railways or long bends. The solution is the use of the so-called "switchback," which uses the same basic construction concept of a stairway, that is, a ramp on one side, a landing, a ramp in the opposite direction, and so on until it reach-

es the peak. The ramp is a steep rise of the rail, a short dead rail, just a bit longer than the train, substitutes the landing. From there, another rail begins again in an opposite direction, always ascending towards the next route inversion. An economic, but slow system, which requires the engineer to change his driving cabin every time. The locals simply call it "El Zig-Zag."

The Hiram Binghman train is formed of only four carriages, all in an elegant blue and gold livery, and it can carry up to 84 passengers. Apart from a kitchen carriage, it comprises two dining cars and an observato-

ry car with a bar. The décor takes the passengers back in time to the luxury trains of the 1920s, even though it must be said that, in reality, such trains never operated on these lines. Both the departure and return trips last around three hours, in which breakfast, various cocktails and dinner of typical local dishes are served before the return to Cuzco in the evening.

For those who cannot, or do not, wish to travel on the Hiram Bingham, there is an excellent alternative. PeruRail offers, on the same line, another more popular but equally interesting train to complete the excursion up to the lost city of the Incas. The train includes a modern panoramic carriage with an almost transparent roof, the "Vistadome," from which one can admire the surrounding Andean peaks, and the charming "Backpacker" car, for travelers with backpacks and sleeping bags, which has the Spartan interior of normal Peruvian carriages. In this way the most curious travelers can get an idea of the Peruvians' method of traveling without having to actually face the real discomforts.

On both carriages, PeruRail provides snacks and beverages for its passengers. These carriages are also used on two other tourist routes, the Sacred Valley – Machu Picchu and Cuzco – Lake Titicaca. PeruRail also offers another train made up of dining cars, lounge cars and observatory cars, and furnished like the European Pullman carriages operating at the start of the 20th century. Together with the new Chinese line that connects Peking to Lasha in Tibet, the line to Lake Titicaca is the highest in the world, with a regular passenger service. The most elevated station is La Raya at 14,000 ft (4313 m).

BIBLIOGRAPHY

Hamilton Ellis, *The pictorial encyclopedia of railways*, Hamlyn, 1968

Peter Lorie & Colin Garrat, *Iron Horse*, 1987

W.J.K. Davies, *Diesel Rail Traction*, Almark, 1973

Dee Brown, *Un fischio nella prateria*, Mondadori, 2000

Wassily Leontief and Paolo Costa, *Il trasporto merci e l'economia italiana*, Marsilio, 1996

Dino Salomone, *La trazione elettrica trifase*, Edizioni Graf, 1976

Fabio Maria Ciuffini, *Sul filo del binario*, Edizioni CAFI, 1988

Dino Salomone, *L'evoluzione della carrozza ferroviaria*, Grafiche Gioos, 1980

Remo Cesarano, *Treni di carta*, Mariotti, 1993

Filippo Tajani, *Storia delle ferrovie italiane*, Garzanti, 1944

Kalla-Bishop, *Italian State Railways Steam Locomotives*, Tourret Publishing, 1986

Carlo Marco, *Locomotive*, Roux Editori, 1890

AA VV, *Ferrovie dello Stato 1900-1940*, Rassegna, 1980

Giovanni Tey, *La locomotiva a vapore*, Duegi Editrice, 2003

Pierangelo Caiti, *Artiglieria ferroviaria e Treni blindati*, Albertelli, 1981

AA VV, *La ferrovia nel 2000*, Duegi Editrice, 1991

INDEX

PHOTO CREDITS

Page 255 Carlos Alvarez/Getty Images

Page 256 NRM/Science & Society Picture Library

Page 257 top and bottom Milepost 92 1/2

Page 258 Milepost 92 1/2

Pages 258-259 Milepost 92 1/2

Pages 260-261 Colin Garratt; Milepost 92 1/2/Corbis

Page 261 top Olivier Douvry/Corbis Sygma/Corbis

Page 261 bottom Marco Bruzzo/Duegi Editrice

Pages 262-263 David Chang/epa/Corbis

Page 263 James Leynse/Corbis

Page 264 James Leynse/Corbis

Pages 264-265 China Photos/Getty Images

Page 265 James Leynse/Corbis

Pages 266-267 Everett Kennedy Brown/epa/Corbis

Page 269 Milepost 92 1/2

Pages 270-271 Michael Yamashita/Corbis

Page 272 Robert Haidinger/Anzenberger/Contrasto

Pages 272-273 Robert Haidinger/Anzenberger/Contrasto

Page 273 Angelo Colombo/Archivio White Star

Page 274 top CuboImages srl/Alamy

Page 274 center Maurice Joseph/Alamy

Page 274 bottom Olycom

Pages 274-275 Robert Haidinger/Anzenberger/Contrasto

Page 276 top Patrick Ward/Corbis

Page 276 bottom Jay Dickman/Corbis

Page 277 top left Patrick Ward/Corbis

Page 277 top right Bernard Annebique/Corbis Sygma/Corbis

Page 277 bottom Angelo Colombo/Archivio White Star

Page 278 David Lefranc/Gamma/Contrasto

Pages 278-279 David Lefranc/Gamma/Contrasto

Page 279 top Bernard Annebique/Corbis Sygma/Corbis

Page 279 bottom Goebel/zefa/Corbis

Pages 280-281 Blickwinkel/Alamy

Page 281 top Angelo Colombo/Archivio White Star

Page 281 bottom Martin Rugner/Agefotostock/Marka

Page 282 Olycom

Pages 282-283 Olycom

Page 283 Angelo Colombo/Archivio White Star

Page 284 top Angelo Colombo/Archivio White Star

Page 284 bottom Toni Anzenberger/Anzenberger/Contrasto

Page 285 top Rhaetian Railway

Page 285 bottom Peter marlow/Magnum Photos/Contrasto

Page 286 top and bottom El Transcantabrico Feve

Pages 286-287 Hubert Stadler/Corbis

Page 287 Angelo Colombo/Archivio White Star

Page 288 GW Travel Limited

Pages 288-289 Wolfgang Kaehler/Corbis

Page 289 top Angelo Colombo/Archivio White Star

Page 289 bottom GW Travel Limited

Page 290 top Lindsay Hebberd/Corbis

Page 290 bottom Angelo Colombo/Archivio White Star

Page 291 Modrow/laif/Contrasto

Page 292 Orient Express Hotels, Trains & Cruises

Page 293 top Angelo Colombo/Archivio White Star

Page 293 bottom Ian Lloyd/Orient Express Hotels, Trains & Cruises

Pages 294-295 Maurice Joseph/Alamy

Page 295 top and bottom Orient Express Hotels, Trains & Cruises

Page 296 top Alain Proust/Rovos Rail

Page 296 bottom Richard Dobson/Rovos Rail

Page 297 top Angelo Colombo/Archivio White Star

Page 297 bottom Peter Rudi-Meyer/Rovos Rail

Pages 298-299 David Lefranc/Gamma/Contrasto

Page 299 top, center and bottom Alain Proust/Rovos Rail

Page 300 top and bottom Angelo Colombo/Archivio White Star

Page 300-301 David Hancock/Anzenberger/Contrasto

Page 301 Sylvain Grandadam/Agefotostock/Marka

Page 302 top Photo High Martel/Via Rail

Page 302 bottom Angelo Colombo/Archivio White Star

Page 303 Matthew G. Wheeler

Page 304 Carl & Ann Purcell/Corbis

Page 305 top Angelo Colombo/Archivio White Star

Page 305 bottom Wolfgang Kaehler/Corbis

Pages 306-307 Alison Wright/Corbis

Page 307 top David McNew/Getty Images

Page 307 bottom Wolfgang Kaehler/Corbis

Page 308 Angelo Colombo/Archivio White Star

Pages 308-309 Chuck Haney/DanitaDelimont.com

Page 309 Lowell Georgia/Corbis

Pages 310-311 Lowell Georgia/Corbis

Page 312 Mel Longhurst/Photoshot

Pages 312-313 Tony Waltham/Robert Harding World Imagery/Corbis

Page 313 top Angelo Colombo/Archivio White Star

Page 313 bottom Stockfolio/Alamy

ACKNOWLEDGEMENTS

The author dedicates this work to his grandfather Giorgio, who sacrificed his life for his work as railwayman.

The author wishes to thank:
Gianfranco Berto, for his help in the overall setting up of the work, and Marco Bruzzo whose exceptional memory has helped me bring into focus some events. To all the staff of the publishing house for the patient way they have followed me.

The Publisher wishes to thank:
Heritage Foundation SBB, Berna, Thomas Koeppel
Jean-Marc Combe, Conservateur du Musée français du chemin de fer de Mulhouse
Colin Nash, Milepost 92 1/2, Newton Harcourt
Malcom Collop
Stefano Paolini

Giuseppe Preianò
Rhaetian Railway AG, Chur, Sandra Beeli
Rail Traction Company Spa, Rome, Miriam Mascolo
El Transcantabrico Feve, Oviedo, Naira Pedregal Marcos
GW Travel Limited, Altrincham, Nichola Absalom
Canadian Pacific Railway, Montréal, R.C. Kennell
Union Pacific Railroad Museum, Council Bluffs (Iowa), John Bromley
Deutsche Bahn AG
DBMuseum Fotosammlung, Nuremberg
Orient Express Hotels, Trains & Cruises
Rovos Rail, Pretoria, Garyth Den
VIA Rail Canada Inc., Montréal
GrandLuxe Rail Journeys, Evergreen (Colorado), Tamra L. Hoppes
Chemins de Fer de Provence, Nizza, Mylène Bénichou
Patentes Talgo S.A., Madrid, Loreto Almodovar
Matthew G. Wheeler
Durango & Silverton Narrow Gauge RR, Durango, Yvonne Lashmett and Andrea Seid
Palace On Wheels Inc., Princeton (New Jersey)
TransEurop-Eisenbahn AG, Basilea

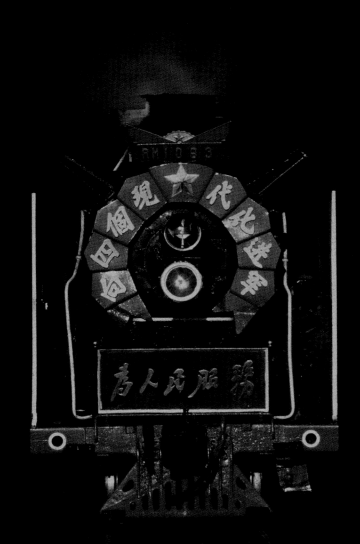